shine

Designed and created by Katty Ibarra and Sylvie Coulange
Written by Jessica Young and Sylvie Coulange
Photography by Scott Winer, Elodie Abadie and Sylvie Coulange
I would never have done it without you Ben. FYM.
Printed in the U.S.A.
© 2017 Sylvie Coulange. All rights reserved.
No portion of this book may be reproduced in any form without permission from the publisher.
For information about bulk purchases address the publisher at: info@faitmaisonlj.com
@fait.maison.lj
First Edition
ISBN 978-0-692-91083-2

shine
food for the soul

Sylvie Coulange

simple
healthy
inspired

The key to change is having faith that when you get rid of the old, something or someone even more magnificent will take its place.

— DANIEL J. LEVITIN

Growing up in the French Caribbean islands, I learned to surf at a young age at my father's side. It was rustic, close to nature, laid back. It is the DNA of who I am and seek to further become.

Surfer, baker, center of the home, I am independent and interested in making my own way in life. Much of what you read here are my own observations about how to live better, starting with what you put into your body.

All that follows is what I have learned by doing both my mistakes and successes. I am a self-taught cook. I began with no prior knowledge or formal training.

My motivation to become a cook was to better nourish my family — my two beautiful boys and my husband, my soulmate. My motivation is Love.

When you go grocery shopping, hand-select ingredients, bring them home, prepare and serve them, you are showing you care.

This book will change the way you cook and the way you live.

Sylvie Coulange.

Dis-moi ce que tu manges, je te dirai ce que tu es.

— JEAN ANTHELME BRILLAT-SAVARIN

— Tell me what you eat, I will tell you what you are.

Once you discover how important healthy food is for the mood, body and brain, it will forever change the way you see food. It brings satisfaction, energy and the means to your own vitality. You can choose to live more creatively, more fully by understanding what constitutes food and how our body uses it.

See food as necessary fuel for the brain. Food provides essential nutrients (carbs, fats, vitamins, minerals, fiber, and proteins) that the body needs in order to properly operate. A well-balanced diet may help protect you from chronic diseases, live a better life and prevent unhealthy impulsive eating.

Prefer quality over quantity. Believe in full fat content foods for richer taste, higher percentage of nutrients (less processed and more natural) and higher satisfaction.

Consume with pleasure and moderation!

Food is energy
Food is vitality
Food is satisfaction

love
plan
focus

In The Kitchen

Having the right tools makes the job easier. It is better to have a few good hard-working utensils than a cluttered kitchen with drawers full of rarely used items.

Cut

    Paring knife
    Curved knife
    6-inch prep knife
    8-inch prep knife
    Serrated knife
    Marble slab - cutting + prep

Prep

    Non-stick rubber spatula
    Slotted spoon
    Wooden spoon
    Vegetable peeler
    Rolling pin
    Wire whisk
    Tongs
    Ladle
    1 small round stainless steel ring

Measure

    Glass measuring cup with handle + pour spout
    1 set of measuring cups
    1 set of measuring spoons
    Food scale

Blend

    Stand mixer
    Immersion hand blender
    Food processor

Cook

    2 stainless steel mixing bowls
    1 small + 1 large saucepans
    1 small + 1 large stainless steel skillets
    1 large stockpot
    1 colander with handles

Bake

    1 round cake pan 8"
    1 square cake pan 9"
    Cake rings 6" + 8"
    1 loaf pan
    1 12-cup muffin pan
    A few silicon molds – any shape
    Waterproof digital thermometer
    Cooking torch
    2 baking sheets
    Silicone baking mats
    Parchment paper
    Wax paper
    16-inch piping bags + tips
    Palette knife

Recipes

Look for the recipes that fit you or your guests' needs using the following acronyms: R (raw) V (vegan: plant-based diet) VEG (vegetarian: diet excluding animal source products but allowing milk, butter, cheese and eggs) DF (dairy-free) GF (gluten-free) NF (nut-free).

morning   17

maple cranberry granola		V	VEG	DF	GF		18
berry smoothie delight	R	V	VEG	DF	GF		20
granola - dark chocolate + seeds		V	VEG	DF	GF	NF	22
chocolate parfait - vegan granola + power bliss balls		V	VEG	DF	GF		24
madeleines			VEG				26
chia pudding		V	VEG	DF	GF		30
chia pudding + mango sorbet		V	VEG	DF	GF		32
chia & chocolate		V	VEG	DF	GF		34
coconut granola		V	VEG	DF	GF		36
financiers			VEG		GF		38
super breakfast bowl	R	V	VEG	DF	GF		40
coconut oatmeal + sautéed peach		V	VEG	DF	GF		44
pear + apple jam		V	VEG	DF	GF	NF	48
oatmeal bowl - almond + pear + bliss balls		V	VEG	DF	GF		50
cinnamon apple parfait		V	VEG	DF	GF		54
coconut & dark chocolate granola		V	VEG	DF	GF	NF	56
banana bread			VEG		GF		58
wild berry cake			VEG				60
date cake			VEG		GF	NF	62
yogurt cake - apple + chocolate			VEG			NF	64

super food   66

breakfast sandwich - roasted tomatoes + avocado + mozzarella		VEG			NF	68
avocado tartines	V	VEG	DF		NF	70
burrata tartines		VEG			NF	71
guacamole	R V	VEG	DF	GF	NF	72
pesto	V	VEG	DF	GF		74
frittata - spinach + basil		VEG	DF	GF		76
roasted tomatoes	V	VEG	DF	GF	NF	78
oeuf cocotte - sautée veggies + roasted tomatoes		VEG	DF	GF	NF	80
oeuf cocotte - mushroom + ham				GF	NF	82
oeuf au plat - sautéed mushrooms		VEG	DF	GF	NF	84
poached egg + avocado toast		VEG	DF		NF	86
lentil salad + hard-boiled egg		VEG	DF	GF	NF	88
kale & Brussel sprouts	V	VEG	DF	GF		90
pistachio dressing	R V	VEG	DF	GF		92
multigrain flatbread + arugula		VEG		GF		92
summer chicken salad				GF		94
wild rice salad + pistachio dressing	V	VEG	DF	GF		98
rice salad + sun dried tomatoes	V	VEG	DF	GF		100
black rice salad + roasted eggplant	V	VEG	DF	GF		102

shine | 11

almond dressing	V VEG DF GF	105
quinoa salad + almond dressing	V VEG DF GF	106
garden salad – kale + herbs	V VEG DF GF	108
tuna + shrimp tartare	NF	110
Caribbean ceviche – mango + vanilla	DF GF NF	112
butternut squash soup – coconut + seeds	V VEG DF GF NF	114
garden soup & pearl couscous	V VEG DF NF	116
pea & mint soup	V VEG DF GF NF	118
leek & potato soup	V VEG DF GF NF	120
miso soup	V VEG DF GF NF	122
lentil & kale soup	V VEG DF GF NF	124
kale & bean soup	V VEG DF GF NF	126
tomato soup	V VEG DF GF	128
creamy tomato pasta	V VEG DF NF	130
shrimp stir-fry + rice noodles	DF GF	132
vegan curry & lemon quinoa	V VEG DF GF	134
zucchini shooters	VEG GF	136
vegan fajitas – black bean puree + guacamole	V VEG DF NF	138
roasted Brussel sprouts	V VEG DF GF NF	140
avocado & kale pasta	V VEG DF NF	142
lemon pasta + burrata cheese	VEG NF	144
pesto pasta + parmesan tuiles	VEG	146
coconut poached fish + mushroom risotto & truffle oil	GF NF	148
dill salmon + almond quinoa	DF GF	150
lemon butter trout + mashed potatoes	GF	152
oven baked halibut + coconut rice	DF GF	154
grilled shrimp + red bell pepper dip	DF GF NF	156
chicken fajitas + guacamole	DF NF	158
chicken tikka masala	DF GF	160
simple breaded chicken + ratatouille	DF	162

gourmandise — 164

just almond butter	R V VEG DF GF	166
magic bliss		168
dark chocolate + granola	R V VEG DF GF	170
sesame bliss balls	V VEG DF GF	172
power bliss balls – matcha + pistachio	V VEG DF GF	174
shiny chocolate		176
pure coconut + chocolate	V VEG DF GF NF	178
coconut magic bliss	GF	180
raw granola bar	R V VEG DF GF	182
vegan cookies	V VEG DF GF NF	184
vegan cake	V VEG DF GF	186
chocolate cups	VEG GF NF	188
moelleux au chocolat	VEG NF	192
caramelized pear & chocolate crumble	VEG	194
creamy vanilla panna cotta + wild berry compote	GF NF	196
nutella® mousse	VEG GF	198
white & dark chocolate bites	VEG GF NF	202

italian meringue	VEG	GF NF	204
unconventional lemon tart			206
wild berry tart			208
macarons - basic recipe	VEG	GF	212
macarons nutella®	VEG	GF	214
macarons fraise	VEG	GF	216
macarons pistache	VEG	GF	218
macarons vanilla	VEG	GF	220

Be content with what you have;
Rejoice in the way things are.
When you realize there is nothing lacking,
The whole world belongs to you.

— LAOZI

Reuse | Repurpose

Too much goes to waste in the kitchen! The recipes that follow have been carefully thought out to help reduce waste by using ingredients in several meals.

Being organized is the key to success. Plan ahead, make notes and create weekly menus to have an overview of what the week will look like.

Planning goes a long way. It is essential for effortless, efficient purchase of needed ingredients that will build your week's meals.

Read the recipe entirely first. Anticipate and make ahead anything that can save you time later on.

Work in a clean and clutter-free environment. Make room around you and clean up as you go. Prefer fresh, organic and top quality ingredients for the most taste and nutrients.

Fresh herbs will make the difference in your dish. Frozen basil and garlic cubes are amazing too!

> Things you take for granted, someone else is praying for.
>
> - MARLAN RICO LEE

morning. *noun.*

the period of time from sunrise to noon.

Break the fast.
Breakfast is essential for a happy mind,
healthy you and a
well-balanced day.

Maple Cranberry Granola

yields 6 to 8 cups

2 cups (180 gr) rolled oats
1 cup (30 gr) brown rice crisp cereal
1 cup (110 gr) whole walnuts
½ cup (83 gr) brown rice flour
½ cup (120 ml) maple syrup

½ tsp salt
1 tsp cinnamon
¼ tsp ginger powder
¼ cup (60 ml) olive oil
½ cup (60 gr) dried cranberries

Preheat the oven to 350F / 180C.
Line a baking sheet with parchment paper or a silicone baking mat.
Combine all the ingredients in a large mixing bowl.
Toss to coat using a wooden spatula.
Spread the mixture evenly on the prepared baking sheet pressing firmly.
Bake 25 minutes in the preheated oven or until golden - do not stir while baking!
Remove from the oven.
Let cool completely before breaking up any large clumps.
Keep in an airtight container for up to 1 month.

vegan | gluten-free

Berry Smoothie Delight
+ granola

serves 1

2 medium bananas
½ cup (55 gr) frozen berries
1 tsp peanut butter powder
¼ cup (60 ml) almond milk

½ tsp chia seeds
+ maple cranberry granola – recipe p. 18
+ almond butter – recipe p. 166

Slice 1 banana and place in the freezer for 15 minutes.
Blend the frozen berries, peanut butter powder, almond milk and frozen banana in a blender until smooth – or use a hand blender.
Stir in the chia seeds.
Slice 1 banana lengthwise. Place in the bottom of a serving jar.
Top with the smoothie. Garnish with fresh granola and almond butter.

raw | vegan | gluten-free

Granola
dark chocolate + seeds

2 ½ cups (225 gr) rolled oats
2 tbsp sesame seeds
2 tbsp pumpkin seeds
½ tsp vanilla powder

¼ cup (60 gr) coconut oil
¼ cup (60 gr) maple syrup
1 cup (175 gr) dark chocolate chips
½ of ¼ tsp salt

Preheat the oven to 375F / 190C.
Line a baking sheet with parchment paper or a silicone baking mat.
Combine oats, sesame seeds, pumpkin seeds, salt, and vanilla powder in a large mixing bowl.
Stir in the oil + maple syrup. Toss to blend using a wooden spatula.
Spread the mixture evenly on the prepared sheet.
Bake in the preheated oven for 25 minutes or until golden.
Remove from the oven and stir in the chocolate chips.
Let the granola cool completely. It will harden as it cools down.
Keep in an airtight container for a few weeks.

vegan | gluten-free | nut-free

Chocolate Parfait
vegan granola + power bliss balls

serves 4

vegan granola:
8 whole pitted dates
1 tsp almond butter - recipe p. 166
1 tbsp coconut oil
¼ cup (20 gr) coconut flakes
½ cup (45 gr) rolled oats
¼ cup (25 gr) sliced almonds
1 tbsp quinoa
1 tsp maple syrup

smoothie:
2 bananas - frozen
1 whole pitted date
1 tbsp unsweetened cocoa powder
1 tbsp peanut butter powder
1 tsp vanilla powder
¼ cup (60 ml) almond milk
+ coconut flakes, buckwheat, flaxseeds, chia seeds
+ power bliss balls – recipe p. 174

To make the granola, pulse all the ingredients in a food processor until combined.
Spoon some of the granola in the bottom of 4 small glass jars. Set aside in the freezer.
To make the smoothie, combine all the ingredients in a blender - or use a hand blender.
Place on the granola.
Add the toppings or more granola.
Serve immediately!

vegan | gluten-free

Madeleines
heart of Nutella®

makes 18

3 eggs – free-range organic
⅔ cup (130 gr) granulated sugar
¼ cup (60 ml) milk
1 tsp vanilla extract
1 ½ cups (210 gr) flour

1 tbsp baking powder
¾ stick (80 gr) butter
Nutella® – cold
+ steel madeleine pan
+ cooking spray

The madeleines will form their "bump" with the temperature shock: the dough will need to be refrigerated overnight and baked in a hot preheated oven.
The traditional steel pan will give the perfect texture to your madeleines.

Start by melting the butter in the microwave.
Place the eggs and sugar in a large mixing bowl. Whisk vigorously until white and bubbly – 1 minute.
Stir in the milk and vanilla extract. Add the flour and baking powder. Whisk from the center out in a slow circular motion until smooth and incorporated. Mix in the butter last.
Refrigerate in an airtight container overnight or at least for 2 hours until cold.
Preheat the oven to 430F / 220C. Lightly coat a steel madeleine pan with non-stick cooking spray.
Transfer the batter to a pastry bag with no tip. Cut off the end and pipe ⅓ of the batter into each cavities. Spoon about 1 tsp of cold Nutella® in the center. Cover with more batter.
Bake in the preheated oven for 10 minutes or until golden.
Let cool completely before removing from the pan.
Transfer to an airtight container. Store at room temperature for up to 4 days.

vegetarian

Proust's muse, no wonder why! These unique little buttery cakes are perfect for busy mornings or in the afternoon with a cup of tea! Browned and crispy on the outside, so moist and soft on the inside, they taste amazing plain! Try them with a coat of your favorite jam too!

s i m p l i c i t y . *noun.*

freedom from complexity.

Ten thousand flowers in spring,
the moon in autumn,
a cool breeze in summer,
snow in winter.
If your mind isn't clouded by
unnecessary things,
this is the best season of
your life.

— WU-MEN

Chia Pudding

serves 4

¼ cup (40 gr) chia seeds
1 cup (240 ml) almond milk
1 vanilla bean
maple syrup

Whisk together chia seeds and almond milk in a bowl.
Cut the vanilla bean lengthwise with a small curved knife.
Scrape the seeds out and add to the chia mixture with 2 tbsp maple syrup.
Stir to combine.
Refrigerate 30 minutes or overnight stirring occasionally.
Spoon the chia pudding into 4 glass jars or any other bowl.
Top with 1 tbsp maple syrup - it will sink to the bottom.
Serve immediately!

vegan | gluten-free

Chia Pudding
+ mango sorbet

serves 4

2 bananas – frozen and sliced
2 cups (480 gr) mango – frozen and diced
½ cup (120 ml) almond milk

chia pudding – recipe p. 30
+ dark chocolate & seeds granola - recipe p. 22
+ 1 fresh mango

Make the chia pudding. Divide among 4 glass dishes.
To make the sorbet, blend all the ingredients in a blender – or use a hand blender.
Place on the chia pudding.
Top with chocolate granola and fresh mango.
Serve immediately!

vegan | gluten-free

Chia & Chocolate

serves 4

chia pudding - recipe p. 30
vegan cookies - recipe p. 184
chocolate smoothie - recipe p. 24

Place some raw vegan cookie crumbs in the bottom of 4 glass dishes.
Top with chia pudding. Refrigerate for 15 minutes.
Make the chocolate smoothie. Add on to the chia pudding.
Garnish with vegan cookie crumbs and serve immediately.
Keep in the fridge for up to 2 days.

vegan | gluten-free

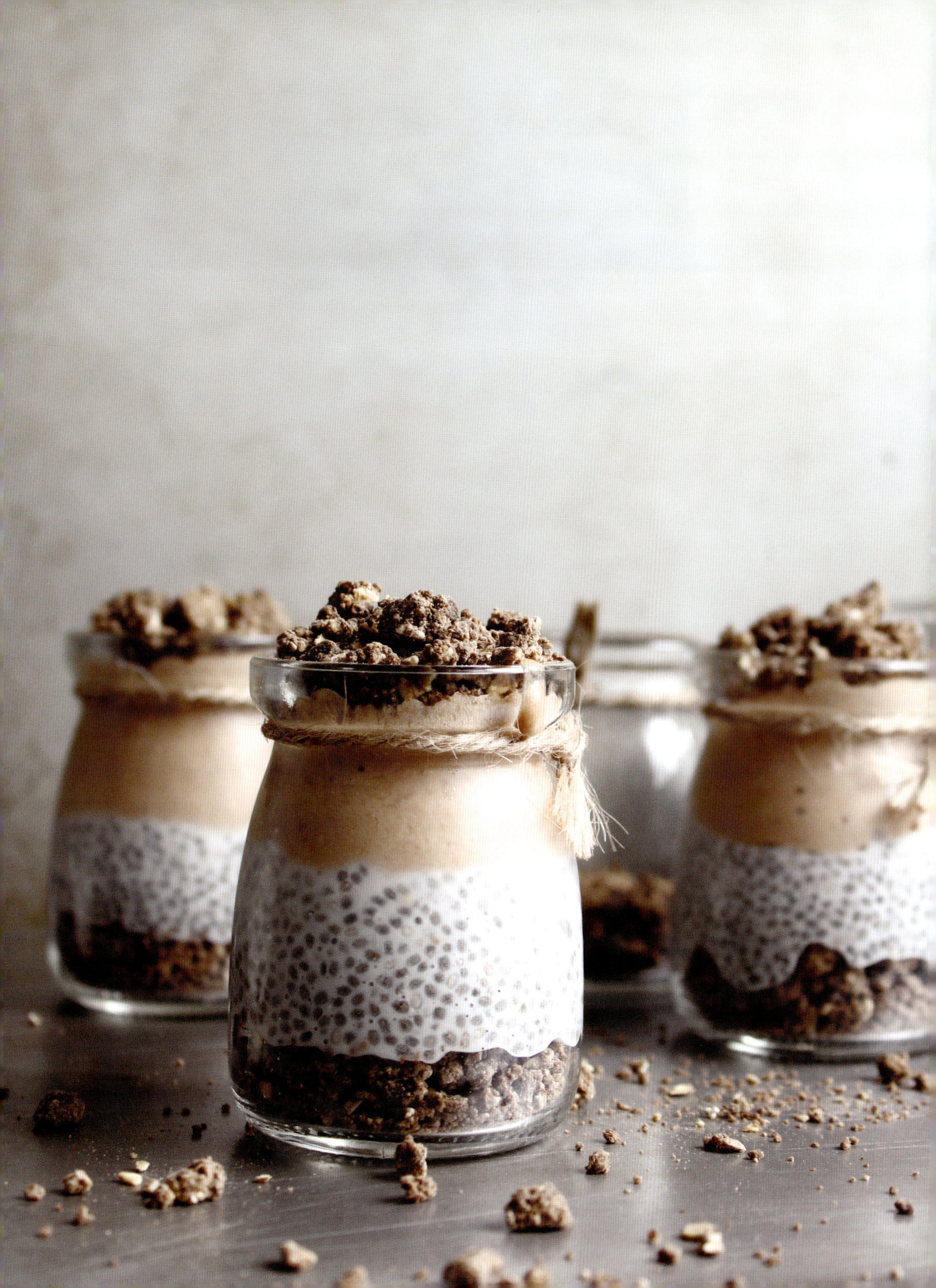

Coconut Granola

1 ¼ cup (100 gr) coconut flakes
1 cup (140 gr) whole almonds
⅓ cup (45 gr) pumpkin seeds
1 ½ cup (135 gr) old fashioned oats

⅔ cup (160 gr) almond butter - recipe p. 166
⅓ cup (80 ml) maple syrup
1 tbsp vanilla extract

Line a 9-inch square cake pan with parchment paper.
Chop the almonds in a food processor. Fold in the rest of the ingredients.
Press the mixture firmly into the prepared pan.
Refrigerate overnight or place in the freezer for a few hours.
Transfer to a glass jar or airtight container.
Keep at room temperature for up to a month.

vegan | gluten-free

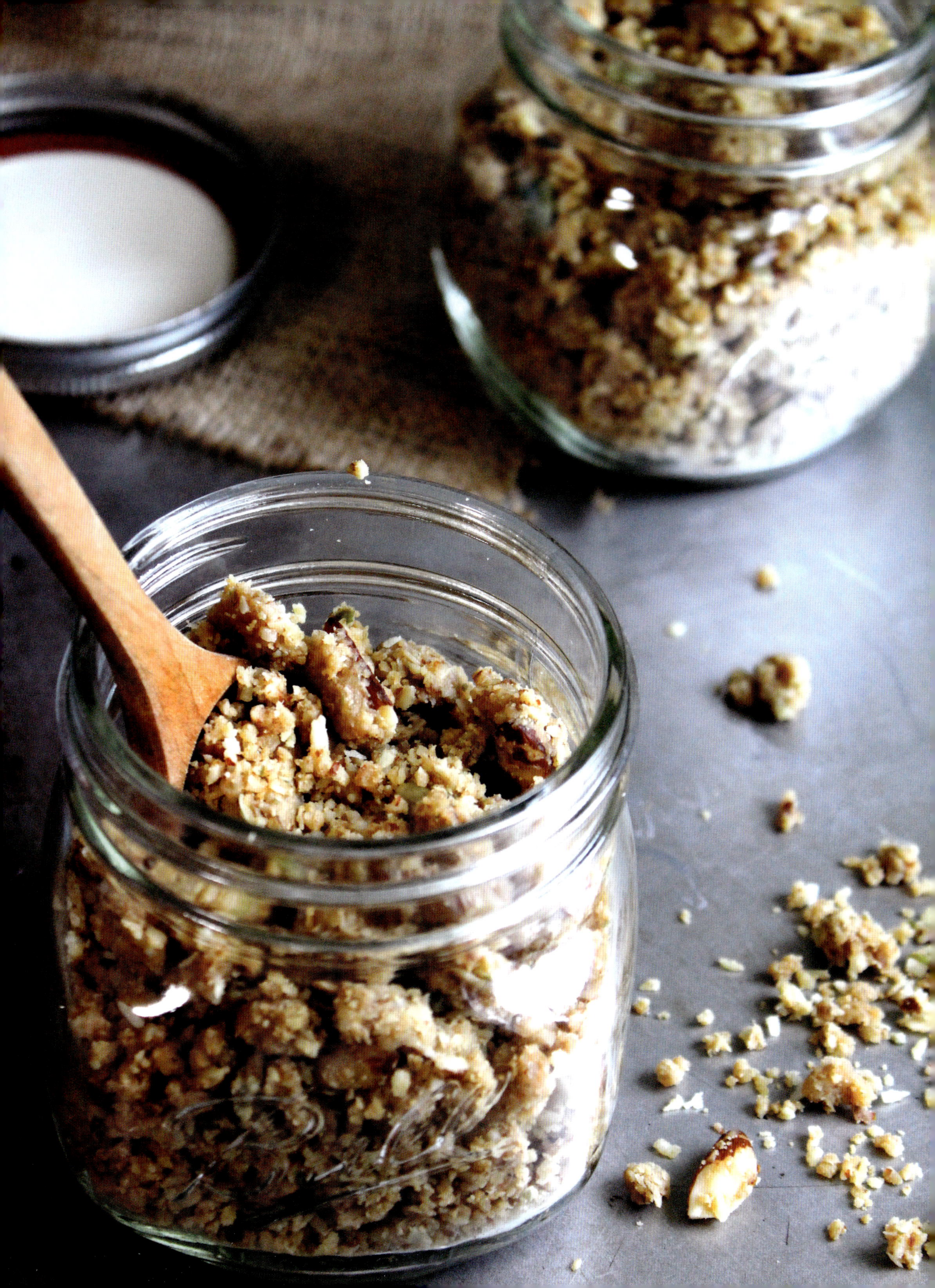

Financiers

Easy and quick to make, these traditional French almond cakes are light, moist and have a unique taste. Replace the flour with brown rice flour for a gluten-free version.

makes 25

3 egg whites
1 cup (125 gr) powdered sugar
¾ cup (75 gr) almond flour
⅓ cup (45 gr) flour

½ cup (100 gr) butter
1 tsp vanilla powder
+ rectangular silicone mold – 20 cavities

Preheat the oven to 390F / 200C.
Make a "beurre noisette" (brown butter): place the butter in a small saucepan.
Cook until golden brown stirring constantly with a whisk. Transfer to a bowl. Set aside to cool.
Combine the egg whites, powdered sugar, almond flour and flour in a large bowl.
Stir in the brown butter. Spoon the batter into the mold - use a piping bag for easy pour.
Bake in the preheated oven for 15 minutes or until nicely golden and a toothpick inserted comes out dry and clean.
Let the cakes cool and store in an airtight container for a few days at room temperature!

vegetarian | gluten-free

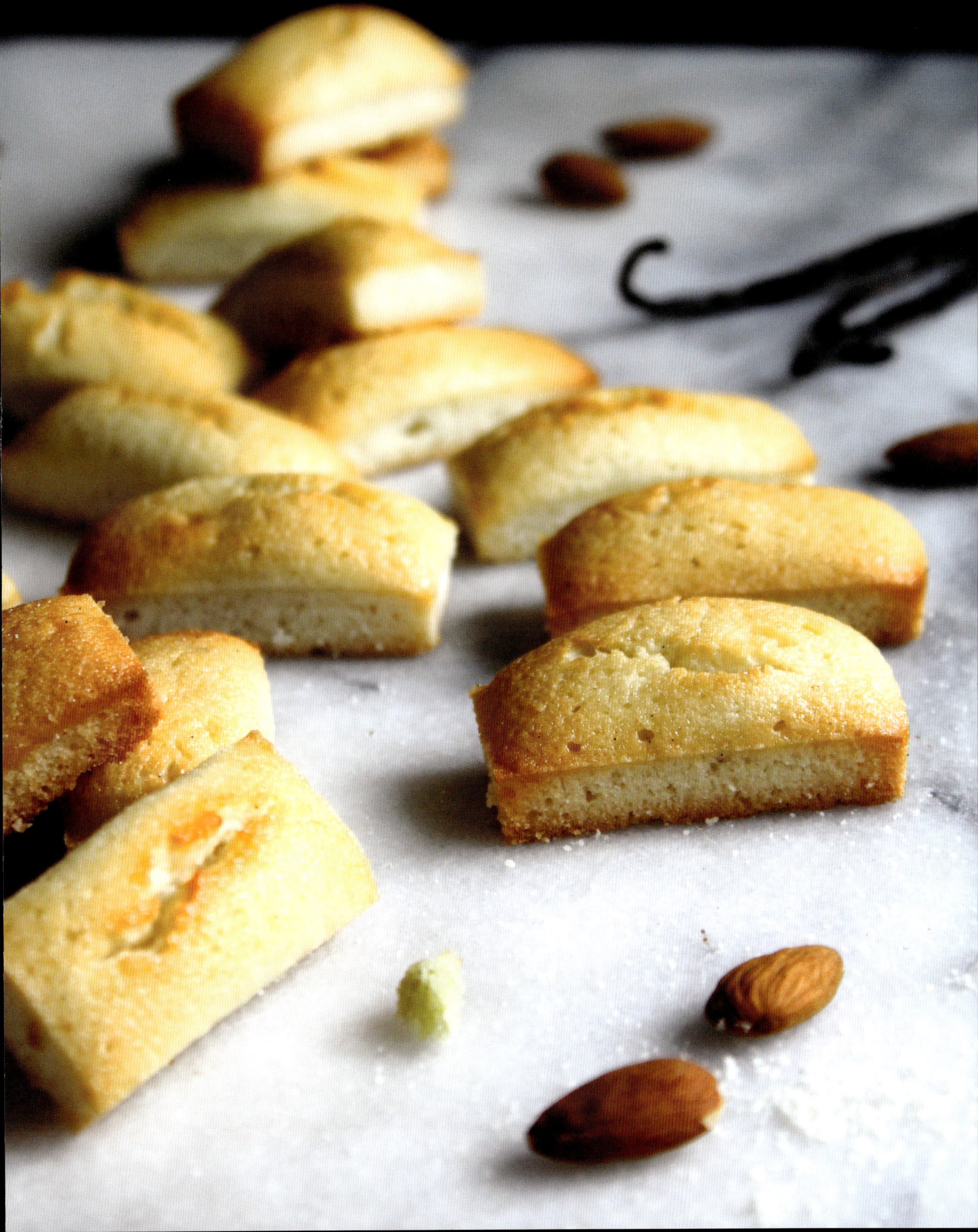

Super Breakfast Bowl

vanilla coconut smoothie
coconut granola
bliss balls
fruits

serves 2

vanilla coconut smoothie:
1 banana – sliced and frozen
½ cup (120 ml) coconut milk - cold
⅓ cup (80 ml) almond milk
1 tsp vanilla powder

+ 1 banana - sliced
+ coconut granola - recipe p. 36
+ sesame bliss balls - recipe p. 172
+ 1 cup (100 gr) frozen berries
+ chia seeds

To make the smoothie, blend all ingredients in a blender until smooth and creamy
- or use a hand blender.
Divide among 2 serving bowls.
Add the toppings or replace with your favorite ones!

raw | vegan | gluten-free

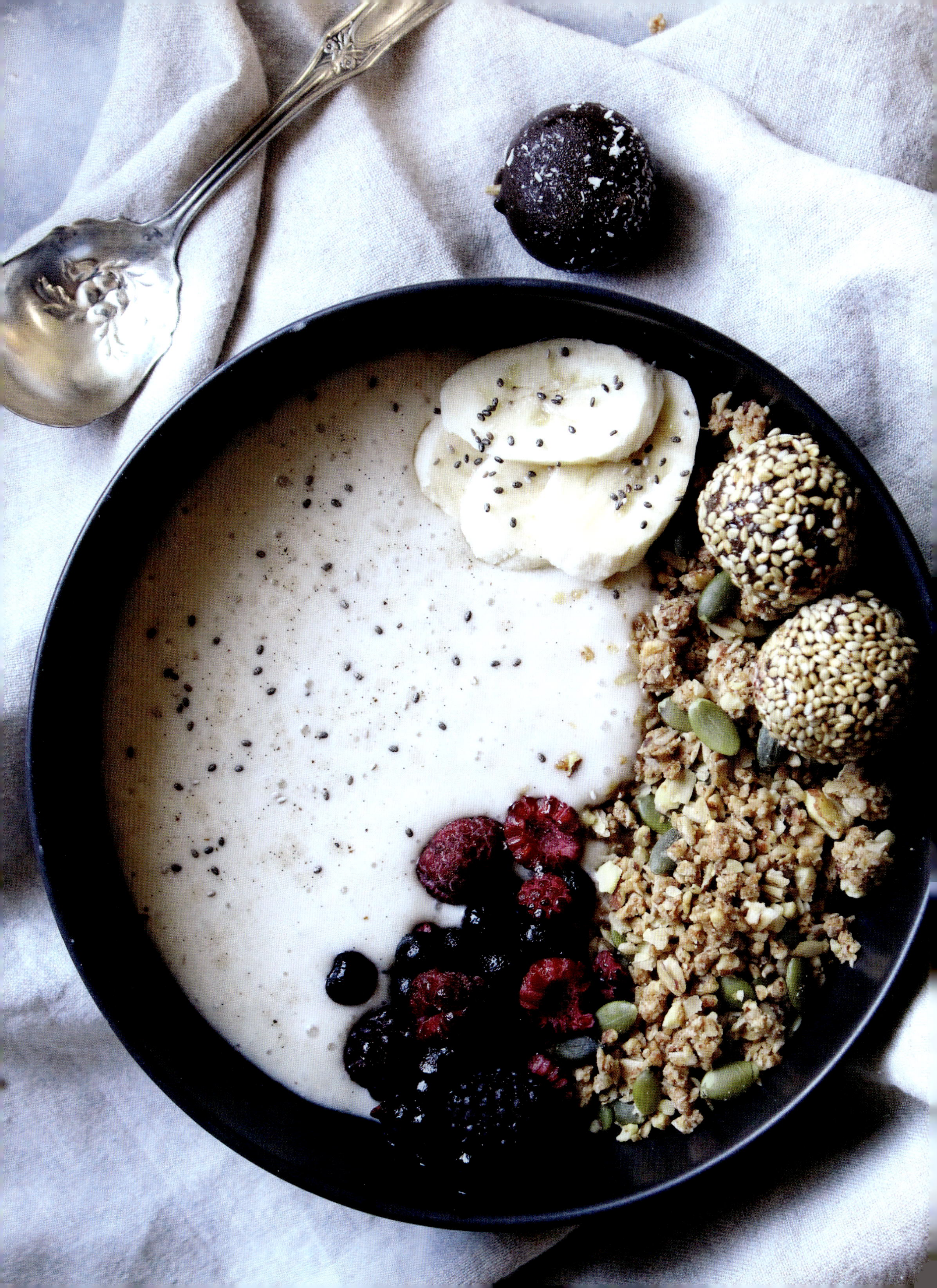

sugar . noun.

a sweet crystalline substance, white when pure, consisting essentially of sucrose obtained from various plants but mainly sugar cane and sugar beet, and used as a sweetener.

All types of sugar provide more or less the same amount of calories and will all be turned into glucose to fuel your body. No matter what kind of sugar, consume in moderation and keep in mind that the healthiest of all is fresh whole fruit!

Here is just an overview of the most natural sweeteners.

<u>Dates and figs:</u> raw, vegan, great source of potassium, copper, iron, magnesium and vitamin B6.

<u>Coconut sugar:</u> raw, vegan, rich in mineral, iron, zinc, calcium, potassium and antioxidants. It contains 70 to 79 % sucrose and only 3 to 9 % of each fructose and glucose.

<u>Maple syrup:</u> vegan, loaded in nutrient, great source of minerals, magnesium, calcium, potassium, zinc and antioxidants. The darker the color, the better!

<u>Raw honey:</u> rich source of vitamins and enzymes, powerful antioxidant. Prefer a darker color which will be richer in flavor. If not raw, it has been pasteurized and loses its health benefits.

<u>Raw cane sugar:</u> wholesome sugar that has not been blended, colored or chemically refined.

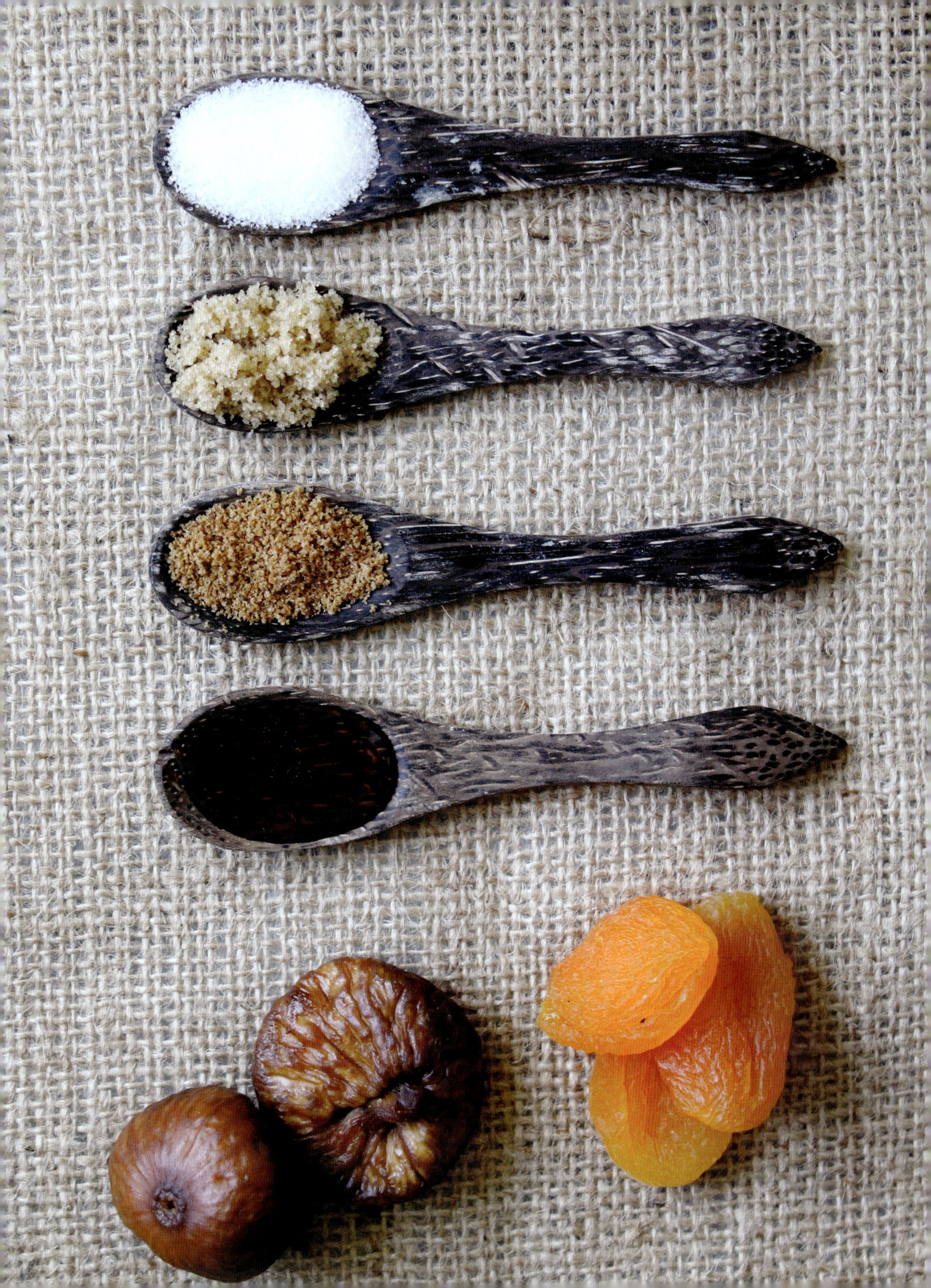

Coconut Oatmeal
sautéed peach

serves 2

½ cup (45 gr) rolled oats
¼ cup (20 gr) unsweetened coconut flakes
1 ½ cup (360 ml) almond milk
½ cup (120 ml) water
coconut oil

1 organic peach – sliced into wedges
+ chopped hazelnuts
+ maple syrup
+ your favorite granola

Place the oats, coconut flakes, almond milk and water in a container with a lid. Refrigerate overnight.
Place the oat mixture in a medium saucepan. Bring to a boil and cook for 5 minutes.
Heat the coconut oil in a small skillet over medium heat. Stir in the sliced peach.
Cook for 8 minutes stirring occasionally with a wooden spatula until soft and nicely browned.
Remove from the heat, stir in the maple syrup.
Divide the oats among two serving bowls. Thin with more milk if it's too thick.
Garnish with warm sautéed peach, granola and chopped hazelnuts.
Top with more maple syrup if needed!

vegan | gluten-free

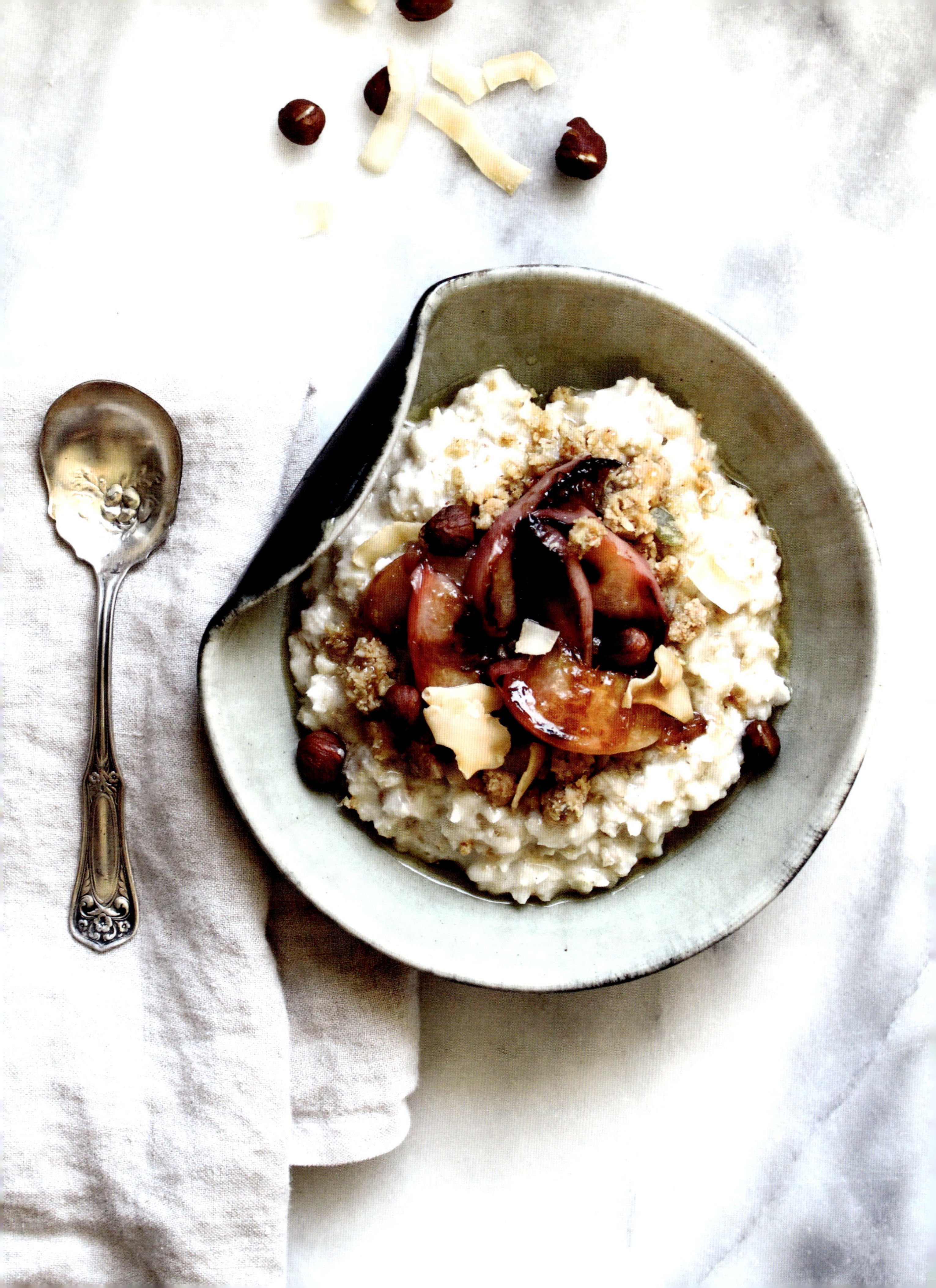

willpower. *noun.*

the ability to control your own
thoughts and the way in which
you behave.

raw power
discipline
determination

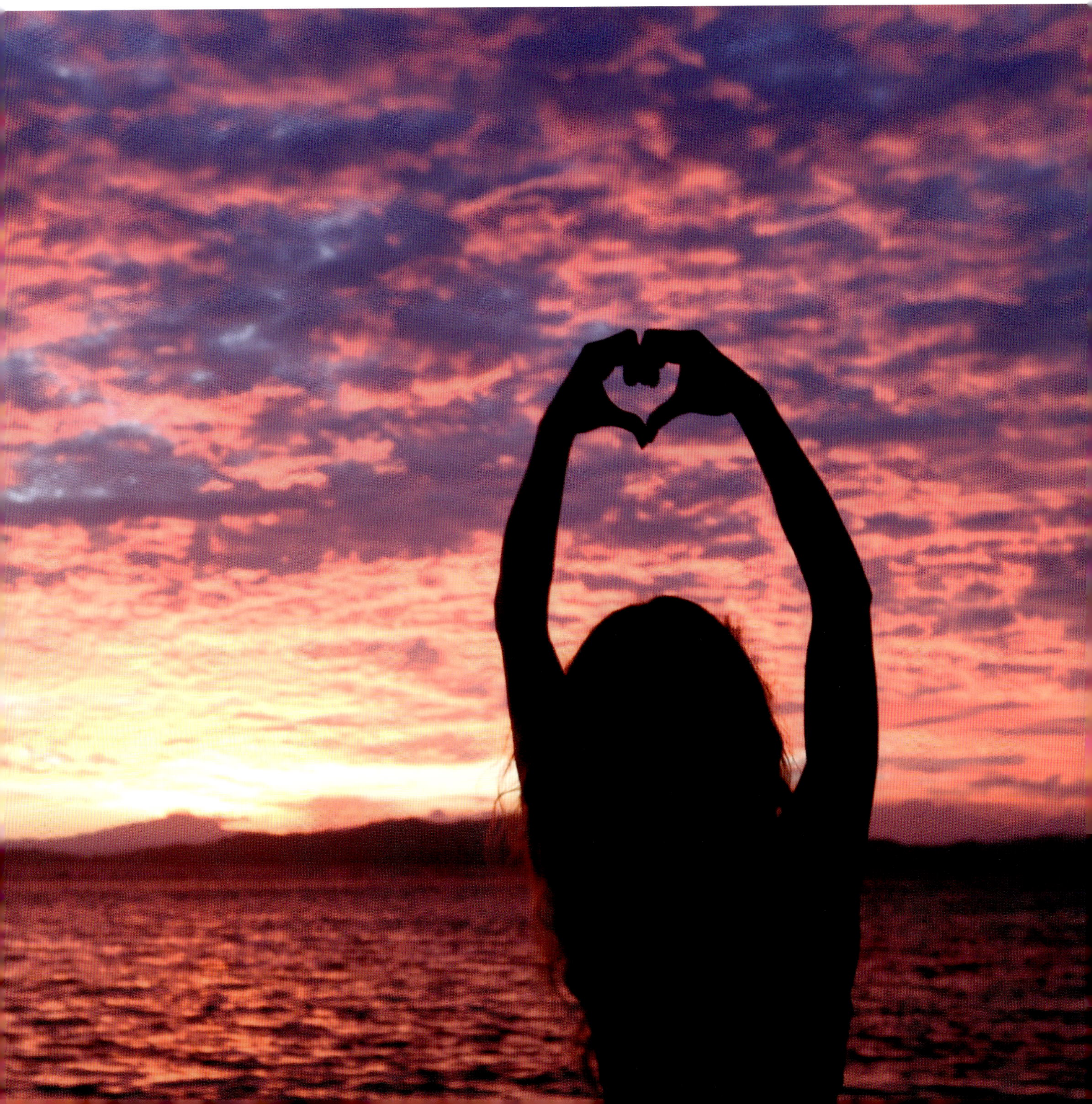

Pear & Apple Jam

makes 1 jar

3 ripe Bartlett pears – peeled and diced
2 Golden Delicious apples – peeled and diced
1 cup (200 gr) granulated sugar + 1 tbsp

1 vanilla bean
1 tsp spiced rum

Day 1 –
Heat 1 tbsp sugar and 1 tsp water in a large skillet over medium heat. Add the diced fruits.
Cook until golden, tossing occasionally – about 5 minutes.
Transfer to a large container. Stir in the rest of the ingredients. Cover and refrigerate overnight.

Day 2 –
Quickly pulse the fruit mixture in a food processor.
Transfer to a heavy pot. Place over medium to low heat.
Bring to a boil and cook until thickened, whisking frequently – about 7 minutes.

Transfer to a glass jar. Let cool completely.
Serve or store in the fridge for up to 2 months.

vegan | gluten-free | nut-free

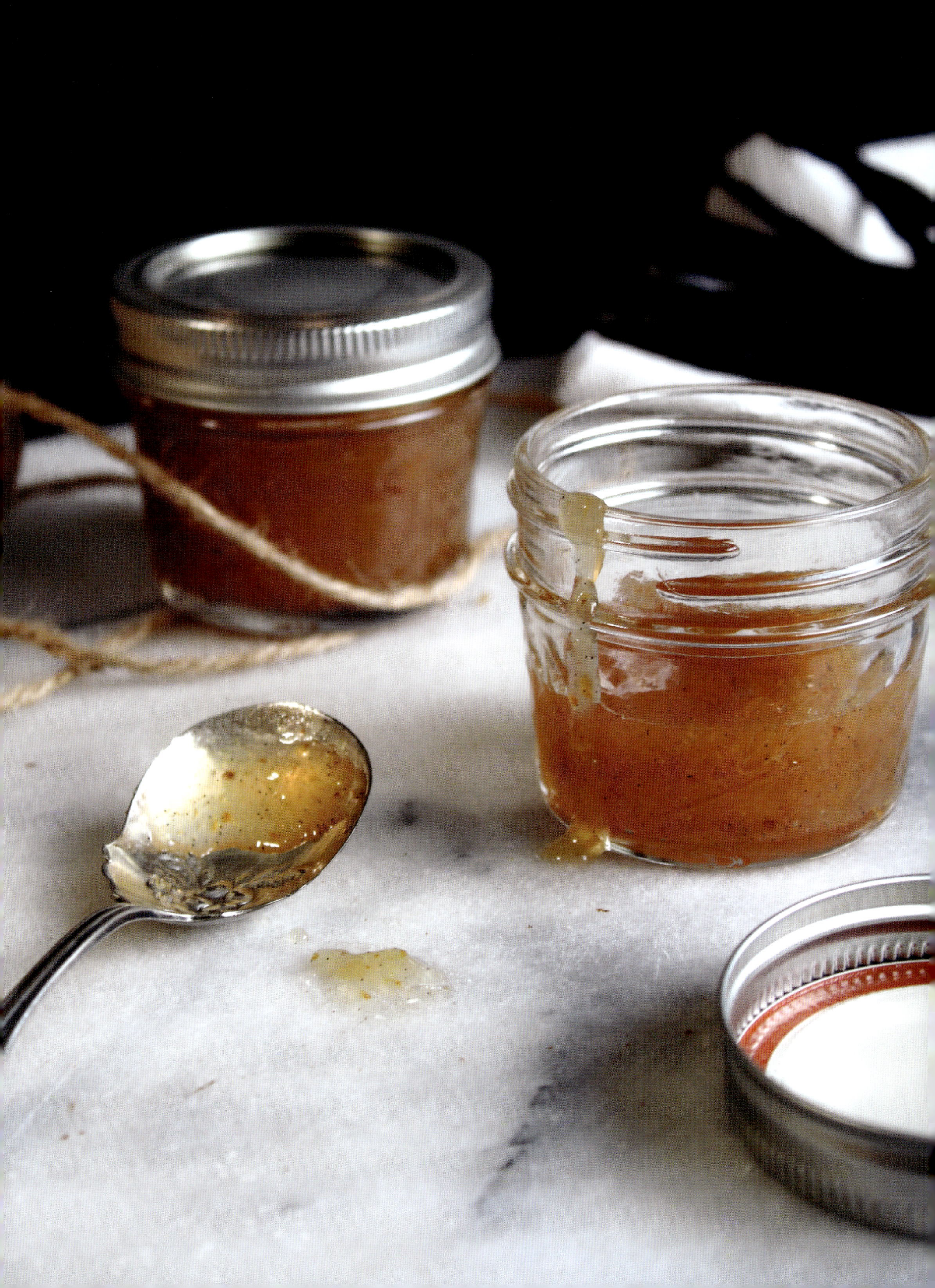

Oatmeal Bowl
almond + pear + bliss balls

serves 2

½ cup (45 gr) old-fashioned oats
1 cup (240 ml) almond milk
1 cup (240 ml) water
pear & apple jam - recipe p. 48
½ cup (60 gr) sliced almonds

almond butter - recipe p. 166
maple syrup
1 pear - diced
+ cinnamon
+ dark chocolate bliss balls - recipe p. 170

Place oats, almond milk and water in a small saucepan over medium heat. Bring to a boil.
Reduce the heat to low and cook for 10 minutes. Remove from the heat.
Stir in 1 tbsp of pear and apple jam - or any other sweeteners.
Divide among 2 serving bowls. Add extra almond milk if you like it creamier.
Quickly toast the sliced almonds: place them in a small skillet over medium heat.
Shake the pan frequently until browned – about 2 minutes. Set aside.
Whisk together 2 tbsp of each: almond butter, water, maple syrup. Place on the oats.
Garnish with diced pears, toasted almonds and a few chocolate bliss balls. Sprinkle with cinnamon.
Serve immediately.

vegan | gluten-free

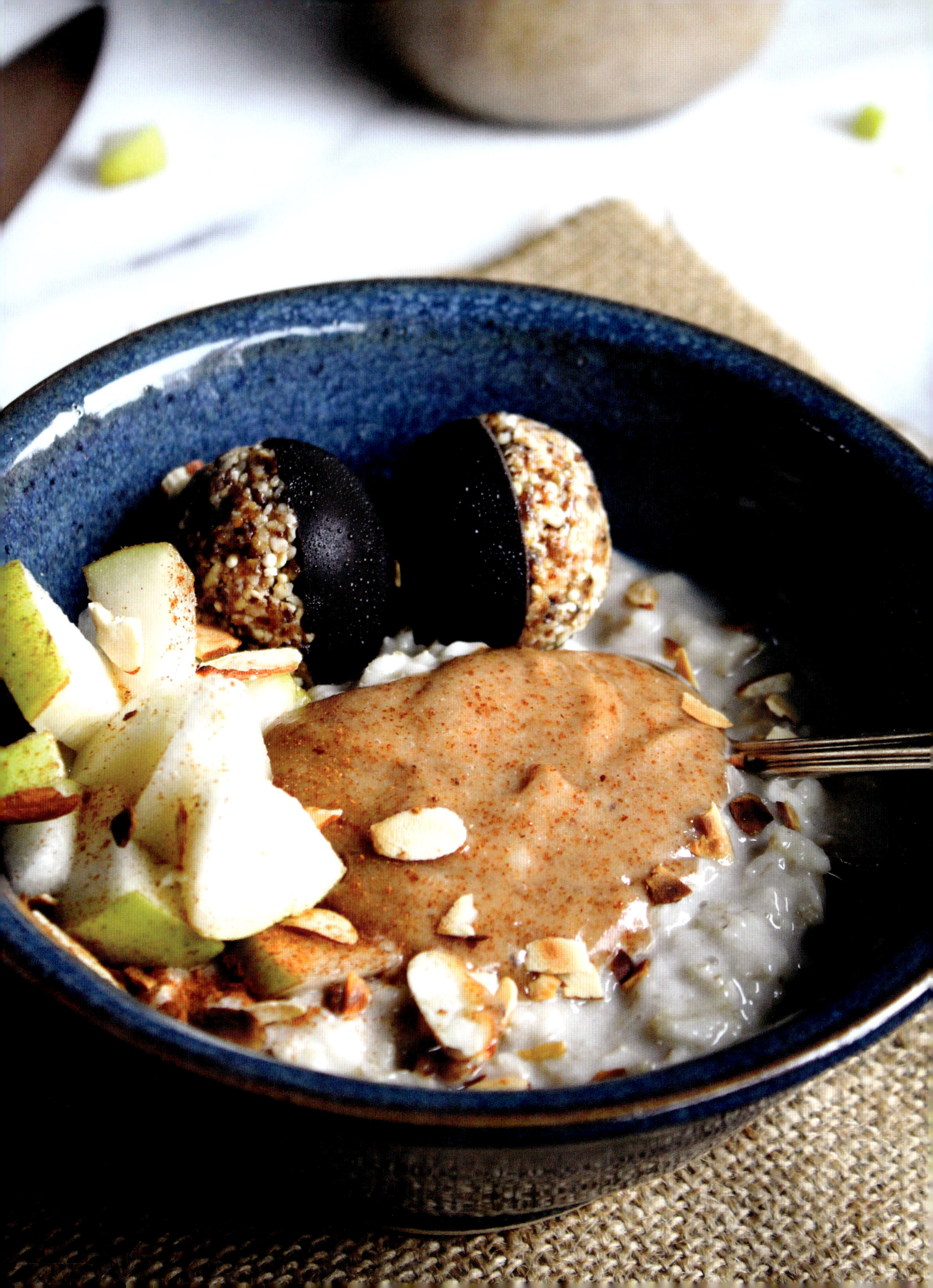

mindful. *adj.*

being conscious, aware.

Mindfulness means paying attention in a particular way: on purpose, in the present moment, and non-judgmentally.

— JON KABAT-ZINN

shine | 53

Cinnamon Apple Parfait

serves 2

1 Golden Delicious apple - cored and diced
1 tsp coconut oil
1 tsp coconut sugar
¼ tsp cinnamon

2 bananas - sliced and frozen
½ cup (120 ml) unsweetened almond milk
1 tsp vanilla powder
+ maple cranberry granola - recipe p. 18

Place the apples and coconut oil in a skillet over medium heat.
Cook until soft, about 6 minutes. Add the sugar and cook 2 minutes more or until golden.
Remove from the pan. Stir in the cinnamon and let cool.
To make the smoothie, blend the bananas, almond milk and vanilla powder in a blender until smooth and creamy - or use a hand blender.
Place the caramelized apples in the bottom of 2 serving glass cups.
Top with the smoothie. Garnish with cranberry granola.
Serve immediately!

vegan | gluten-free

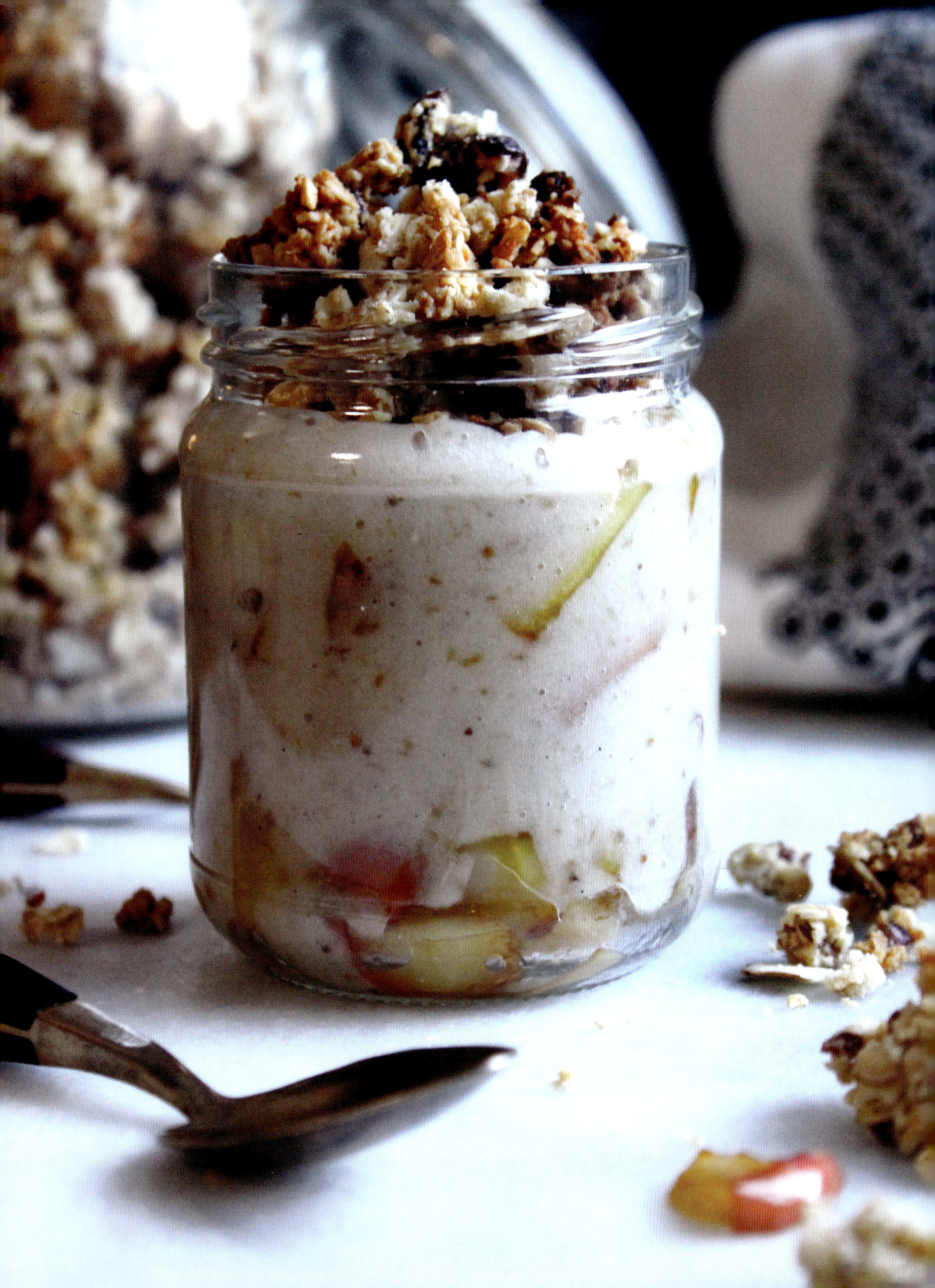

Coconut & Dark Chocolate Granola

2 cups (180 gr) rolled oats
¼ cup (40 gr) raw buckwheat groats
¼ cup (35 gr) flaxseed
¼ cup (40 gr) chia seeds

½ cup (45 gr) toasted coconut chips
½ cup (120 ml) maple syrup
1 tbsp coconut oil
1 cup (175 gr) dark chocolate chips

Preheat the oven to 375F / 190C.
Line a baking sheet with parchment paper or a silicone baking mat.
Combine oats, buckwheat, flaxseeds, chia seeds and coconut chips in a large bowl.
Add the maple syrup and coconut oil, stir well.
Spread the mixture evenly on the prepared baking sheet.
Bake in the preheated oven for 30 minutes or until golden.
Remove from the oven and stir in the chocolate chips.
Let the granola cool completely before storing in a glass container.

vegan | gluten-free | nut-free

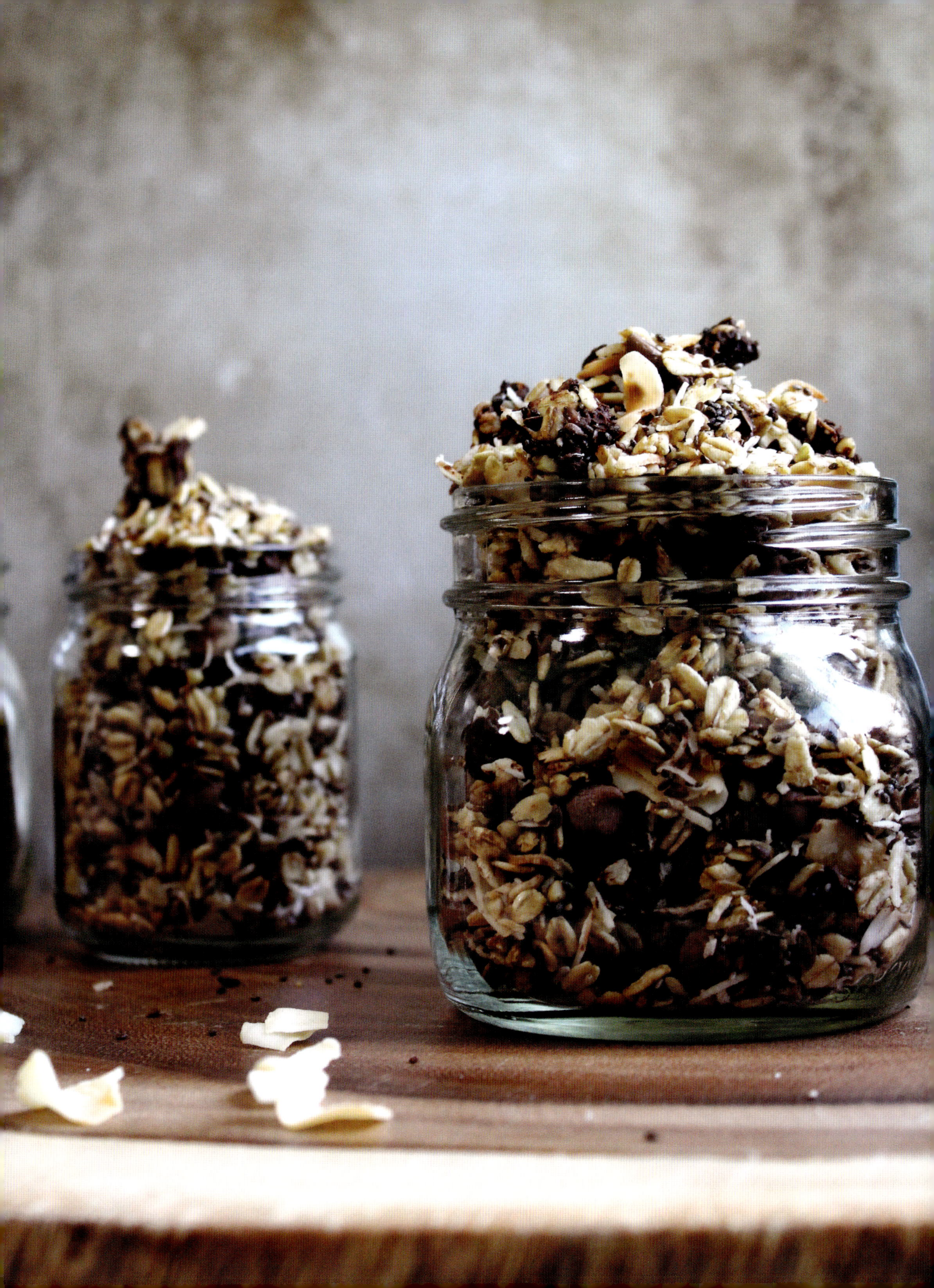

Banana Bread
+ spiced rum

makes 1

½ cup (60 gr) roughly chopped walnuts
½ cup (110 gr) butter – soft
⅔ cup (160 ml) maple syrup
2 eggs – free-range organic

2 large ripe bananas
3 tbsp spiced rum
1 ¼ cup (205 gr) brown rice flour
1 tsp baking powder

Preheat the oven to 390F / 200C.
Place the walnuts in a baking pan. Roast in the preheated oven for 10 minutes. Set aside.
Place the butter in the bowl of an electric mixer with the whip attachment. Beat for 1 minute.
Add the maple syrup and continue to mix until just combined – 30 seconds.
Stir in the eggs, one at a time mixing well after each addition.
Roughly mash the bananas with a fork. Add to the dough along with the rum.
Beat until just incorporated.
Stir in the flour, baking powder and walnuts on low speed until combined.
Coat a loaf pan with non-stick cooking spray. Add the dough and bake in the preheated oven for 45 minutes or until a toothpick inserted comes out clean and the cake has a nice golden color.
Let the bread cool before removing from the pan.
Serve warm or keep in the fridge for a few days.

vegetarian | gluten-free

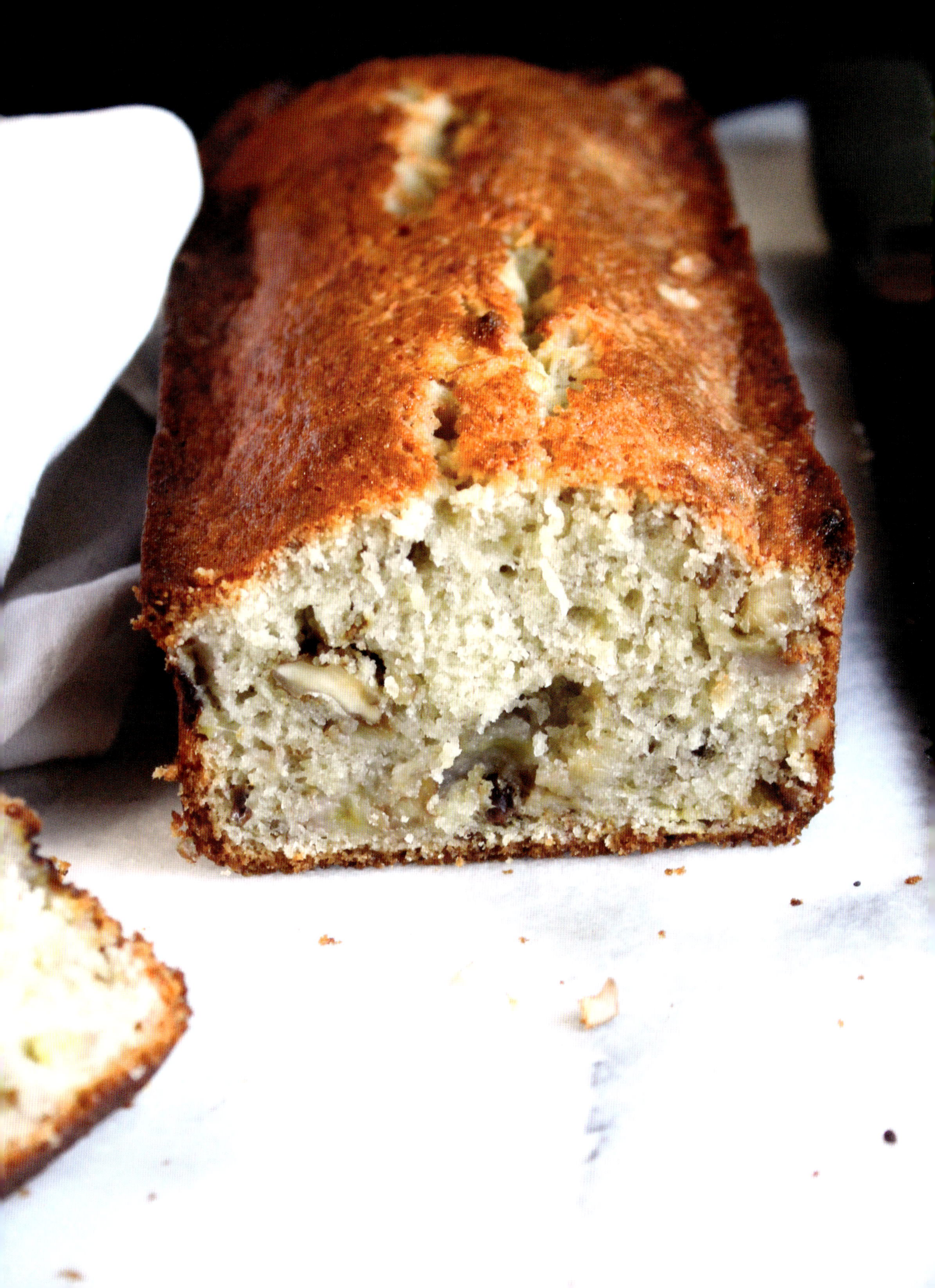

Wild Berry Bread

makes 1

½ cup (50 gr) almond flour
1 cup (140 gr) flour
1 tsp baking soda
1 ½ tsp baking powder
½ cup (100 gr) granulated sugar
½ cup (100 gr) butter - at room temperature

2 eggs – free-range organic
¾ cup (180 ml) almond milk
1 tsp vanilla extract
¼ cup (40 gr) almond paste – raw marzipan
1 cup (100 gr) frozen organic berries
½ cup (55 gr) sliced almonds + more to coat

Preheat the oven to 375F / 190C. Coat a loaf pan with non-stick cooking spray.
Combine almond flour, flour, baking soda, baking powder in a large mixing bowl.
Place the sugar and butter in the bowl of an electric mixer with the whip attachment.
Beat at medium speed until combined – 2 minutes.
Add the eggs, one at a time, beating a few seconds at medium speed in between each addition.
Mix in ½ of the flour mixture and then stir in the almond milk and vanilla extract on low speed.
Add the rest of the flour and mix until incorporated.
Place the almond paste in a small bowl and melt in the microwave - 10 seconds.
Stir in the batter along with the frozen berries and sliced almonds using a wooden spatula.
Pour the batter into the prepared pan. Sprinkle evenly with more sliced almonds.
Bake in the preheated oven for 50 minutes or until a toothpick inserted in the center comes out clean and the cake has a nice golden color.
Let the cake cool completely in the fridge before removing from the pan.
Store in the fridge for a few days.

vegetarian

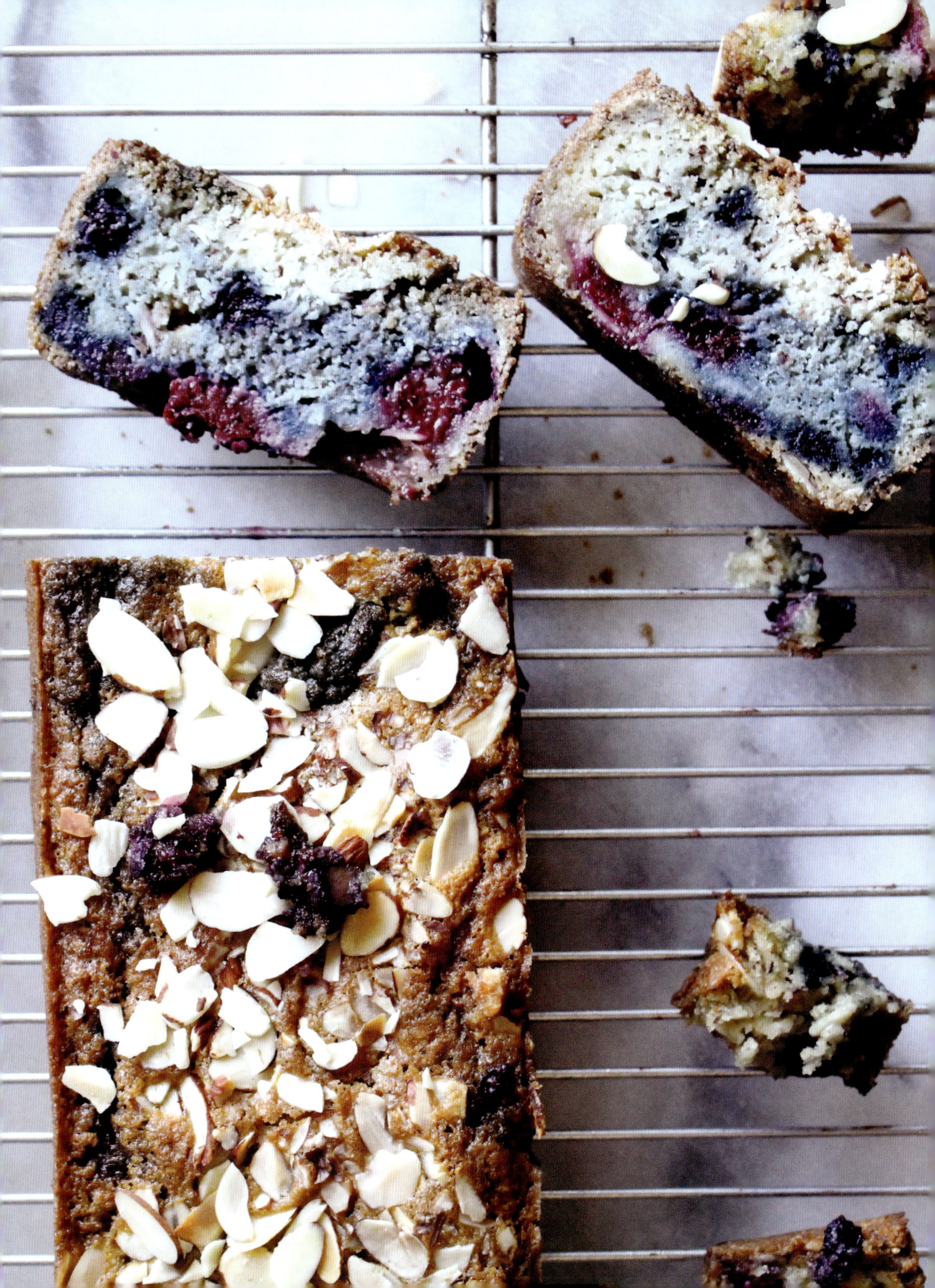

Date Cake

makes 1

1 ¾ cup (250 gr) whole pitted dates
1 ¼ cup (300 ml) boiling water
1 tsp baking soda
1 cup (150 gr) brown rice flour

1 tsp baking powder
¼ cup (60 gr) butter
½ cup (70 gr) coconut sugar
2 eggs – free-range organic

Preheat the oven to 390F / 200C. Coat a loaf pan with non-stick cooking spray.
Place the dates, boiling water and baking soda in the bowl of a food processor.
Leave undisturbed for 30 minutes.
Add the rest of the ingredients and pulse until combined – 30 seconds.
Transfer the dough to the prepared pan.
Bake in the preheated oven for 30 minutes or until a toothpick inserted comes out clean.
Let the cake cool before removing from the pan.
Serve warm or keep in the fridge for a few days.

vegetarian | gluten-free | nut-free

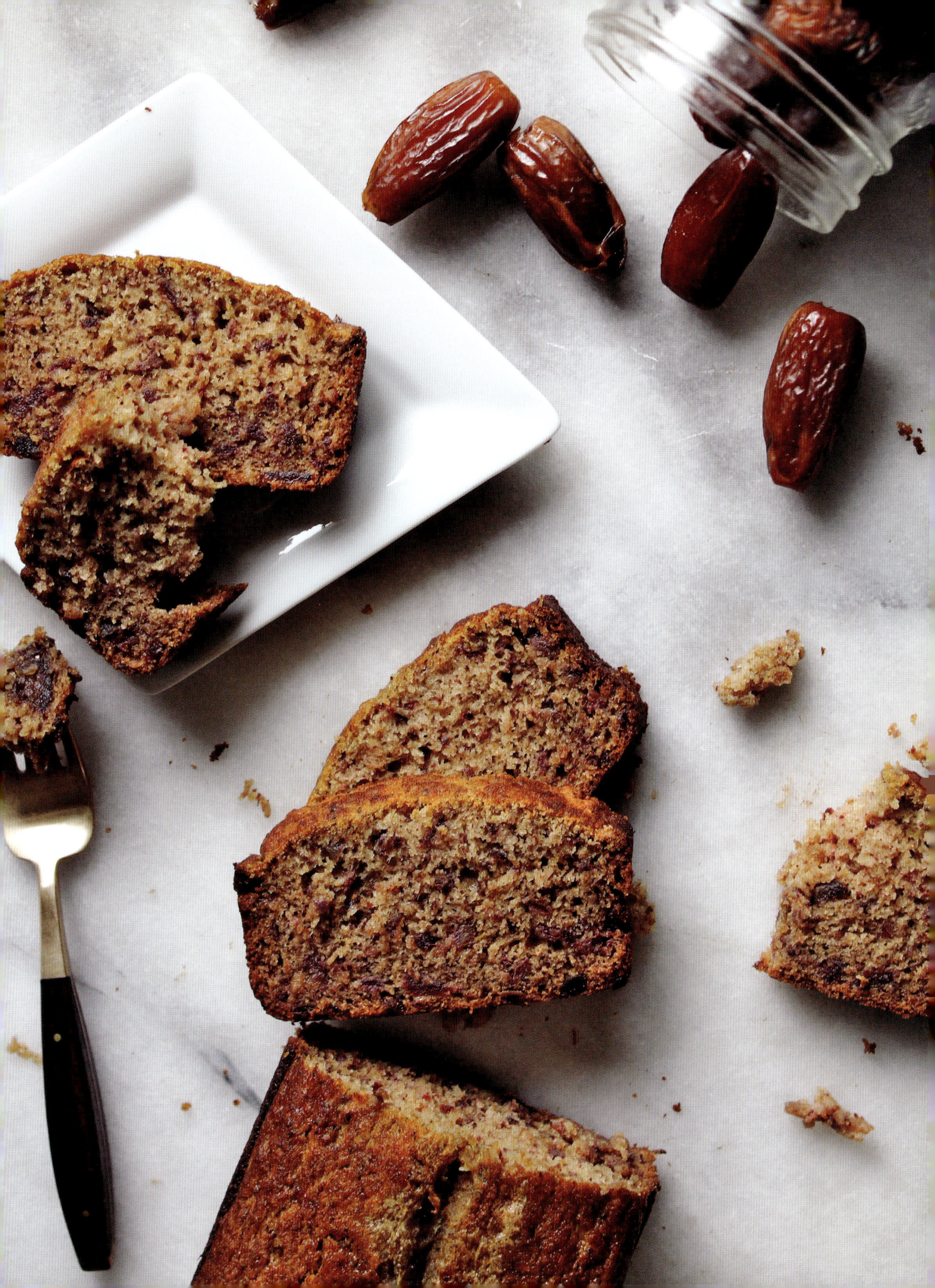

Yogurt Cake
apple + chocolate

makes 1

1 cup (285 gr) vanilla Greek yogurt
3 eggs – free-range organic
¾ cup (150 gr) granulated sugar
½ tsp vanilla extract
1 ½ cups (210 gr) flour

2 tsp baking powder
½ cup (120 ml) vegetable oil
3 small apples – peeled, cored and diced
¾ cup (130 gr) dark chocolate chips

Preheat the oven to 350F / 180C. Generously butter a loaf pan.
Whisk together the yogurt, eggs, sugar and vanilla in a large mixing bowl until well blended.
Sift together the flour and baking powder in a different bowl. Slowly whisk into the wet ingredients.
Fold in the oil using a rubber spatula. Stir until incorporated.
Mix in the apples and chocolate chips.
Transfer the batter to the prepared pan.
Bake for about 45 minutes, or until golden brown.
A cake tester placed in the center of the cake will come out clean.
Let cool completely before removing from the pan.
Keep tightly wrapped at room temperature for up to 3 days.

vegetarian | nut-free

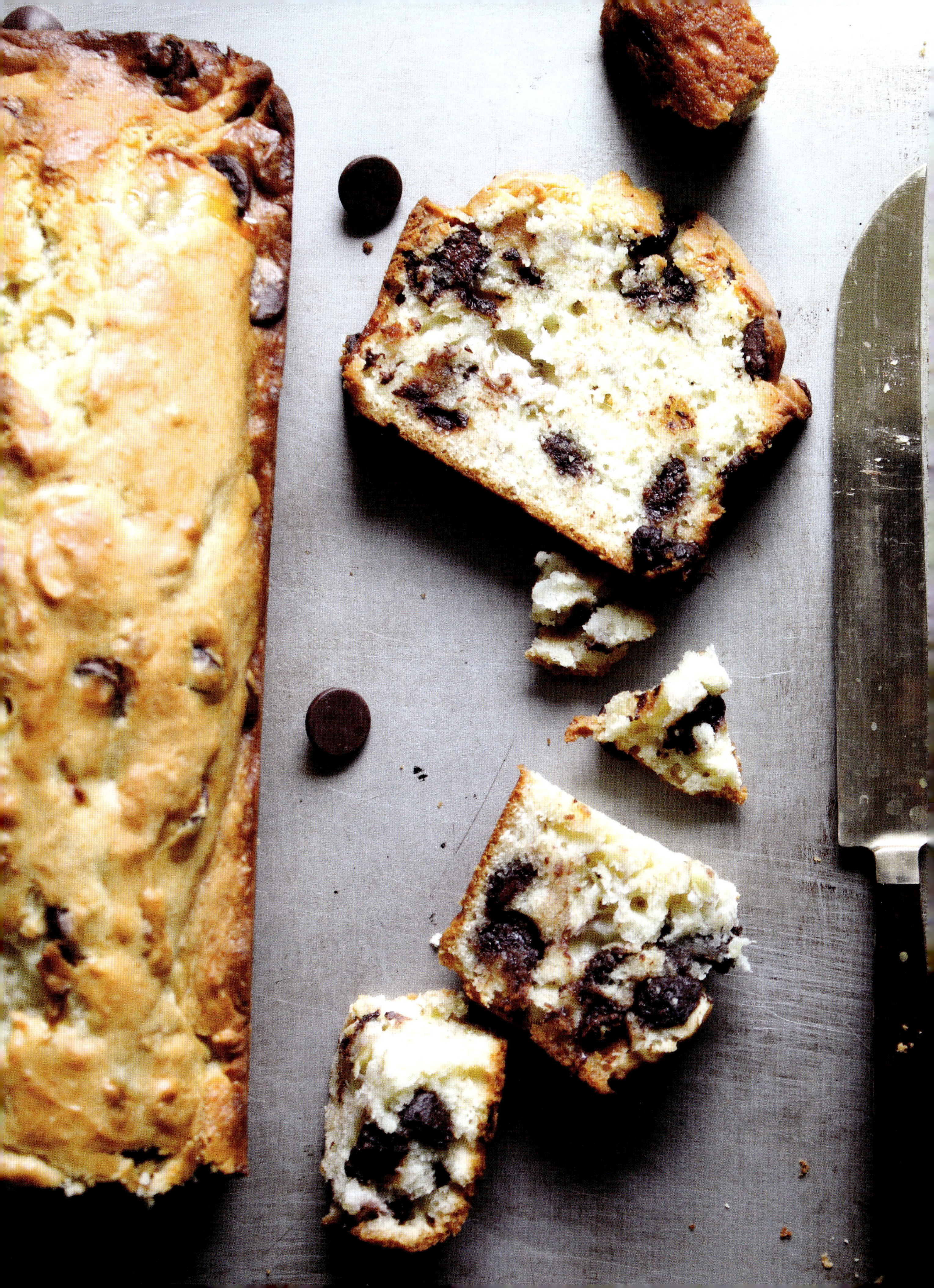

superfood. *noun.*

a nutrient-rich food
considered to be especially
beneficial for health
and well-being.

Fresh herbs give a unique taste to your food and offer amazing health benefits.
bottom to top: mint | chives | rosemary | thyme | dill | frozen basil cubes

Breakfast Sandwich
roasted tomatoes + avocado + mozzarella

serves 2

1 ripe avocado - halved and pitted
the juice of ½ a lemon
1 tsp lemon pepper
2 everything bagels

½ mozzarella ball - thinly sliced
20 fresh basil leaves
roasted tomatoes – recipe p. 78

Make the roasted tomatoes first.
Mash the avocado with a fork in a small bowl. Stir in the lemon juice and lemon pepper.
Toast the bagels.
Place the mozzarella slices onto both halves of the bagels.
Top with basil leaves and roasted tomatoes.
Spread some of the mashed avocado on the other halves and place on top of the roasted tomatoes.
Wrap tightly with plastic wrap. Slice in half using a long serrated knife.
Remove the plastic wrap and enjoy!

vegetarian | nut-free

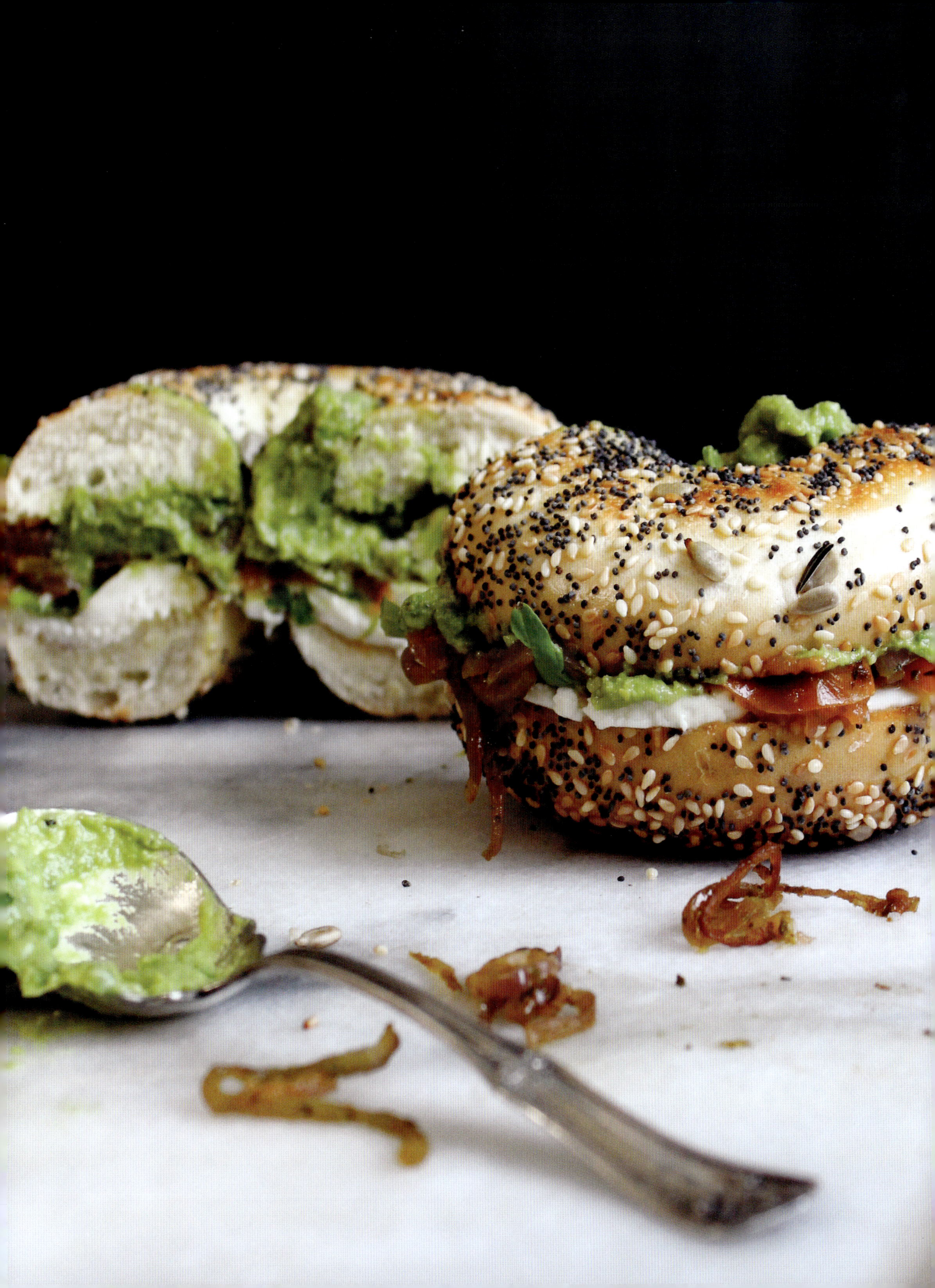

Avocado Tartines

Halve, pit and slice 1 avocado. Squeeze ½ lemon juice on each side, sprinkle with 1 tsp lemon pepper and crushed red pepper. Remove the skins and place on 2 slices of toasted multigrain bread. Top with fresh basil and serve.

vegan | vegetarian | dairy-free | nut-free

Burrata Tartines

Use a vegetable peeler to shave ½ of a cucumber into wide thin ribbons.
Place in a colander with 1 tsp salt.
Let sit for 20 minutes. Rinse thoroughly, drain and press in the colander with your hands to remove any excess water. Blot dry with paper towels. Tear 1 burrata ball and sprinkle over 2 slices of toasted multigrain bread. Season to taste. Add the cucumber ribbons.
Sprinkle with crushed pink peppercorn.

vegetarian | nut-free

Guacamole

serves 4

2 ripe avocados – halved and pitted
the juice of 1 lemon
1 tbsp lemon pepper
5 cherry tomatoes – finely chopped

1 tbsp finely chopped jalapeno pepper
1 tbsp fresh chopped cilantro
salt

Scoop out the avocado flesh with a spoon. Place in a large bowl with the lemon juice. Mash with a fork. Stir in the lemon pepper and add more salt if needed. Fold in the tomatoes, jalapeno pepper and cilantro. Toss to blend. Refrigerate for 20 minutes and then serve.

raw | vegan | gluten-free | nut-free

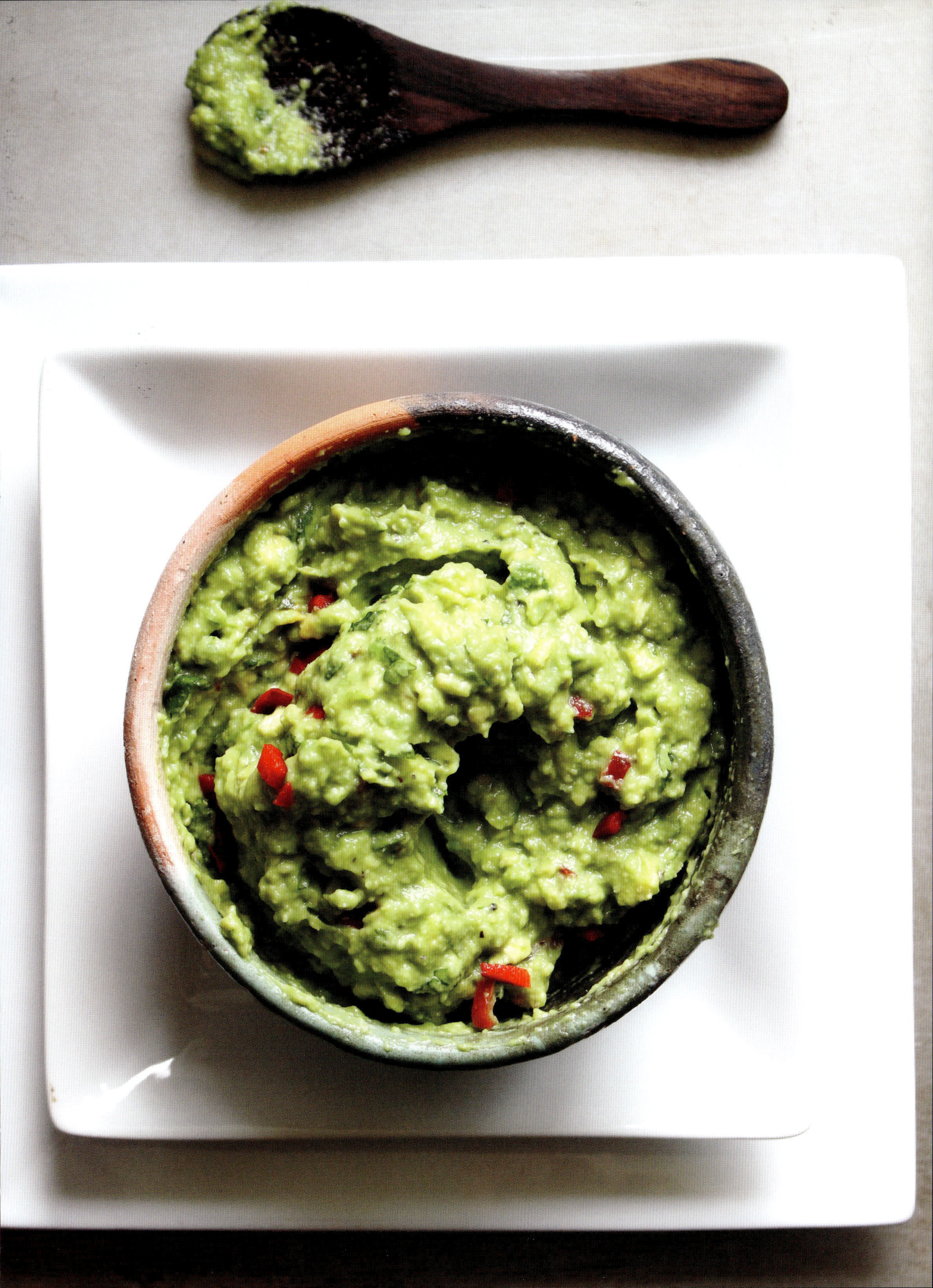

Pesto

8 tbsp pine nuts
1 garlic clove
1 cup (40 gr) fresh chopped basil

1 frozen basil cube
½ cup (120 ml) olive oil
½ tsp salt

Place the pine nuts in a pan over medium heat.
Toast until golden, stirring occasionally - about 3 minutes.
Pulse all the ingredients in a food processor until combined and smooth.
Transfer to a jar.
Refrigerate for a few months.

vegan | gluten-free

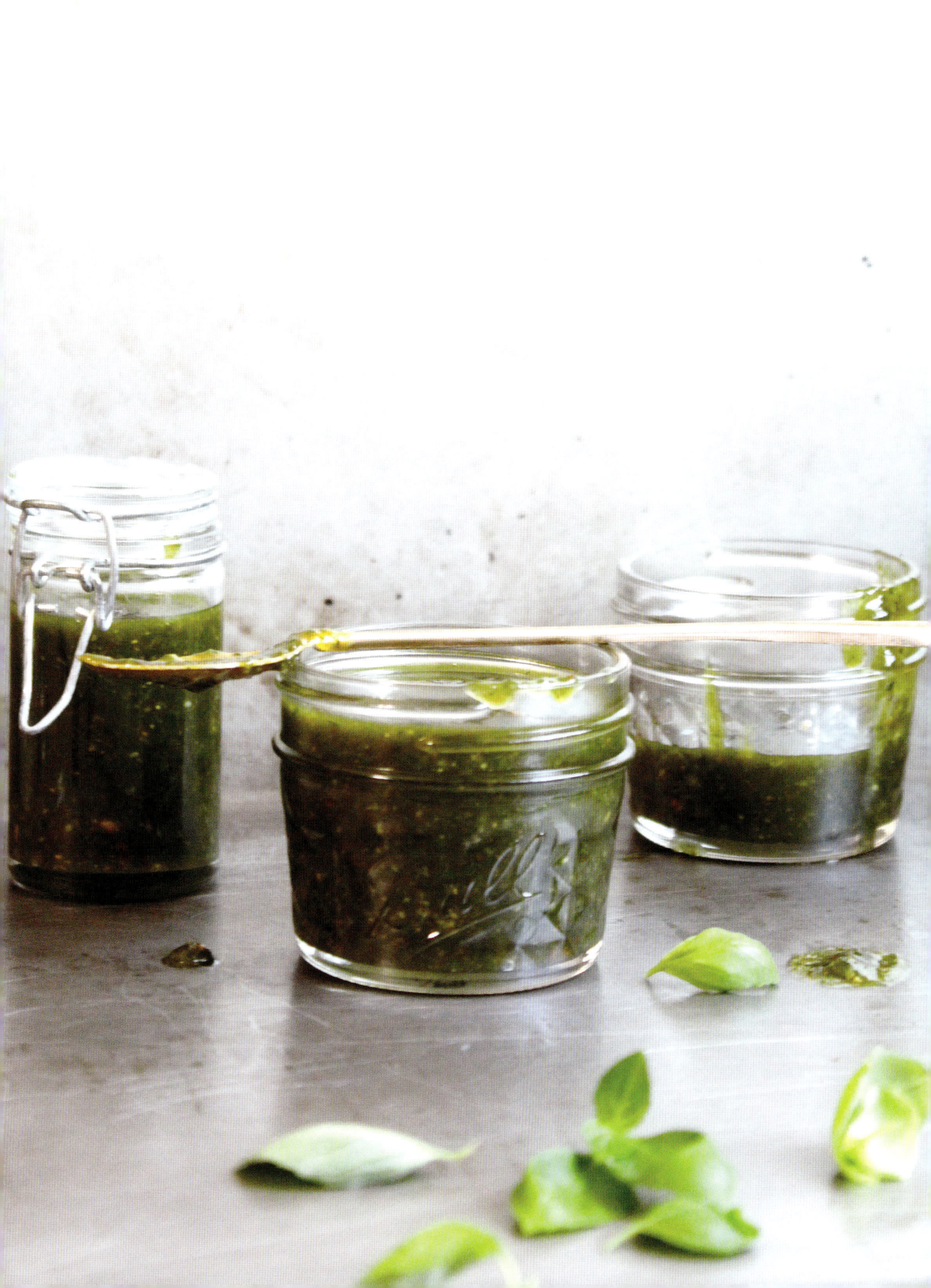

Frittata
spinach + basil

serves 2

5 baby potatoes - peeled and halved
4 large eggs – free-range organic
pesto - recipe p. 74
½ cup (80 gr) frozen spinach

a handful of fresh basil leaves
salt + pepper
+ olive oil cooking spray

Bring a pot of salted water to a boil. Add the potatoes and cook until tender – about 15 minutes.
Beat the eggs with 1 tbsp pesto in a mixing bowl.
Season to taste with salt and pepper.
Stir in the potatoes and spinach.
Coat a medium size pan with olive oil cooking spray. Place over medium to low heat.
Add the egg mixture and cook for about 6 minutes, stirring occasionally.
Transfer to a serving plate. Garnish with fresh basil.
Serve immediately.

vegetarian | dairy-free | gluten-free

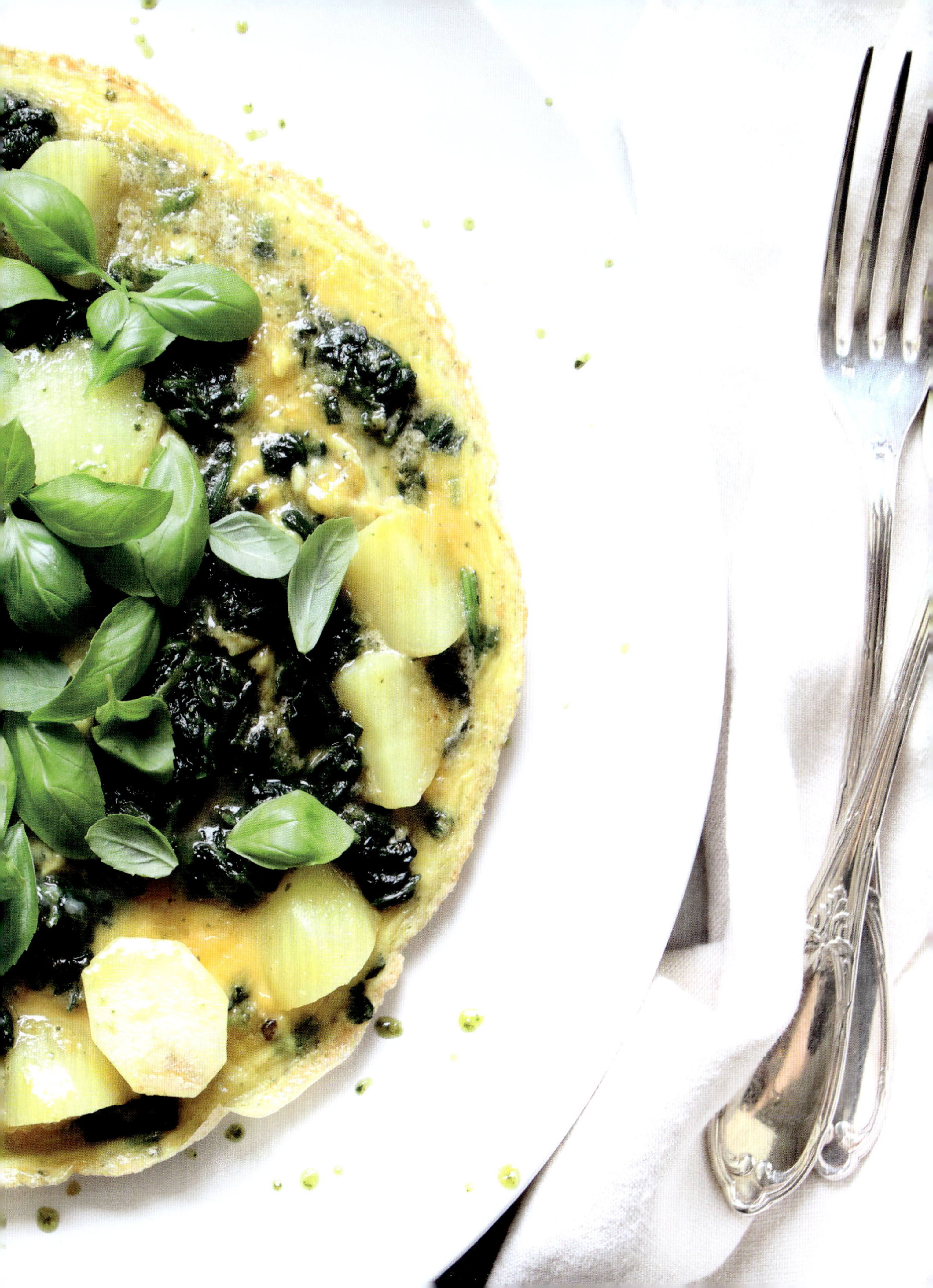

Roasted Tomatoes

serves 2

25 cherry tomatoes
2 oz. (60 gr) red onion - thinly sliced
1 tbsp olive oil

½ tsp salt
pepper to taste

Preheat the oven to 450F / 230C.
Line a baking sheet with parchment paper.
Place all the ingredients in a mixing bowl. Toss to coat.
Transfer to the prepared baking pan.
Roast in the preheated oven for about 25 minutes.

vegan | gluten-free | nut-free

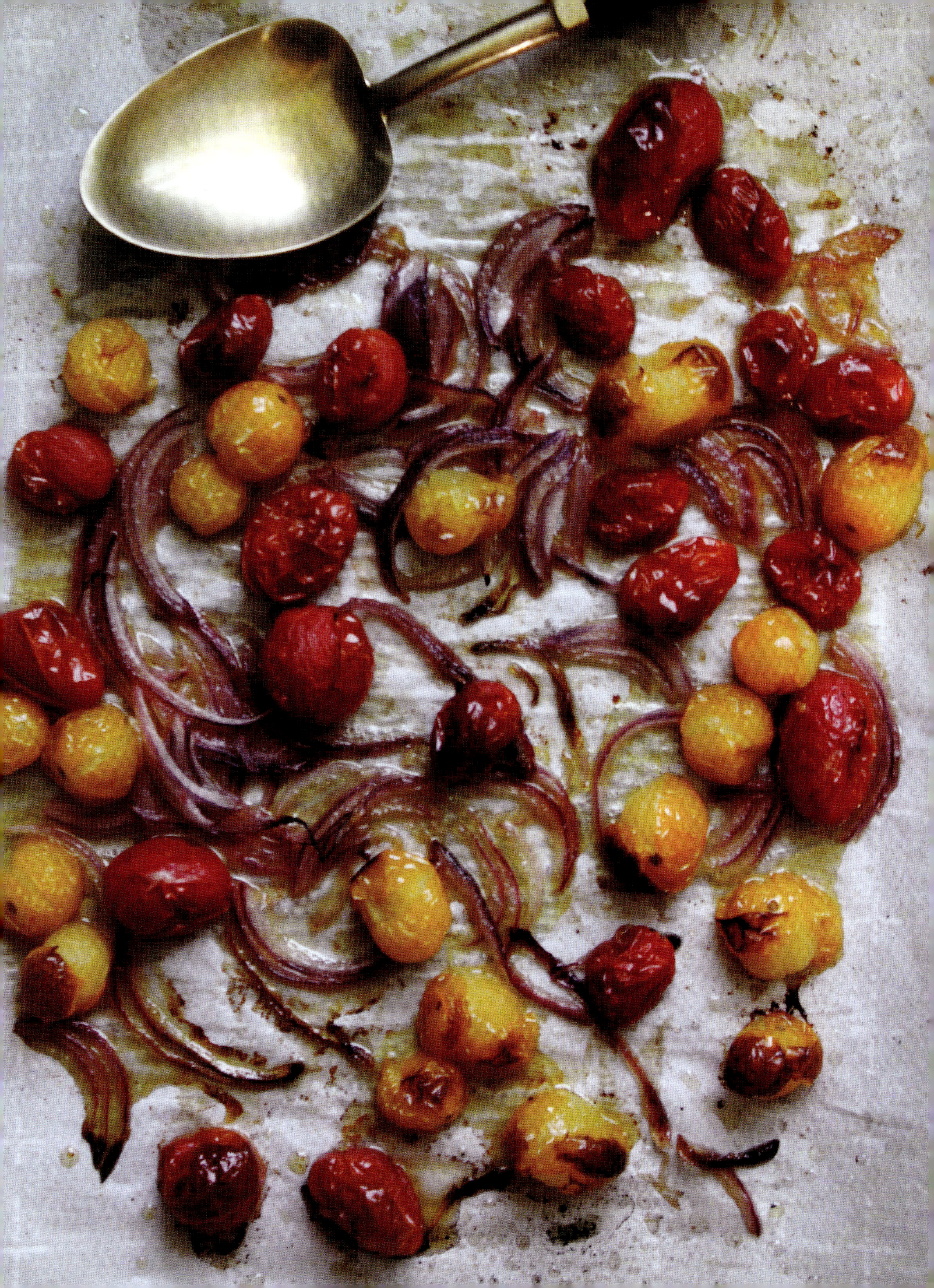

Oeuf Cocotte
sautéed veggies + roasted tomatoes

serves 4

8 eggs – free-range organic
olive oil
roasted tomatoes – recipe p. 78
½ red bell pepper – diced small
3 white mushrooms – thinly sliced

1 Roma tomato – diced small
1 tbsp garlic powder
½ cup (120 ml) water
salt + pepper

Make the roasted tomatoes first.
Place 1 tbsp olive oil in a skillet over medium heat. Stir in the onions and cook until nicely browned, stirring occasionally – about 4 minutes. Add the red bell pepper, mushroom, tomato, garlic powder and water. Season to taste with salt and pepper.
Cook over medium heat until tender – about 20 minutes.
Place the veggies into 4 serving ramekins. Carefully crack 2 eggs on top.
Season with salt and pepper.
Bake at 356F / 180C until the whites are set but the yolks still runny – about 12 minutes.
Serve right away garnished with roasted tomatoes.

vegetarian | dairy-free | gluten-free | nut-free

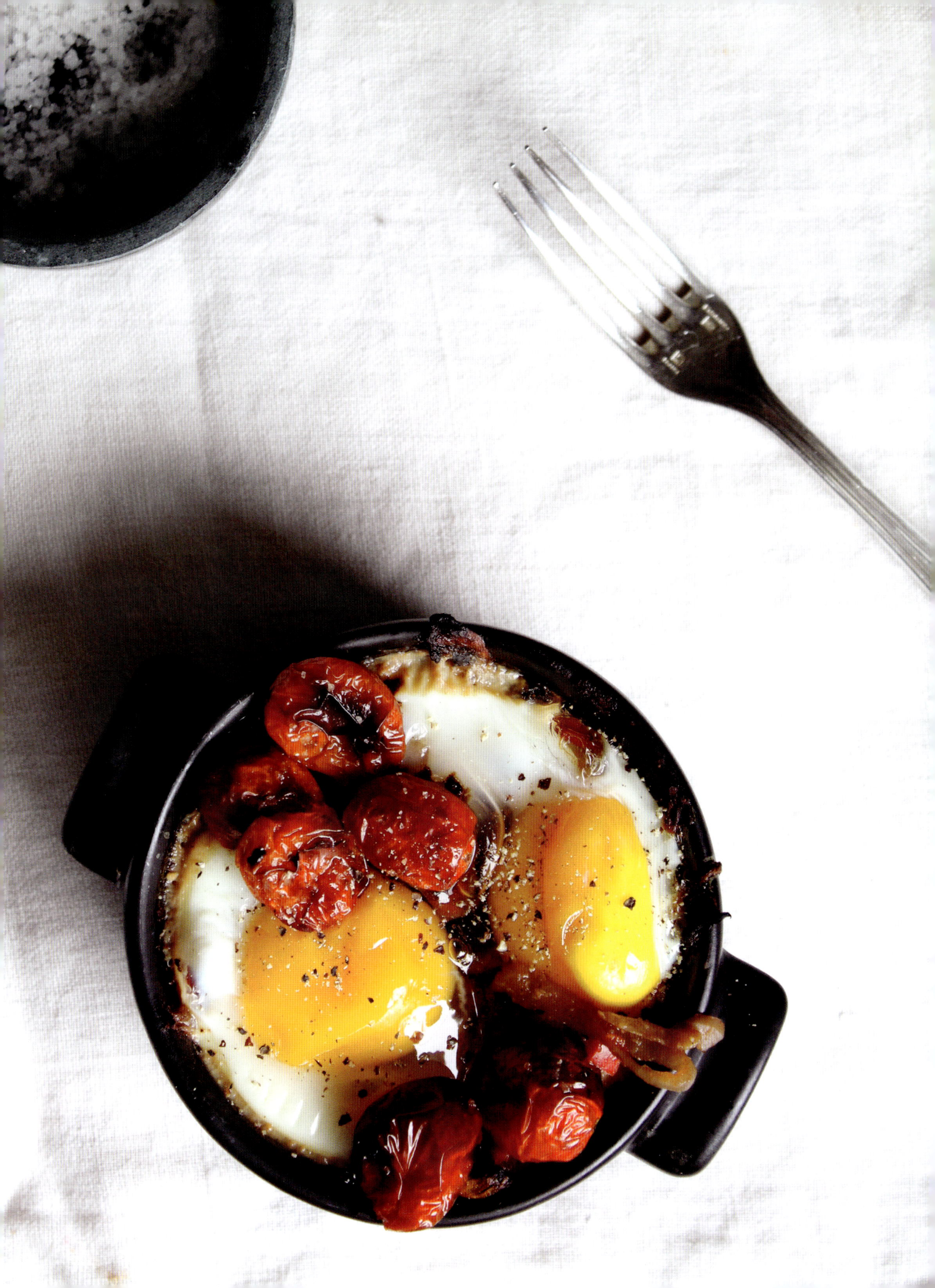

Oeuf Cocotte
mushroom + ham

serves 2

4 white mushrooms – cleaned and sliced
½ cup (75 gr) cooked ham - diced
⅓ cup (80 ml) heavy cream
1 tbsp fresh chopped chives

1 tbsp fresh chopped parsley
2 eggs - free-range organic
1 tbsp butter
salt + pepper

Preheat the oven to 390F / 200C.
Melt the butter in a small pan over medium heat. Stir in the mushrooms.
Cook 6 minutes, stirring occasionally. Add the ham and cook 1 minute more.
Mix in the heavy cream, chives, parsley. Remove from the heat. Season to taste.
Divide the mushroom mixture among 2 serving dishes. Carefully crack the egg on top. Sprinkle with a pinch of salt and pepper. Bake in the preheated oven for 15 minutes or until the egg whites are set.
Serve immediately with toasted bread.

gluten-free | nut-free

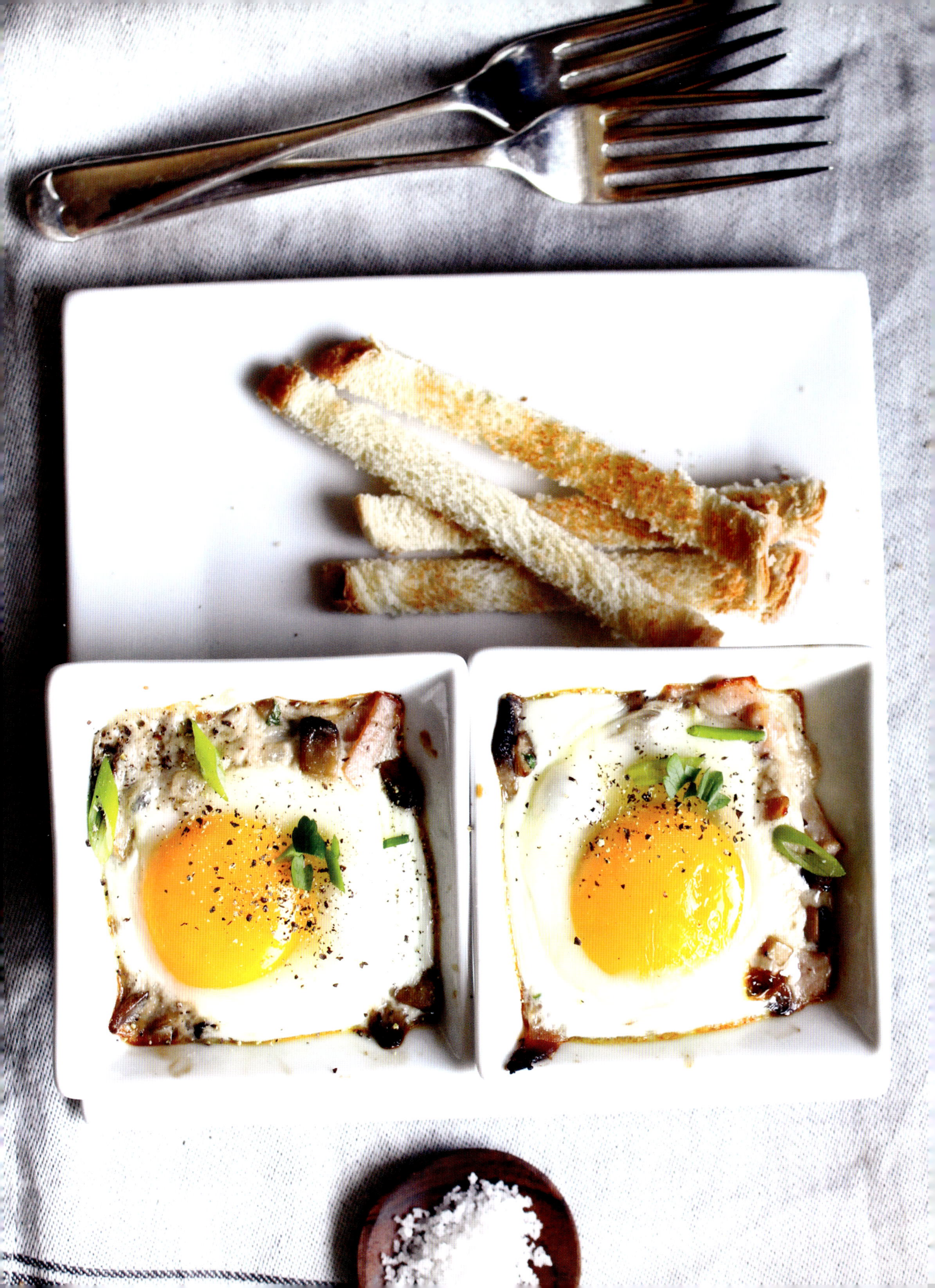

Oeuf au Plat
+ sautéed mushrooms

serves 2

1 bunch of enoki mushrooms
5 oyster mushrooms
2 oz. (60 gr) red onion - thinly sliced
2 eggs – free-range organic
olive oil

1 tbsp balsamic vinegar
salt + pepper
2 cups (150 gr) mixed salad greens
1 tbsp fresh chopped chives

Gently clean and cut the oyster mushrooms into smaller pieces.
Chop off the dirty ends of the enoki mushrooms. Gently rinse under cold water.
Heat 1 tbsp olive oil in a pan over medium heat. Add the red onions and cook for about 4 minutes, stirring constantly. Add the mushrooms, leave untouched for one minute. Flick the pan to toss.
Continue to cook 30 seconds. Remove from the heat, season to taste. Set aside.
Coat a skillet with non-stick cooking spray and place over high heat for a minute.
Reduce the heat to medium low.
Crack the eggs, one at a time into the pan and cook until the whites are firm.
Combine 2 tbsp olive oil, balsamic vinegar and a pinch of salt in a mixing bowl. Stir in the greens.
Divide among 2 serving plates. Top with sautéed mushrooms and sprinkle with chopped chives.
Serve with your sunny side up egg.

vegetarian | gluten-free | nut-free

Proven to lower the risks of cancer, excellent immune system booster, Enoki mushrooms are a rich source of important nutrients - proteins, fibers, vitamins, antioxidants.
They are very fragile and don't hold up well to heat. A quick dry-pan roasting - under 2 minutes - brings out the most umami.

Poached Egg
+ avocado toast

serves 2

3 cups (60 gr) fresh spinach
1 cup (40 gr) fresh basil
15 cherry tomatoes - halved
2 tbsp olive oil
1 tbsp balsamic vinegar
1 frozen basil cube

salt + pepper
multigrain bread
1 avocado – pitted and halved
2 tbsp white wine vinegar
2 eggs - free-range organic

Combine olive oil, balsamic vinegar, frozen basil cube and a pinch of salt in a large mixing bowl.
Stir in the spinach, fresh basil and tomatoes.
Toast 2 slices of multigrain bread.
Scoop out the avocado flesh. Mash on a plate with a fork.
Season to taste with salt and pepper and spread on the toasts.
Bring a large pot of water to a boil. Add the white wine vinegar and 1 tbsp salt.
Reduce the heat to low.
Crack one egg at a time into a small bowl and drop into the water in a quick motion.
Let cook undisturbed for 5 minutes. Scoop the eggs out with a slotted spoon.
Gently place on the avocado toasts. Season to taste and serve with a side of spinach salad.

vegetarian | dairy-free | nut-free

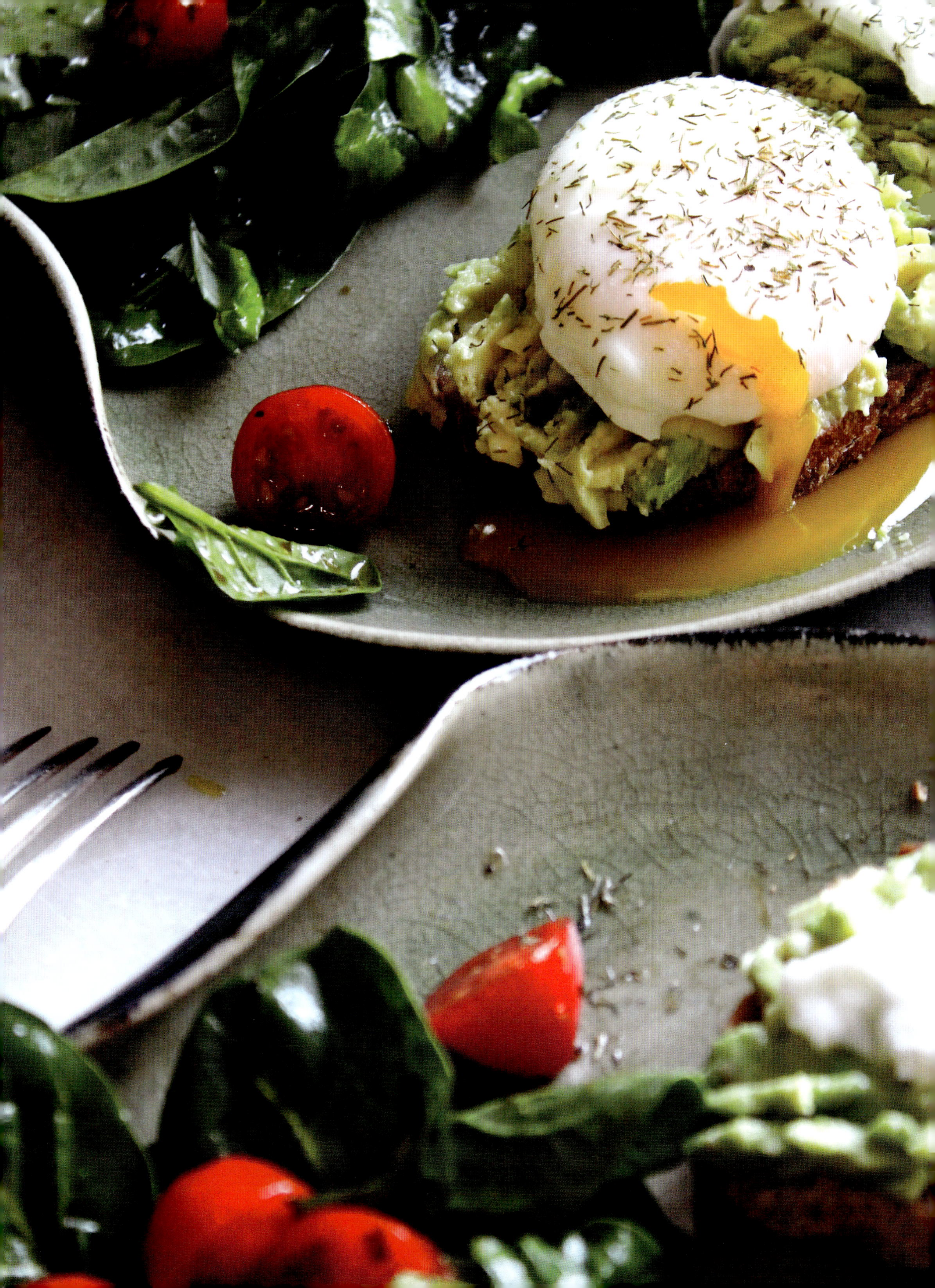

Lentil Salad
+ hard-boiled egg

serves 2

2 eggs – free-range organic
½ cup (85 gr) frozen lima beans
½ zucchini – thinly sliced
1 cup (30 gr) chopped kale
1 tbsp olive oil
1 tbsp white wine vinegar

1 tbsp cumin powder
a pinch of cayenne pepper
a pinch of salt
1 x 15 oz. (425 gr) can of lentils – rinsed and drained
1 tbsp pumpkin seeds

Place the eggs in a pot, cover with water and bring to a boil.
Reduce the heat to low, cook for 8 minutes. Add the frozen lima beans and cook for 2 minutes more.
Transfer to a colander under cold running water to stop the cooking. Peel the eggs.
Coat a large skillet with non-stick cooking spray. Place over medium heat. Add the zucchini and cook for about 2 minutes. Flip on the other side and continue to cook 2 minutes or until nicely grilled on both sides. Turn off the heat. Add the chopped kale and leave untouched for a few minutes.
Combine olive oil, white wine vinegar, cumin, salt and cayenne pepper in a large bowl.
Stir in the lentils, lima beans, kale and sautéed zucchini.
Transfer to a serving bowl. Sprinkle with pumpkin seeds and serve with hard-boiled eggs.

vegetarian | dairy-free | gluten-free | nut-free

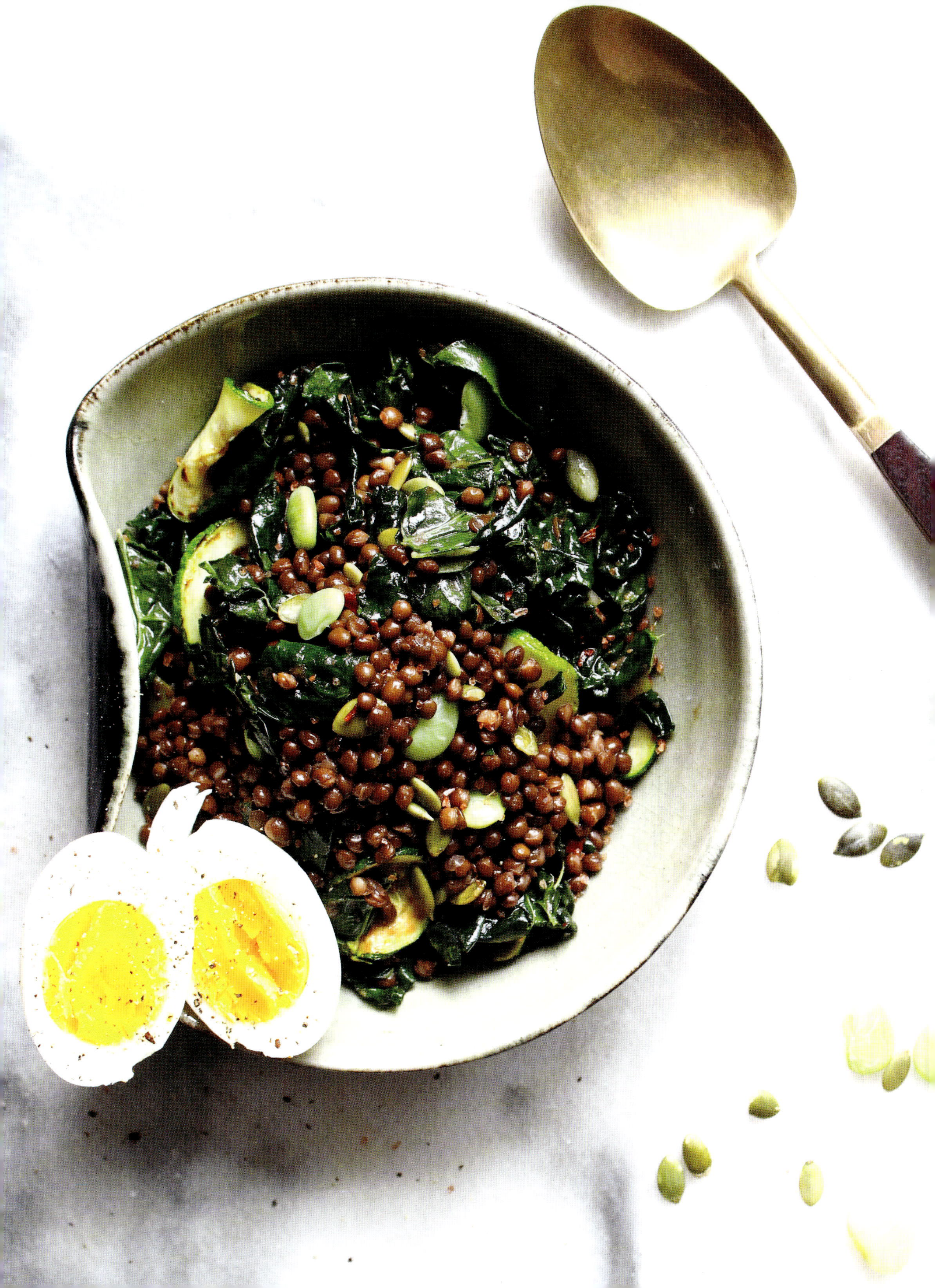

Kale & Brussel Sprouts
French vinaigrette

serves 4

roasted Brussel sprouts - recipe p. 140
1 bunch of kale
2 tbsp olive oil
1 tbsp red wine vinegar
1 tsp Dijon mustard
the juice of ½ a lemon
2 cups (150 gr) chopped mixed salad greens
½ cup (20 gr) broccoli sprouts
10 sun-dried tomatoes – chopped
1 tbsp fresh chopped parsley
1 avocado – pitted, peeled and diced
⅓ cup (50 gr) whole cashews
crushed red pepper
salt

Make the roasted Brussel sprouts first.
Rinse, drain and chop the kale.
Combine olive oil, red wine vinegar, Dijon mustard and a pinch of salt in a large mixing bowl.
Squeeze in the lemon juice. Whisk to blend.
Add the kale, greens, broccoli sprouts, sun-dried tomatoes and parsley. Toss to coat.
Garnish with roasted Brussel sprouts, avocado and cashews. Top with crushed red pepper.
Serve immediately!

vegan | gluten-free

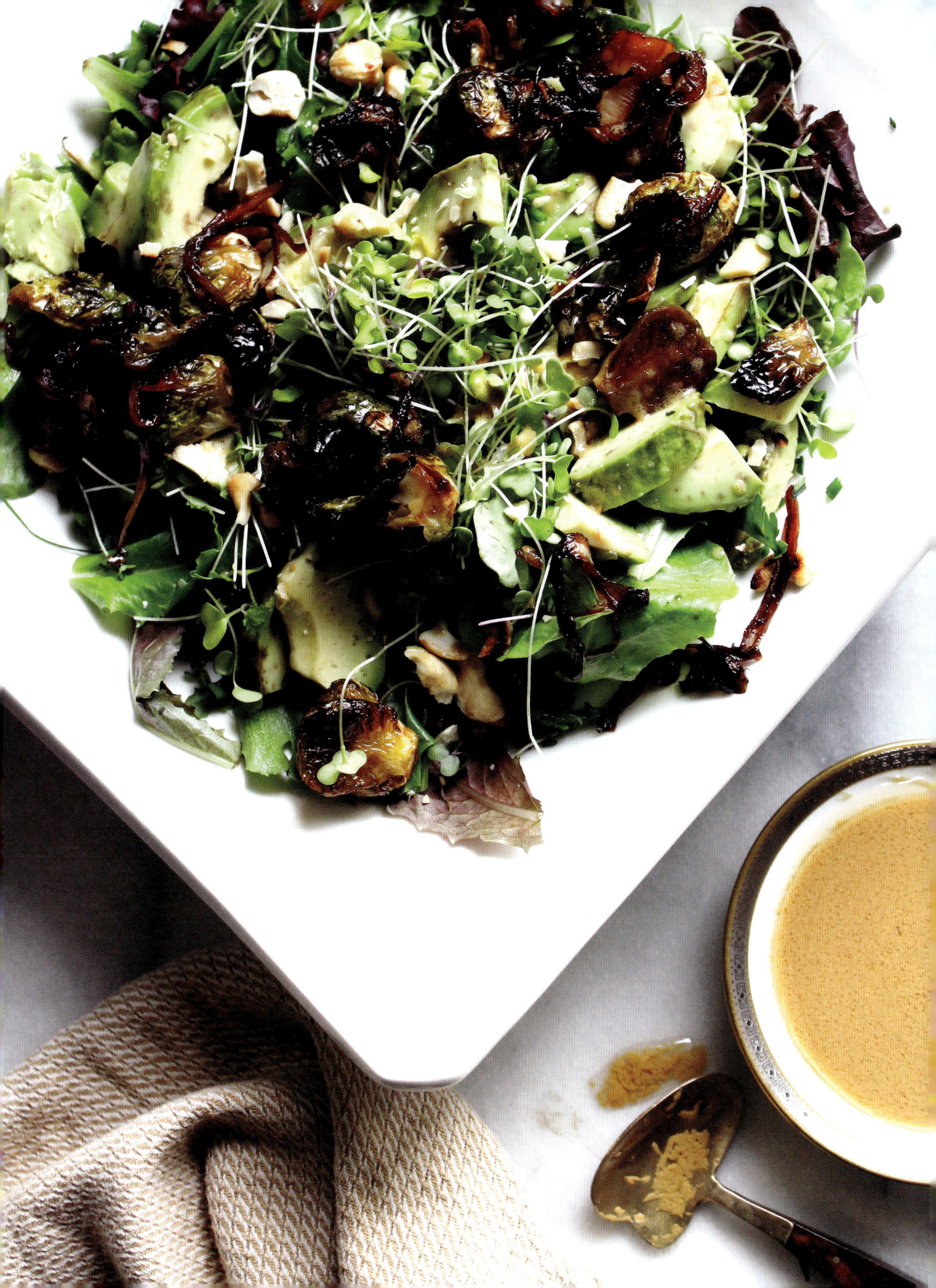

Pistachio Dressing

1 tsp fennel seeds
¼ tsp coriander powder
½ tsp cumin powder
2 tbsp fresh chopped rosemary
¼ cup (5 gr) fresh chopped parsley

1 tsp salt
¾ cup (180 ml) olive oil
1 cup (150 gr) whole pistachios
¼ tsp red crushed pepper

Pulse all the ingredients in a food processor until combined.
Transfer to a glass jar. Keep in the fridge for a few weeks.

raw | vegan | gluten-free

Multigrain Flatbread
+ arugula

Place a multigrain flatbread on a hot grill pan for a few minutes.
Remove from the pan and spread 2 tbsp of the pistachio dressing evenly on top.
Garnish with 2 cups (40 gr) arugula, halved cherry tomatoes and parmesan shavings.
Serve immediately!

vegetarian | gluten-free

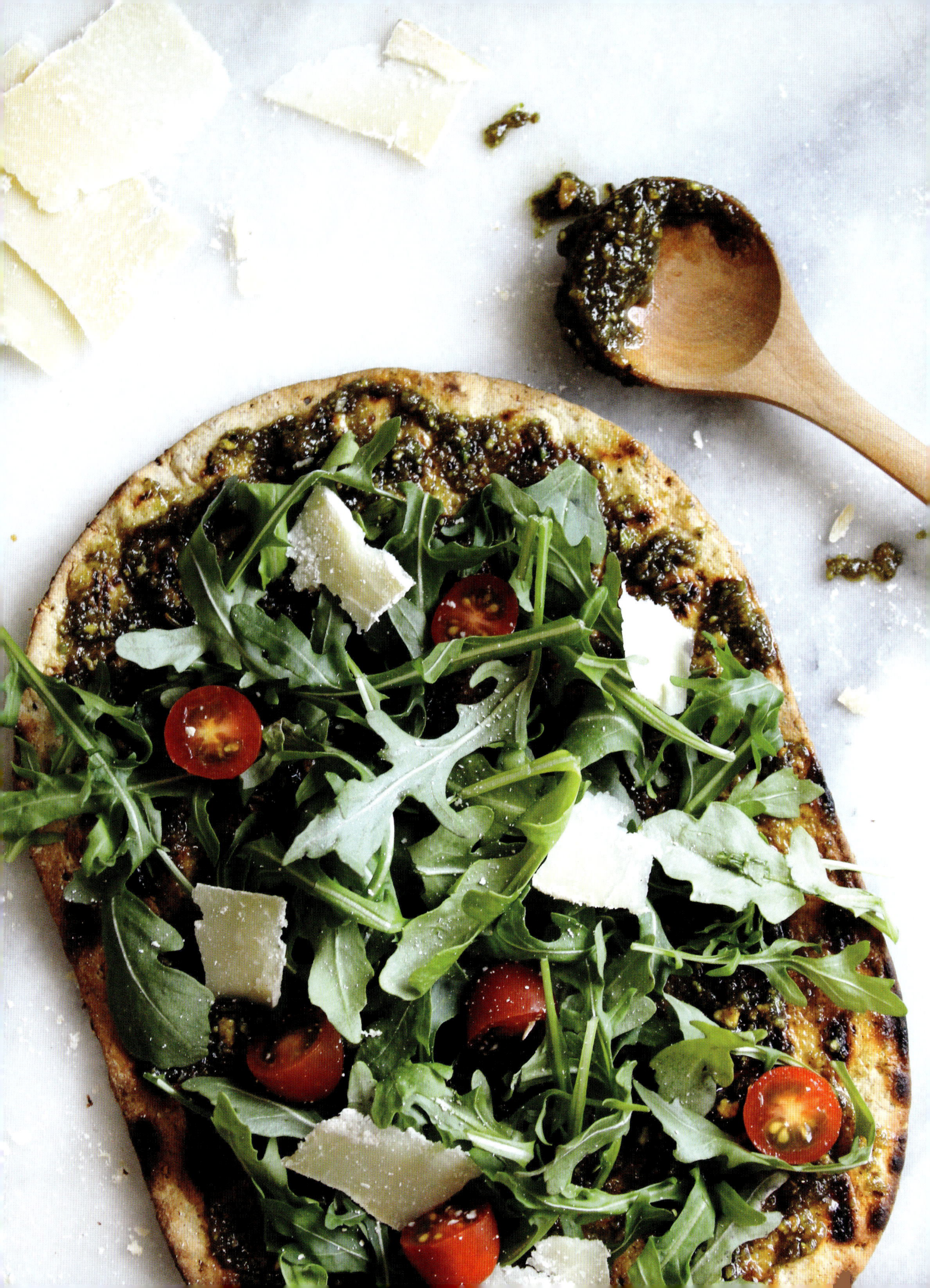

Summer Chicken Salad

serves 4

2 chicken breasts - farm-raised organic
2 tbsp pistachio dressing - recipe p. 92
1 egg - free-range organic
4 cups (300 gr) mixed salad greens
1 avocado - pitted, peeled and diced
20 cherry tomatoes - halved

3 tbsp olive oil
2 tbsp balsamic vinegar
salt
+ crushed red pepper
+ parmesan shavings

Preheat the oven to 430F / 220C. Line a baking sheet with parchment paper.
Pulse the chicken, pistachio dressing and egg in a food processor. Shape into bite-size balls.
Place on the prepared baking sheet. Refrigerate for 20 minutes.
Bake in the preheated oven until cooked through - about 15 minutes.
Whisk together olive oil, balsamic vinegar and a pinch of salt in a large mixing bowl. Stir in the greens.
Transfer to a serving plate. Top with chicken meatballs, avocado and tomatoes.
Garnish with crushed red pepper and parmesan shavings.

gluten-free

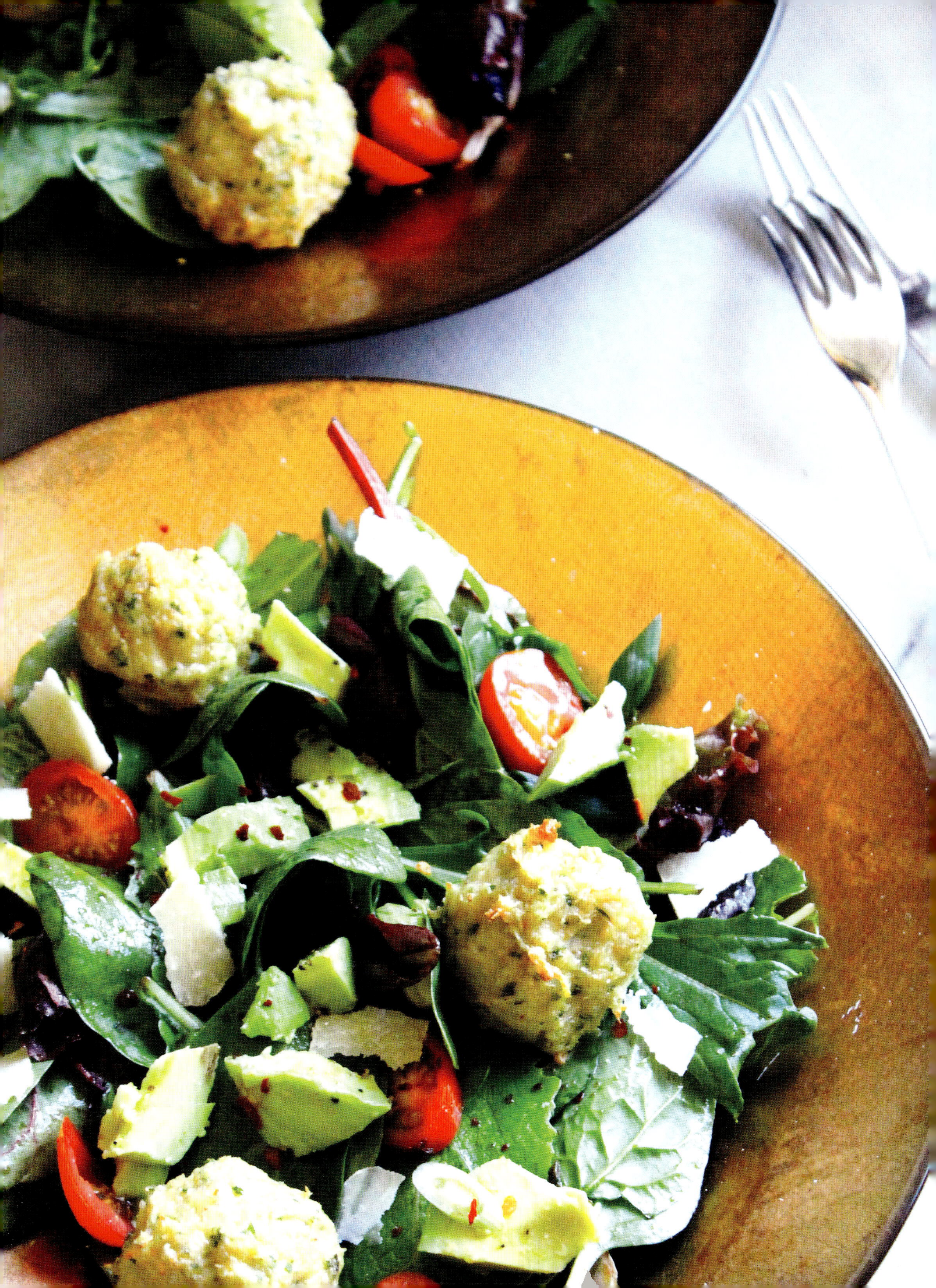

Rice

Rice comes in many varieties and is considered a staple food.

Low in calorie, gluten-free and high in carbohydrates, it provides fast and instant energy.

Here is a list of the most popular forms:

White rice – it is a refined grain that has been processed and stripped from its natural nutrients. Often times polished to give it an appealing white color. It is however usually enriched in certain vitamins. It is found in 3 grains:

- **long:** most common type of rice. It is fluffy and dry, with separate grains when cooked. It is also the most forgiving! Use in side dishes, pilafs and salads - basmati, jasmine rice.
- **medium:** similar to short-grain rice. It becomes chewy and sticky when cooked. Use in your paellas - Valencia, Bomba.
- **short:** this grain shows the highest percentage of amylopectin, the starch that makes rice sticky. Best for risottos, sushi, pudding - Arborio.

Instant rice – it is normal white rice that has been pre-cooked and dehydrated. It is therefore more processed, less nutritious and more expensive.

Brown rice – it is a healthy whole grain food where only the outermost layer of the grain has been removed. Brown rice is more natural and less processed. It is lower in calories and more nutritious. It shows higher content of fiber, vitamins and minerals. It also has a lower glycemic index but requires longer cooking time.

Wild rice – it is a whole grain food, highly nutritious. Wild rice is an excellent source of protein, minerals, dietary fibers and vitamin B. It is however one of the most expensive kind of rice due to its intensive labor to harvest. This type of grain takes longer to cook.

Black rice – it is high in nutritional value and a great source of iron, vitamin E and antioxidants. The dark color is due to an excess of anthocyanin, a powerful antioxidant.

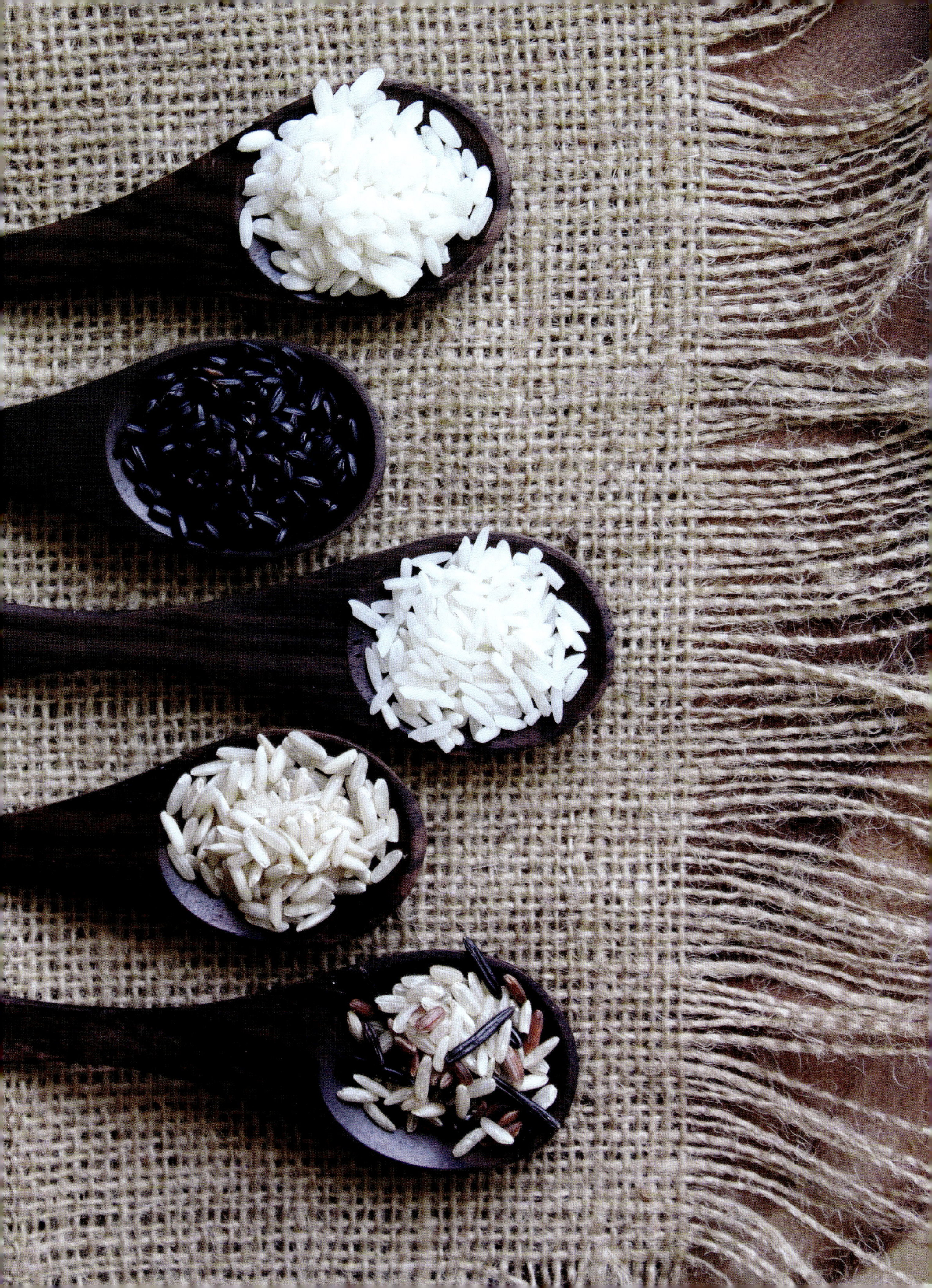

Wild Rice Salad
+ pistachio dressing

serves 4

1 cup (200 gr) wild rice
1 small broccoli head – cut into small florets
3 tbsp pistachio dressing – recipe p. 92

1 cup (20 gr) arugula
2 tbsp fresh chopped parsley
⅓ cup (50 gr) roughly chopped pistachios

Place 2 cups of water in a medium size pot and bring to a boil. Add ½ tsp salt and the rice.
Reduce the heat to low, cover and cook until tender – about 30 minutes.
Remove from the heat. Transfer to a bowl. Let cool completely.
While the rice is cooking, bring a large pot of salted water to a boil.
Add the broccoli florets and cook until tender – about 10 minutes.
Drain and rinse under cold running water.
Add to the rice with the pistachio dressing, arugula, parsley and pistachios. Toss to combine.
Refrigerate until needed!

vegan | gluten-free

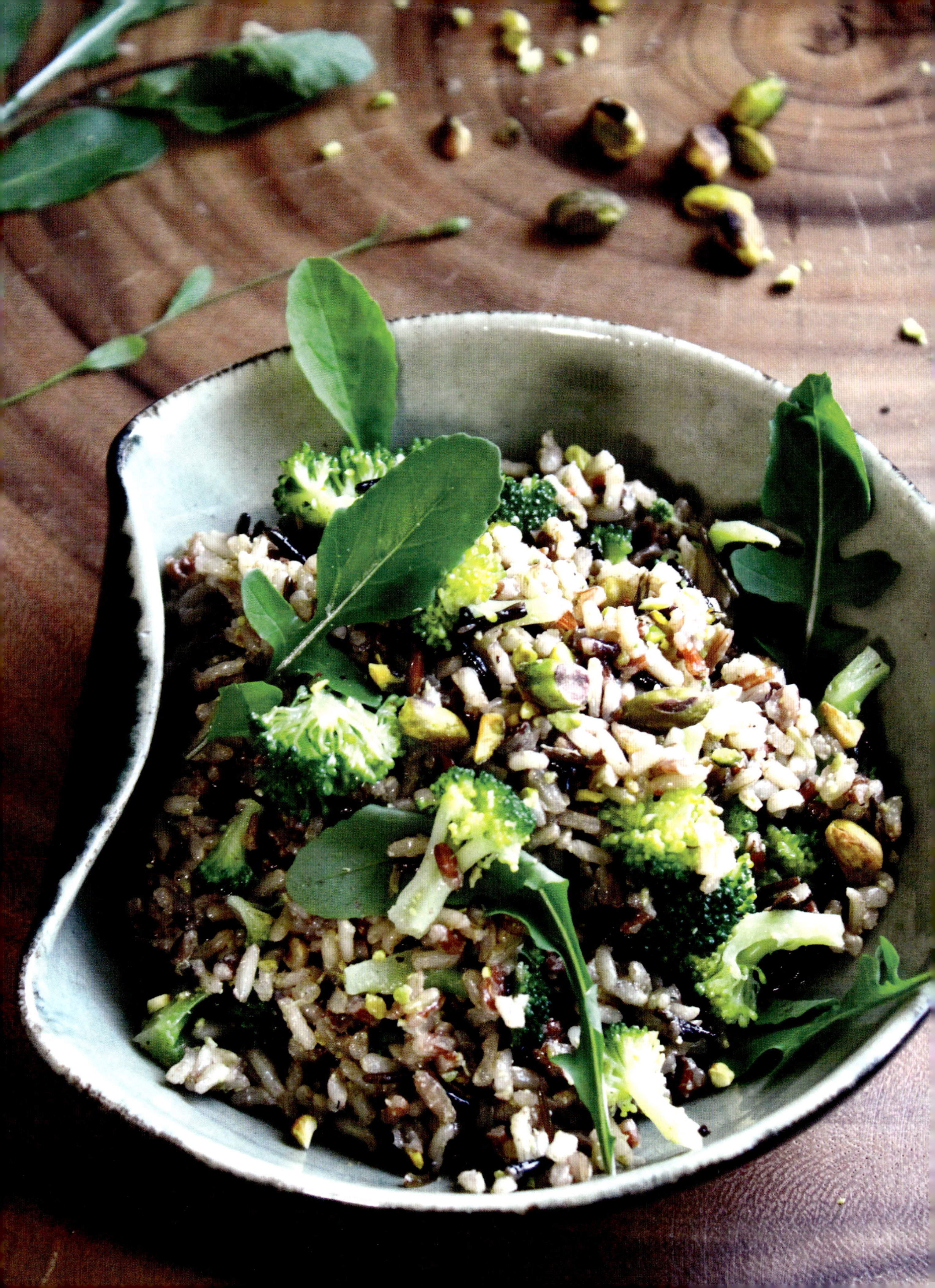

Rice Salad
+ sun dried tomatoes

serves 4

1 cup (200 gr) white rice - long grain
2 tbsp pine nuts
3 tbsp pesto – recipe p. 74

20 cherry tomatoes - quartered
10 sun-dried tomatoes – chopped
½ cup (30 gr) fresh chopped basil

Cook the rice according to the package instructions.
Place the pine nuts in a small skillet over medium heat.
Toast for a few minutes, stirring frequently until golden – about 3 minutes. Set aside.
Place the pesto in a large mixing bowl. Thin with 1 tbsp water if too thick.
Stir in the rice, cherry tomatoes, sun dried tomatoes, fresh basil and pine nuts.
Toss to coat.
Transfer to a serving bowl and refrigerate until needed.

vegan | gluten-free

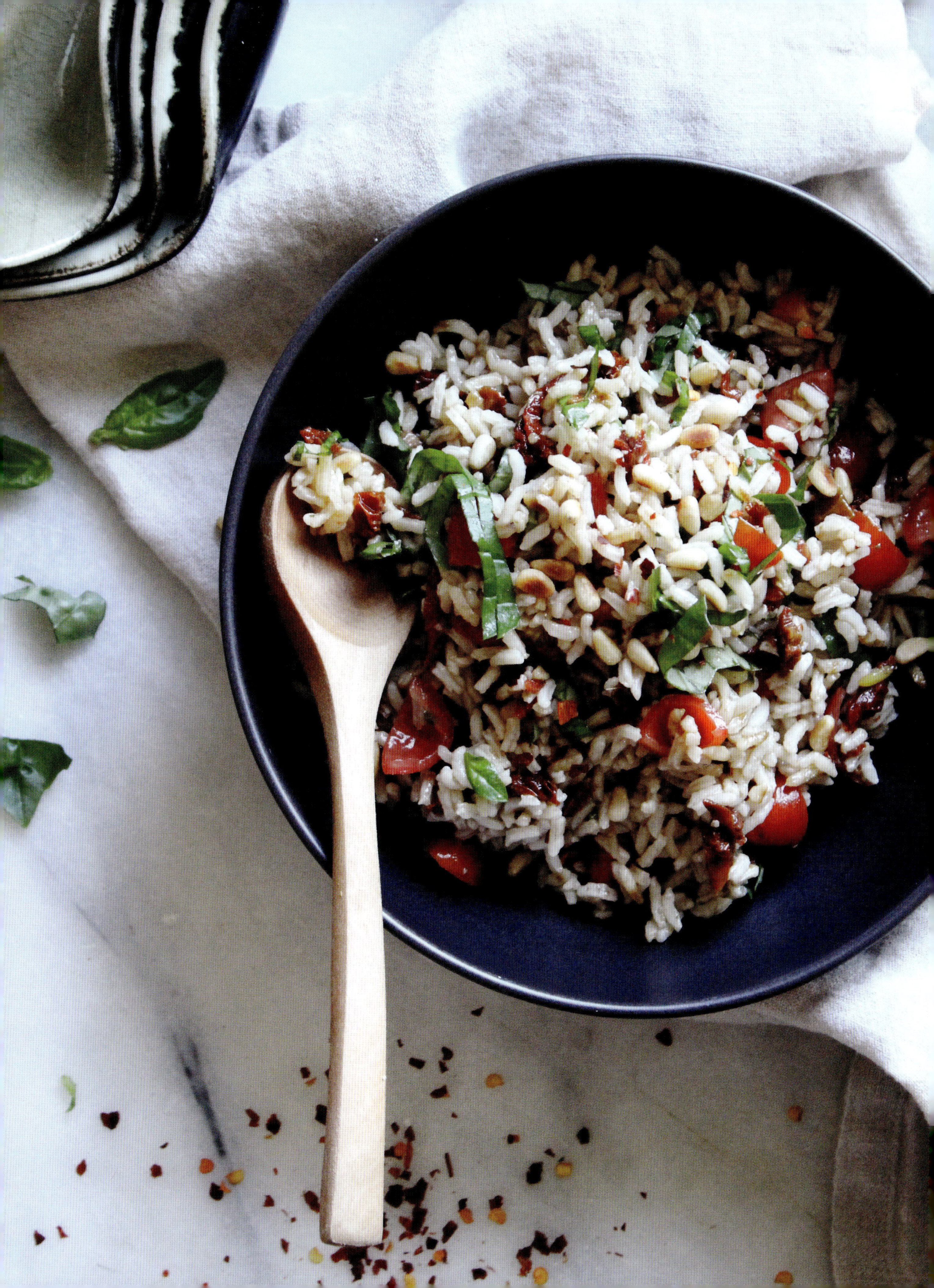

Black Rice Salad
+ roasted eggplant

serves 4

1 red bell pepper – halved and seeded
1 small eggplant – diced
1 cup (200 gr) black rice
3 tbsp almond dressing – recipe p. 105
1 cup (20 gr) arugula

2 tbsp fresh chopped parsley
2 tbsp fresh chopped mint
⅓ cup (40 gr) chopped almonds
salt + pepper

Preheat the oven to 450F / 230C.
Line a baking sheet with parchment paper or silicone baking mat.
Place the red bell peppers cut side down on the prepared pan. Spread the diced eggplant on the same pan, next to the peppers, in a single layer. Roast in the preheated oven, undisturbed, for 25 minutes or until the skins of the peppers are charred and wrinkled and the eggplant nicely browned.
Remove from the oven, let cool completely. Peel off the peppers skins and chop.
Bring 3 cups of water to a boil in a saucepan. Add 1 tsp of salt and the rice.
Reduce the heat to low, cover and cook until tender- about 30 minutes.
Remove from the heat. Rinse under cold running water, drain and place in a mixing bowl.
Stir in the eggplants, red bell peppers, almond dressing, arugula, parsley, mint and chopped almonds.
Toss to combine. Season to taste with salt and pepper.
Refrigerate until needed.

vegan | gluten-free

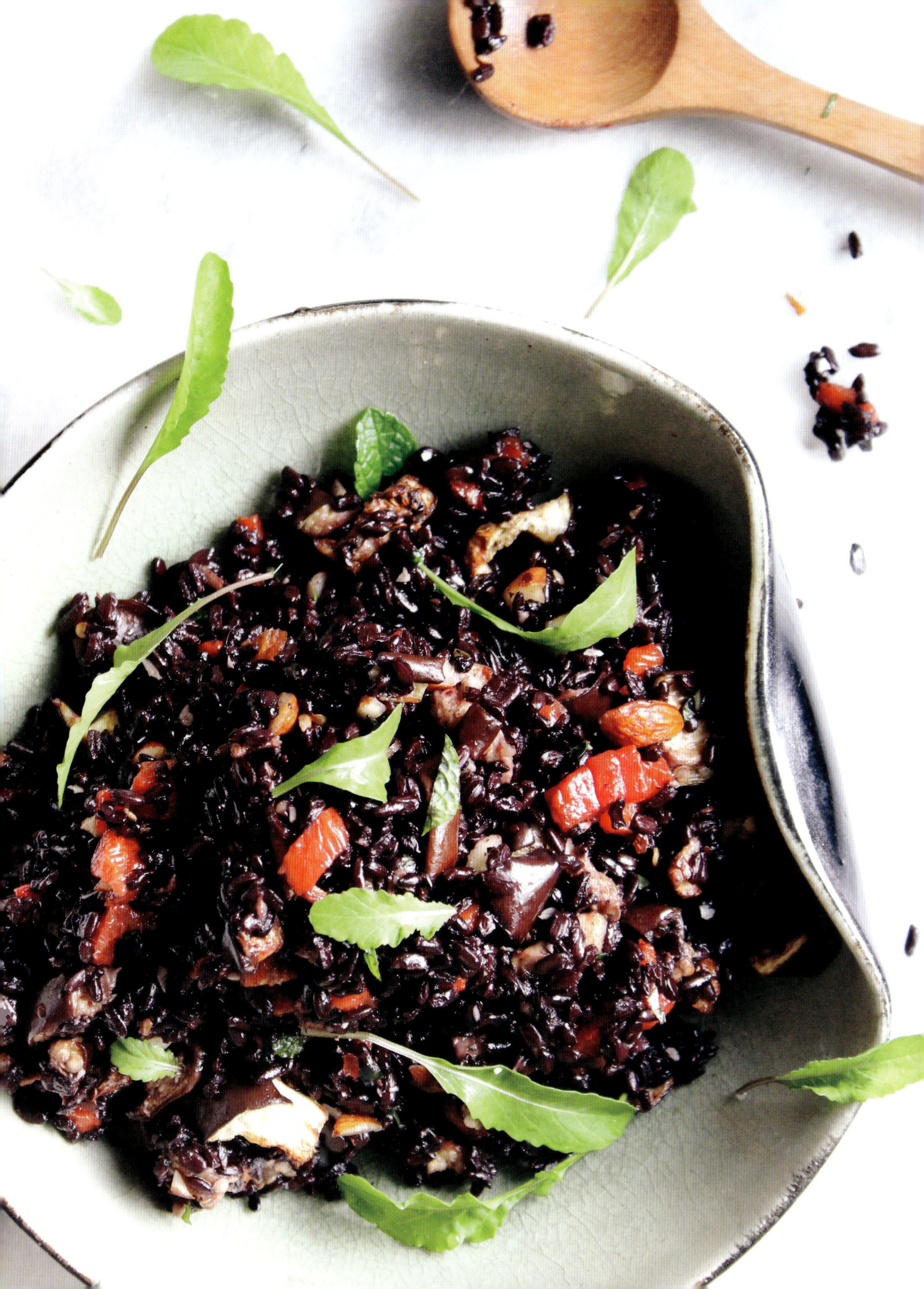

Whole grains, seeds and legumes are amazing energy boosters and are packed with vital nutrients. Great source of fiber, magnesium, potassium and iron they help fight diseases and should be consumed daily.

Popular grains, seeds and legumes include but are not limited to:

Barley	Chia	Beans
Buckwheat	Flax	Chickpeas
Bulgur	Hemp	Lentils
Farro	Pumpkin	Peanuts
Quinoa	Sunflower	Peas
Millet	Sesame	Tofu
Oats	Wheat Germ	Nuts

Almond Dressing

¼ cup (20 gr) sliced almonds
⅓ cup (160 ml) almond oil
1 tsp Dijon mustard

1 tbsp red wine vinegar
1 tbsp balsamic vinegar
½ tsp salt

Place the almonds in a skillet over low heat. Toast until golden, stirring occasionally.
Chop in a food processor. Set aside.
Whisk together almond oil, Dijon mustard, red wine vinegar, balsamic vinegar and salt in a large bowl.
Stir in the almonds.
Transfer to a glass jar.
Keep in the fridge for a few weeks.

vegan | gluten-free

Quinoa Salad
+ almond dressing

serves 2

1 cup (170 gr) quinoa
1 cup (20 gr) fresh chopped arugula
4 tbsp fresh chopped mint
¼ cup (30 gr) sliced almonds

¼ cup (40 gr) whole almonds
⅓ cup (80 gr) chickpeas – rinsed and drained
2 tbsp almond dressing – recipe p. 105
1 avocado – pitted and diced

Place 2 cups of water and the quinoa in a saucepan. Bring to a boil.
Cook until the quinoa is tender and the water is absorbed, about 15 minutes.
Transfer to a large mixing bowl with the arugula, mint, sliced + whole almonds and the chickpeas.
Season with almond dressing. Toss to blend.
Top with avocado and refrigerate until needed.
Serve chilled.

vegan | gluten-free

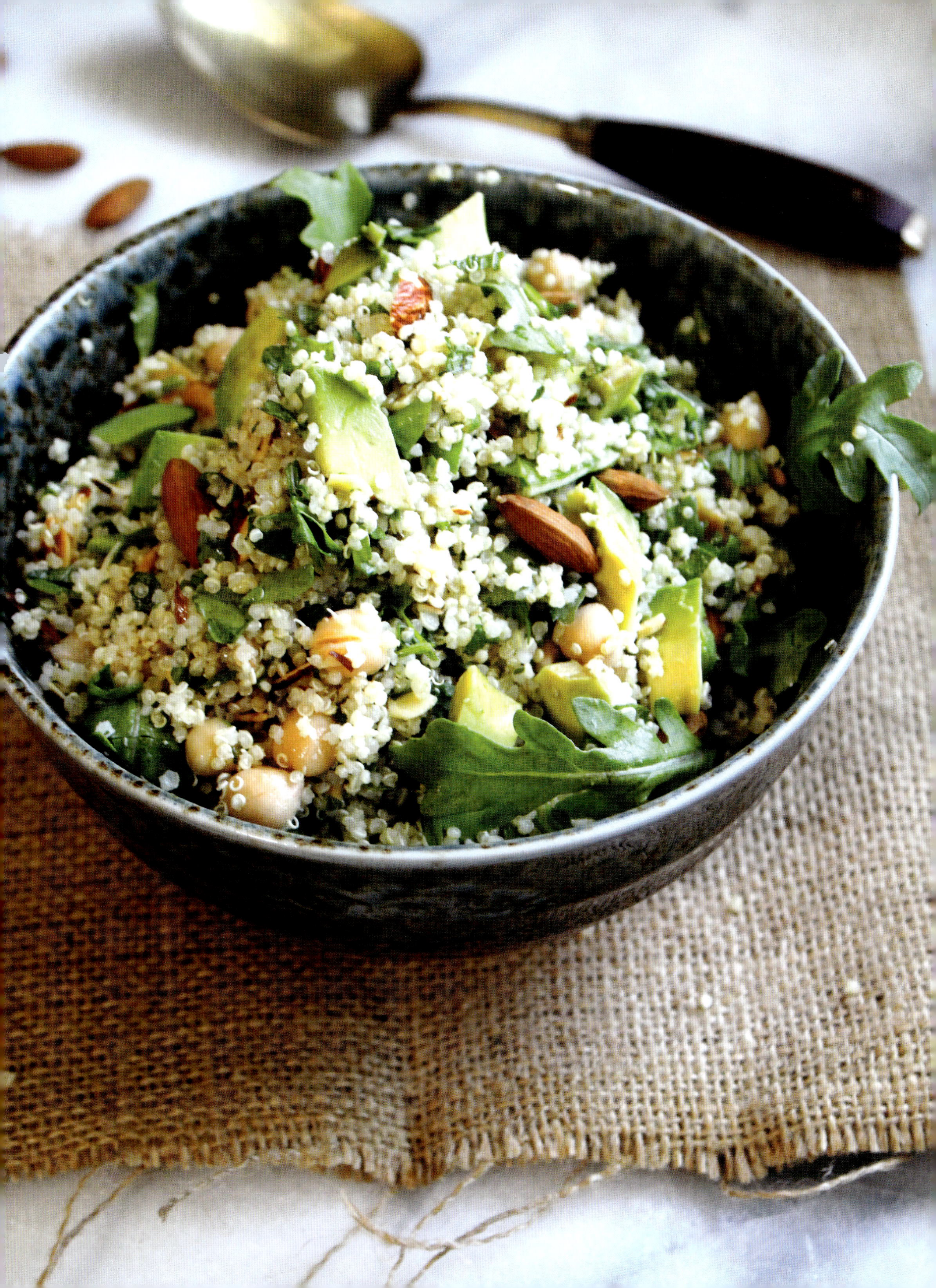

Garden Salad
kale + herbs

serves 4

1 cup (20 gr) fresh arugula
1 cup (30 gr) fresh chopped kale
1 cup (20 gr) fresh spinach
1 cup (10 gr) fresh dill sprigs
⅓ cup (40 gr) sliced almonds

almond dressing - recipe p. 105
1 small broccoli - stem removed and chopped
10 cherry tomatoes
1 small jalapeno pepper - seeded and finely chopped
½ cup (60 gr) cranberries

Wash the arugula, kale, spinach and dill in a large bowl of cold water. Spin dry in a salad spinner.
Place the almonds in a skillet over medium heat. Toast until golden, shaking the pan occasionally.
Place the greens in a large bowl. Season with almond dressing.
Add the broccoli, tomatoes and jalapeno. Toss to blend.
Garnish with cranberries. Top with toasted almonds.
Serve immediately.

vegan | gluten-free

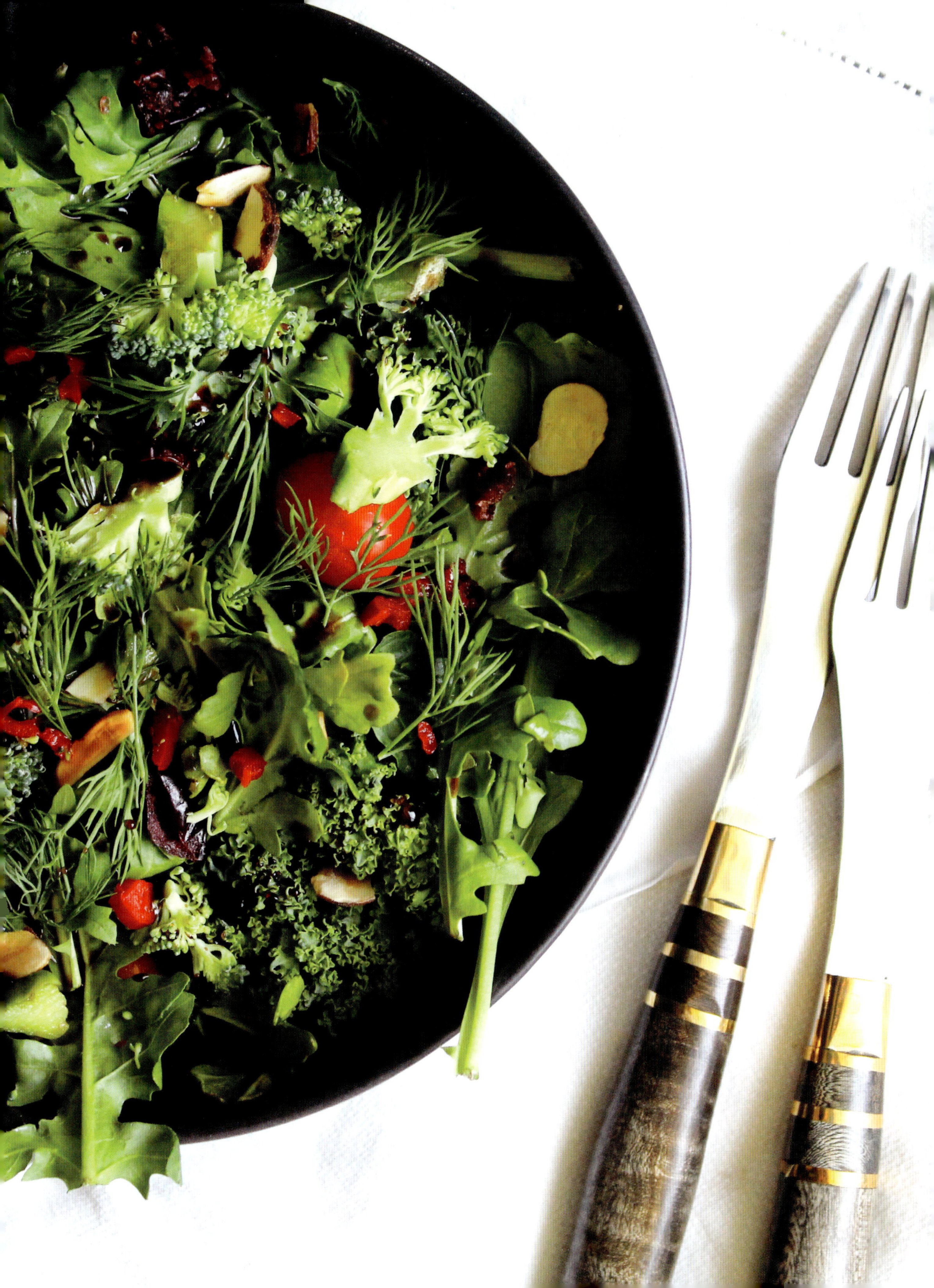

Tuna & Shrimp Tartare

serves 2

½ lbs. (230 gr) sushi grade ahi tuna – diced
6 medium shrimp – cooked, peeled and diced
1 tbsp sesame oil
1 tbsp soy sauce
1 avocado – pitted, peeled and diced

1 tbsp wasabi sauce
toasted sesame seeds
+ sliced ginger
+ 1 small round stainless steel ring

Combine tuna, shrimp, sesame oil and soy sauce in a mixing bowl. Season to taste.
Place the avocado in a separate bowl with the wasabi sauce. Carefully toss to combine.
To serve, place a small round stainless steel ring on a plate. Add ¼ of the tuna mixture, gently packing it down. Top with ½ of the avocado mixture and another layer of the tuna mixture.
Sprinkle with toasted sesame seeds.
Refrigerate for 15 minutes.
Serve cold with sliced ginger and a side of greens + crackers.

nut-free

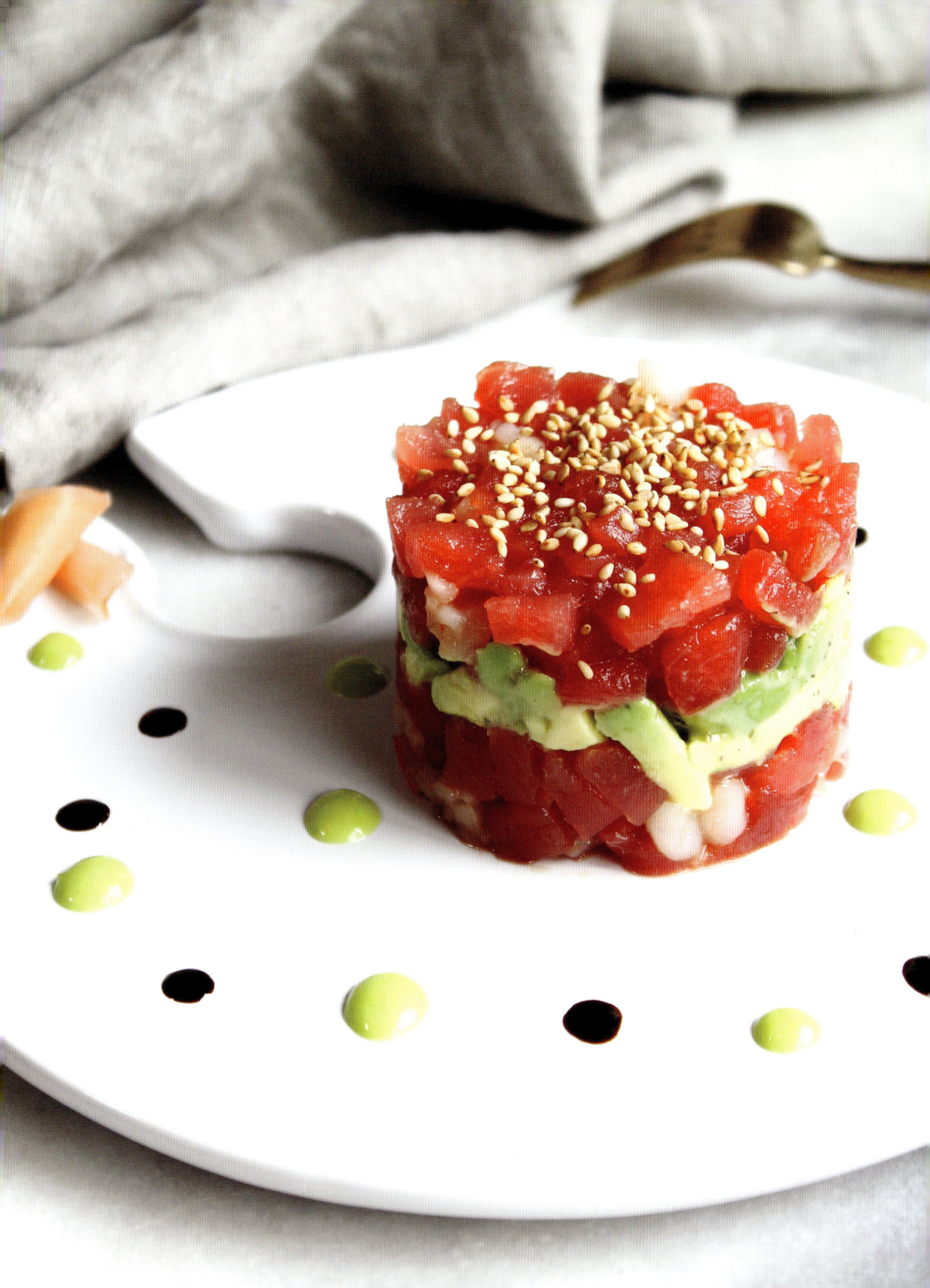

Caribbean Ceviche
mango + vanilla

serves 4

1 fresh swordfish steak - diced
1 mango – peeled and diced
1 vanilla bean
3 tbsp olive oil

1 lemon
1 tbsp chopped chives
salt + pepper

Halve the vanilla bean lengthwise. Scrape the seeds out and place in a small mixing bowl. Whisk in the olive oil, the zest of the lemon and squeeze in the juice as well. Season to taste. Toss in the swordfish, mango and chives. Cover and refrigerate ½ hour.
Serve with a side of basmati rice!

dairy-free | gluten-free | nut-free

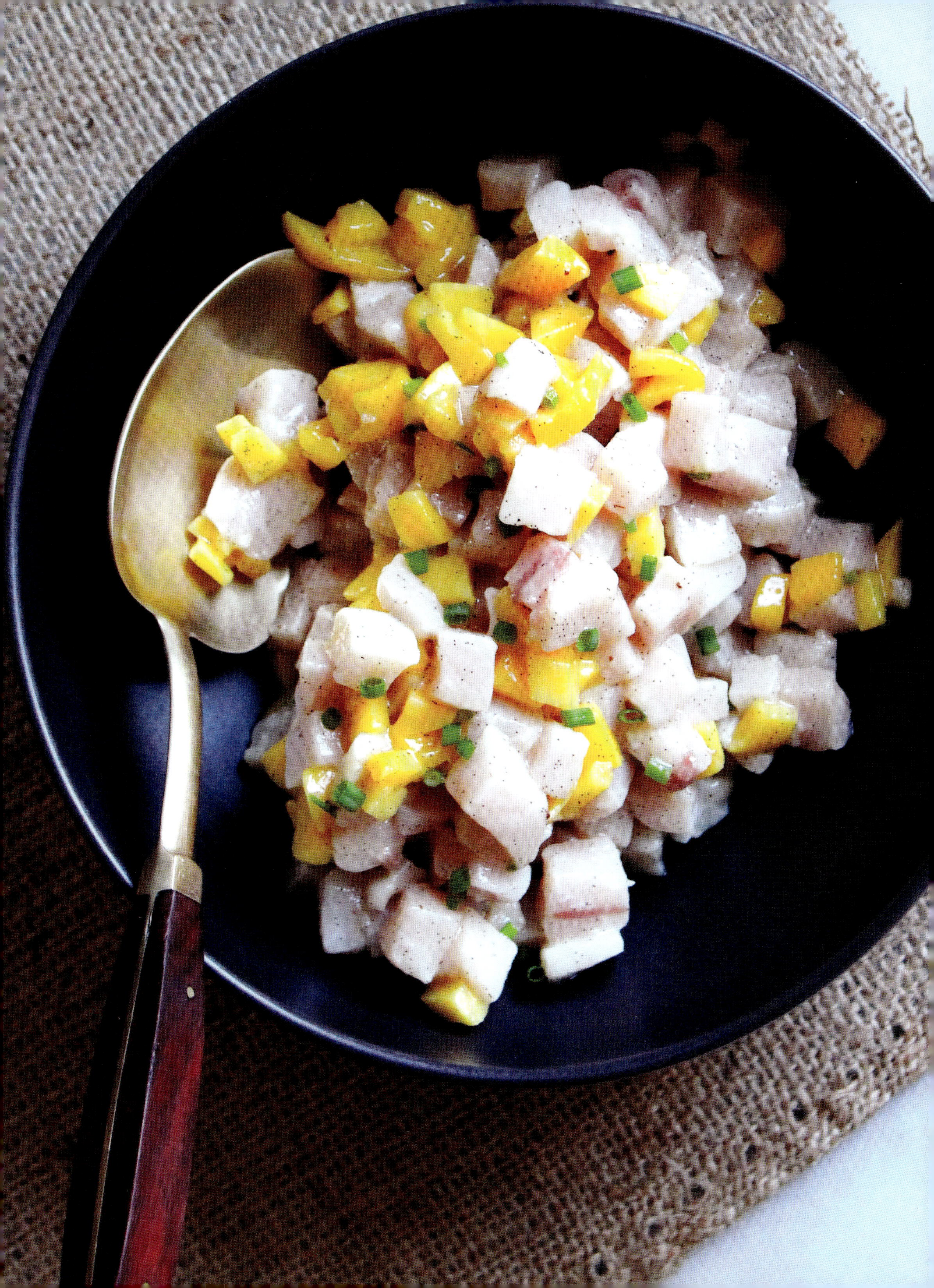

Butternut Squash Soup
coconut + seeds

serves 4

1 lbs. (454 gr) butternut squash – peeled, seeded and diced
7 oz. (200 gr) white potato – peeled and diced
1 cup (240 ml) vegetable broth
3 tbsp coconut milk

¼ tsp grated nutmeg
1 tbsp curry powder
salt + pepper
sunflower seeds

Bring a large pot of salted water to a boil.
Add the vegetables and cook until tender, about 30 minutes.
Drain and place in the bowl of a food processor.
Add the vegetable broth, coconut milk, nutmeg and curry powder. Blend until smooth.
Season to taste.
Serve immediately topped with sunflower seeds and a touch of coconut milk.

vegan | gluten-free | nut-free

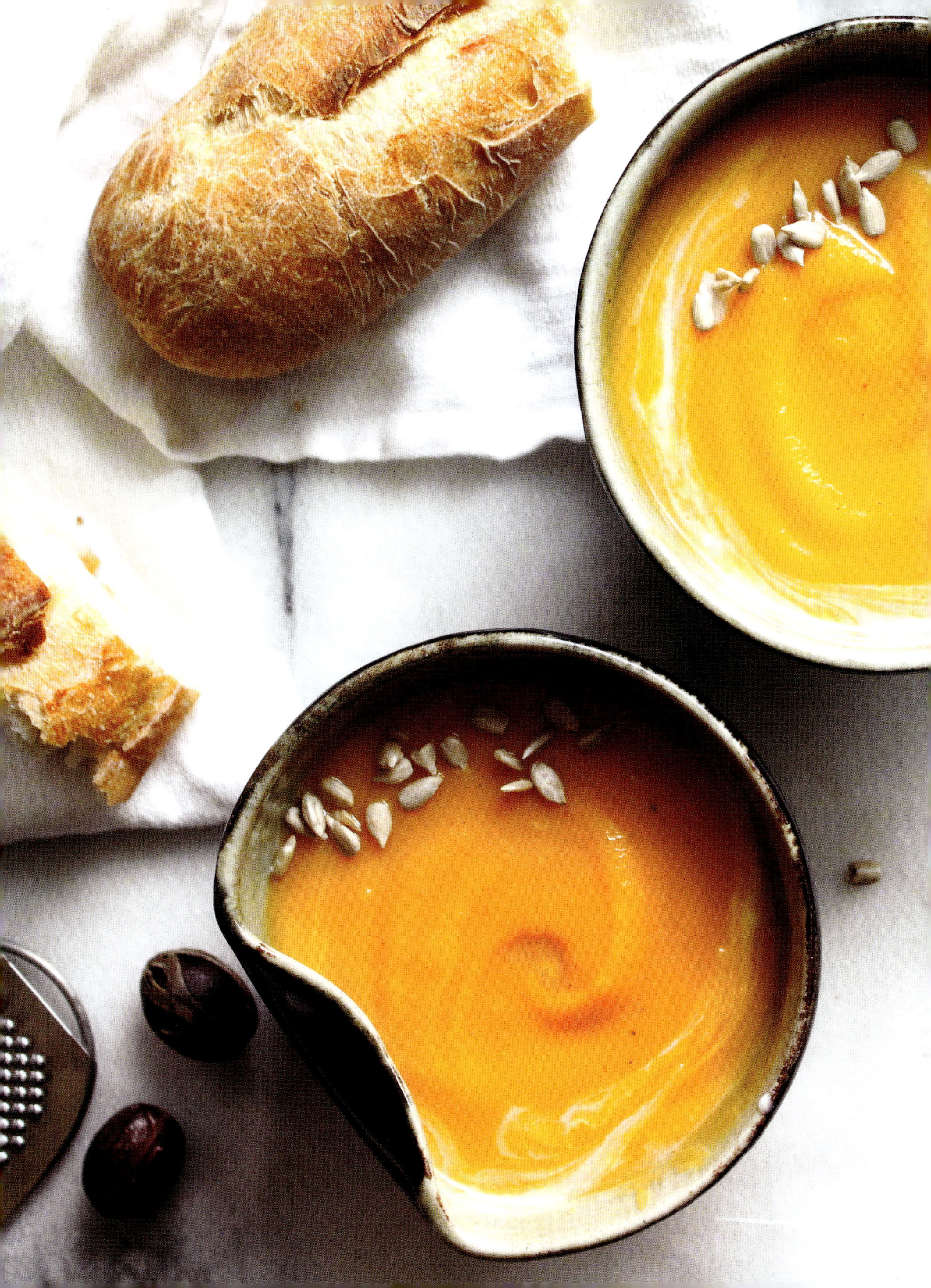

Garden Soup & Pearl Couscous

serves 4

2 medium carrots
2 celery stalks
2 Roma tomatoes
1 tsp olive oil
2 garlic cloves - peeled and thinly sliced

2 frozen basil cubes
1 cup (170 gr) pearl couscous
4 cups (1 L) vegetable broth
½ cup (75 gr) frozen green peas
a few fresh basil leaves

Rinse, peel and cut the carrots, celery and tomatoes into 0.4 in / 1 cm dice.
Heat the olive oil with the garlic and basil cubes in a large pot over medium heat – 1 minute.
Add the carrots and celery. Cook for 2 minutes, stirring occasionally.
Stir in the pearl couscous, tomatoes and vegetable broth.
Continue to cook uncovered for 10 minutes.
Add the green peas and cook 2 minutes more. Remove from the heat.
Pour evenly in individual bowls. Add a few fresh basil leaves.
Serve immediately!

vegan | nut-free

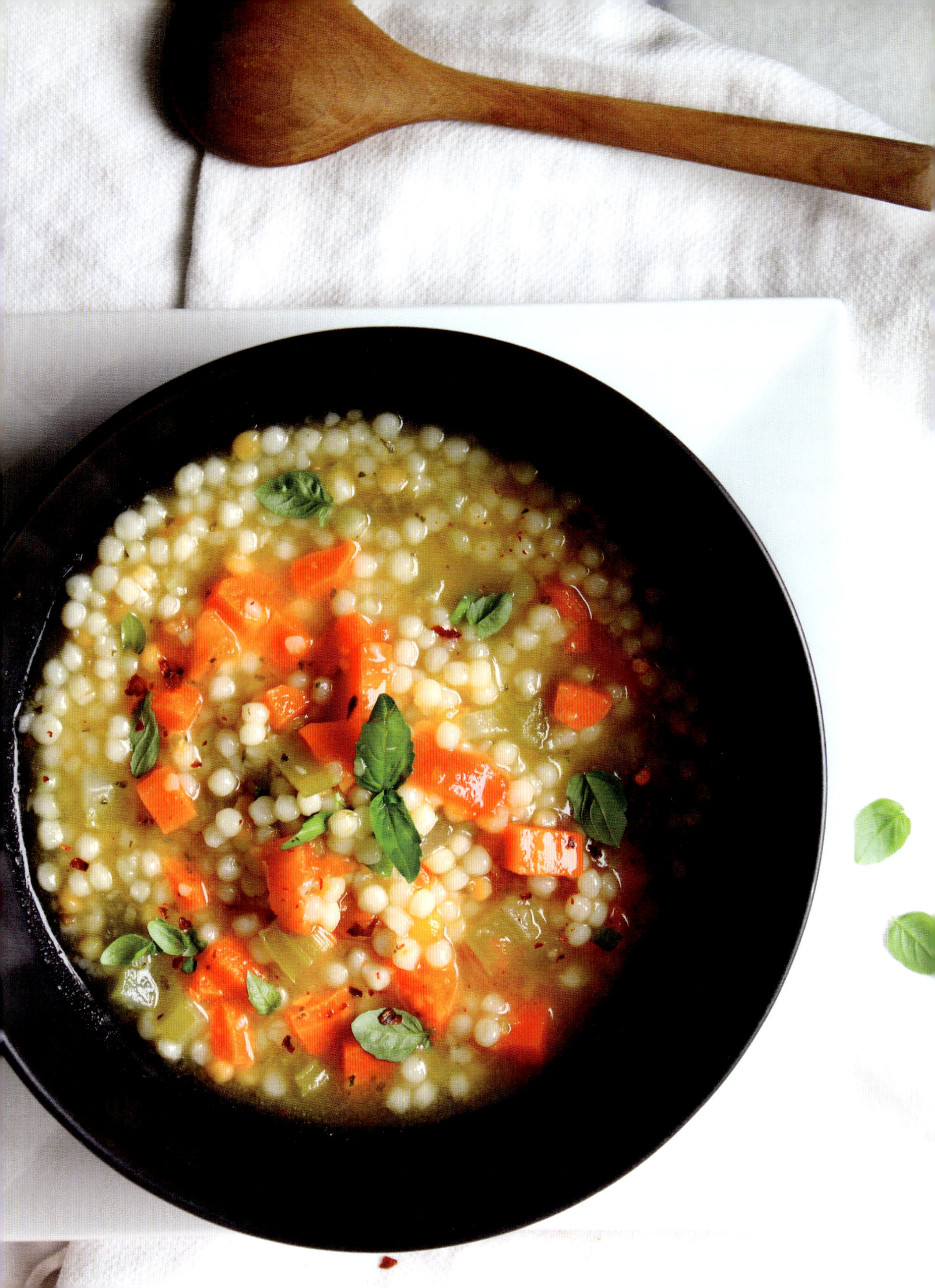

Pea & Mint Soup

serves 4

1 celery stalk - chopped
2 small white potatoes - diced
3 cups (720 ml) vegetable broth
1 cup (150 gr) frozen green peas

1 cup (120 gr) edamame
1 cup (30 gr) fresh mint leaves + more to serve
freshly ground pepper

Place the celery, potatoes and broth in a large pot over medium heat.
Bring to a boil. Cook until the potatoes are soft – about 15 minutes.
Add the frozen green peas and edamame. Cook 5 minutes more.
Place in the bowl of a food processor. Add the mint and blend until smooth – 2 minutes.
Transfer to a serving bowl.
Garnish with fresh mint leaves.
Serve immediately.

vegan | gluten-free | nut-free

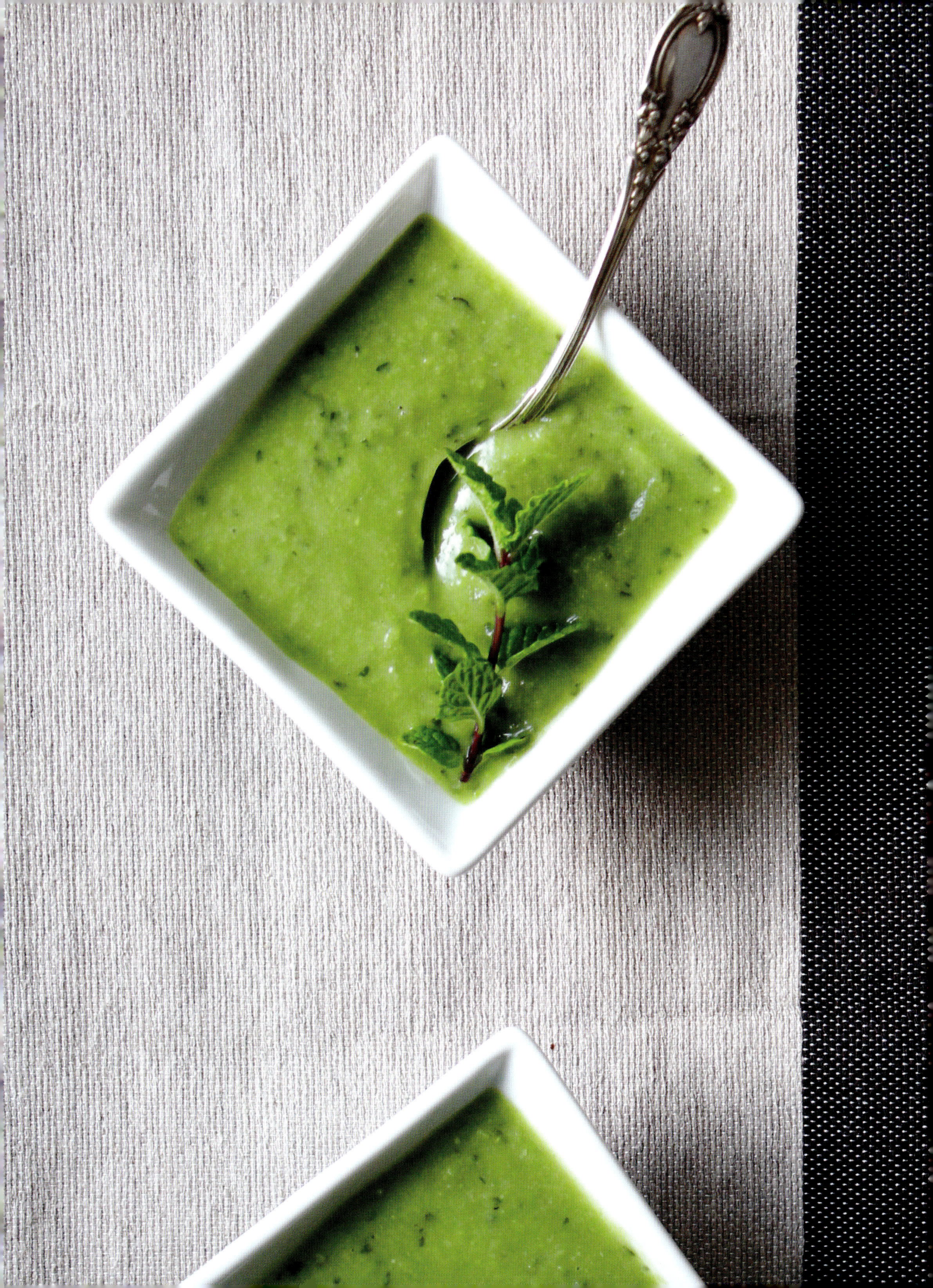

Leek & Potato Soup

serves 4

3 leeks – darker part removed
1 large Yukon potato – peeled and chopped
2 cups (500 ml) vegetable broth
1 cup (250) water

fresh thyme
olive oil
freshly ground pepper

Clean and finely chop the leeks. Place in a large pot over medium heat with the potatoes and 1 tsp olive oil. Cook for 5 minutes, stirring frequently. Add vegetable broth and water.
Bring to a boil and cook for 30 to 40 minutes.
Place in the bowl of a food processor. Blend until smooth.
Divide among 4 serving dishes. Drizzle with olive oil.
Garnish with fresh thyme and freshly ground pepper.
Serve immediately!

vegan | gluten-free | nut-free

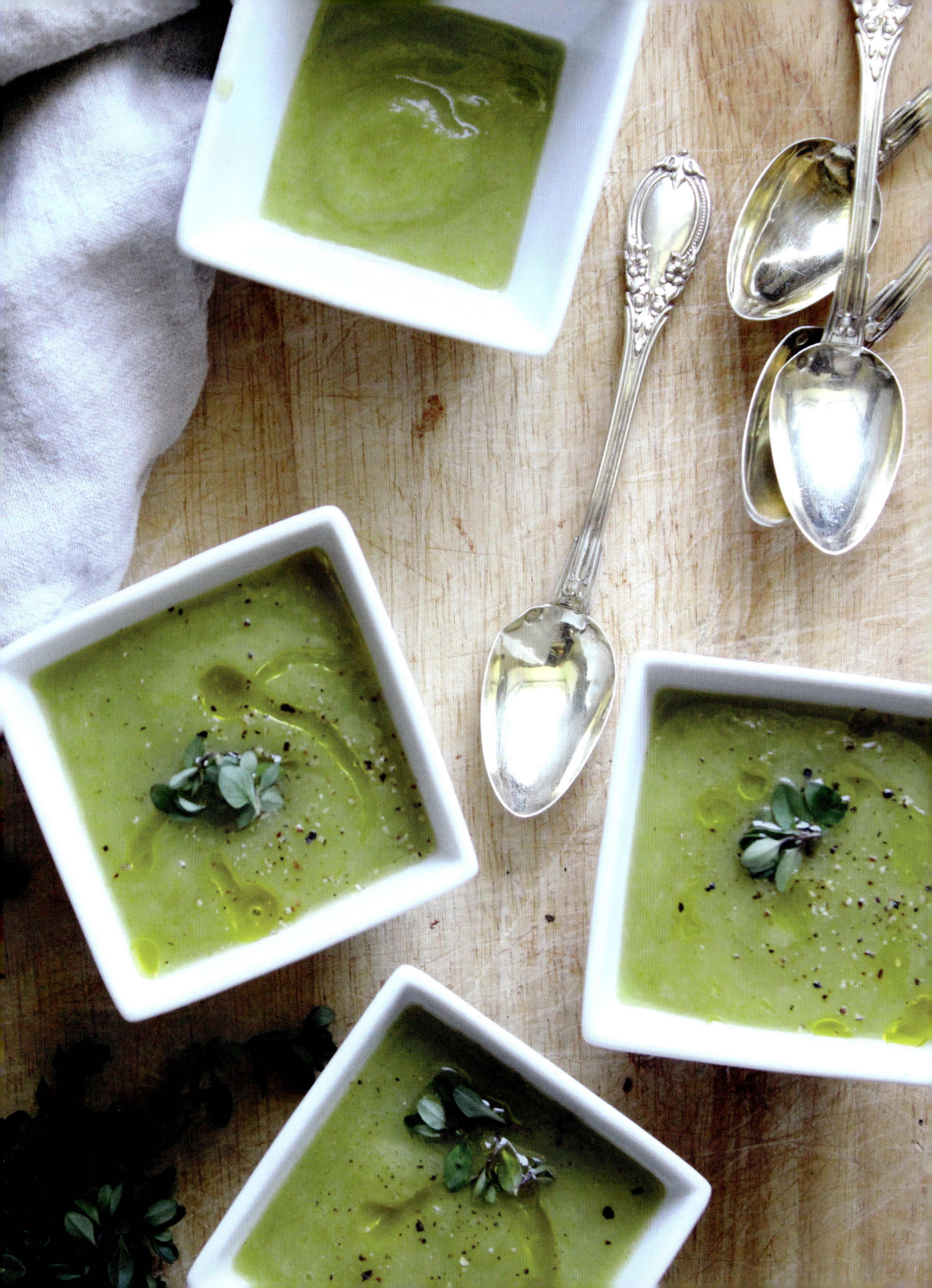

Miso Soup

serves 4

1 rice noodle bundle – or any clear noodle
3 cups (720 ml) water
1 cup (240 ml) vegetable broth
2 tbsp miso paste
sesame oil
1 oz. (30 gr) onion – thinly sliced

4 white mushrooms – thinly sliced
1 baby bok choy – cleaned and stem removed
10 sugar snaps – finely chopped
¼ cup (10 gr) fresh chopped coriander
1 tbsp sesame seeds

Bring the water and broth to a boil in a large pot. Stir in the miso paste. Remove from the heat.
Add the noodles, cover and leave untouched for 20 minutes.
Heat 1 tsp of sesame oil in a skillet. Add the onions and mushrooms.
Cook for 5 minutes on low heat, stirring occasionally.
Remove from the heat. Stir in 1 more tsp sesame oil and a pinch of salt.
Place the bok choy leaves, sautéed mushrooms, sugar snaps and coriander in the pot containing the noodles. Quickly reheat and divide among 4 serving bowls.
Serve immediately garnished with sesame seeds.

vegan | gluten-free | nut-free

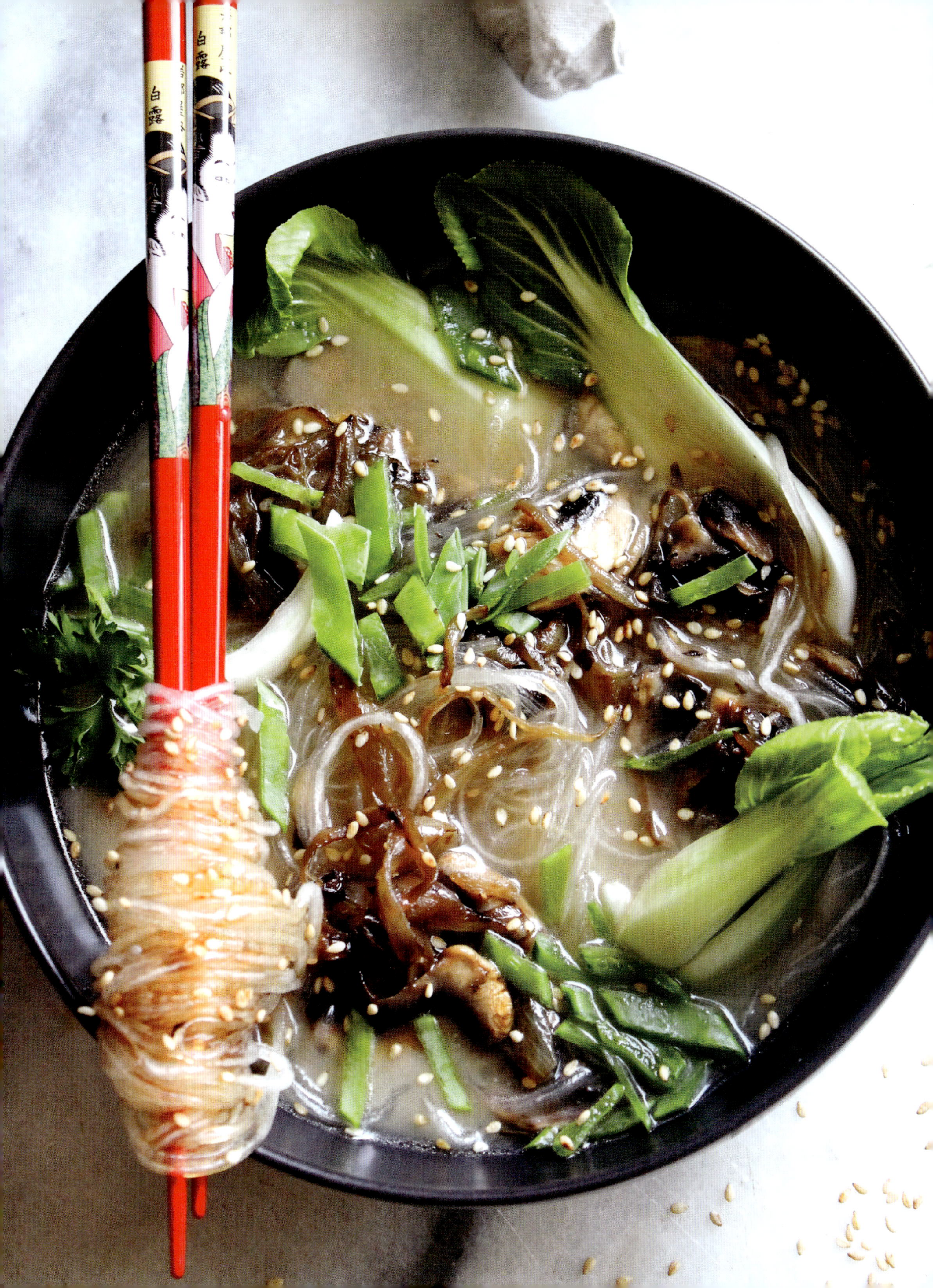
白露

Lentil & Kale Soup

serves 4

1 cup (200 gr) dry lentils
2 carrots - diced
2 celery stalks - diced
2 garlic cloves - thinly sliced

4 cups (1 L) vegetable broth
2 Roma tomatoes - peeled and diced
1 cup (30 gr) chopped kale + more to serve
+ arugula, sunflower seeds

Heat 1 tsp olive oil in a large saucepan over medium heat. Stir in the garlic, carrots, celery and lentils. Cook for 2 minutes. Add the broth. Bring to a boil and cook for 20 minutes over medium heat. Add the tomatoes. Cook 10 minutes more. Remove from the heat, stir in the chopped kale.
Pulse the mixture in a food processor until smooth - about 3 minutes.
Transfer to 4 serving bowls.
Garnish with fresh arugula and kale. Sprinkle with sunflower seeds.
Serve immediately.

vegan | gluten-free | nut-free

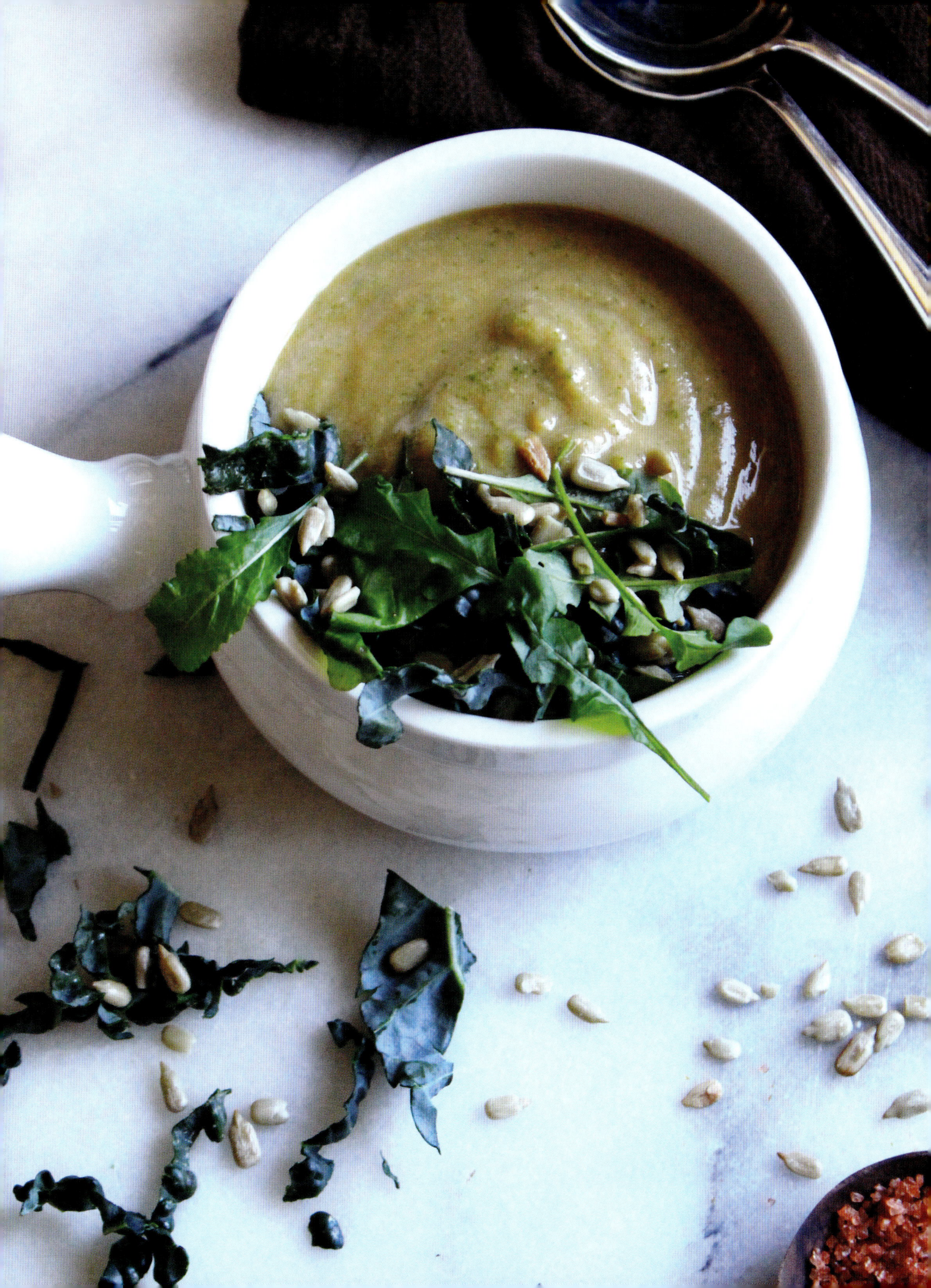

Kale & Bean Soup

serves 4

2 carrots - diced
2 celery stalks - diced
4 cups vegetable broth

1 cup (30 gr) chopped kale
1 lbs. (454 gr) canned white beans - rinsed and drained
1 tbsp olive oil

Heat the olive oil in a pot over medium heat. Stir in the carrots and celery. Cook for 2 minutes.
Add the broth and beans. Cook until the vegetables are tender - about 15 minutes.
Remove from the heat, stir in the chopped kale.
Cover and leave untouched for 10 minutes.
Divide among 4 serving bowls.
Serve immediately!

vegan | gluten-free | nut-free

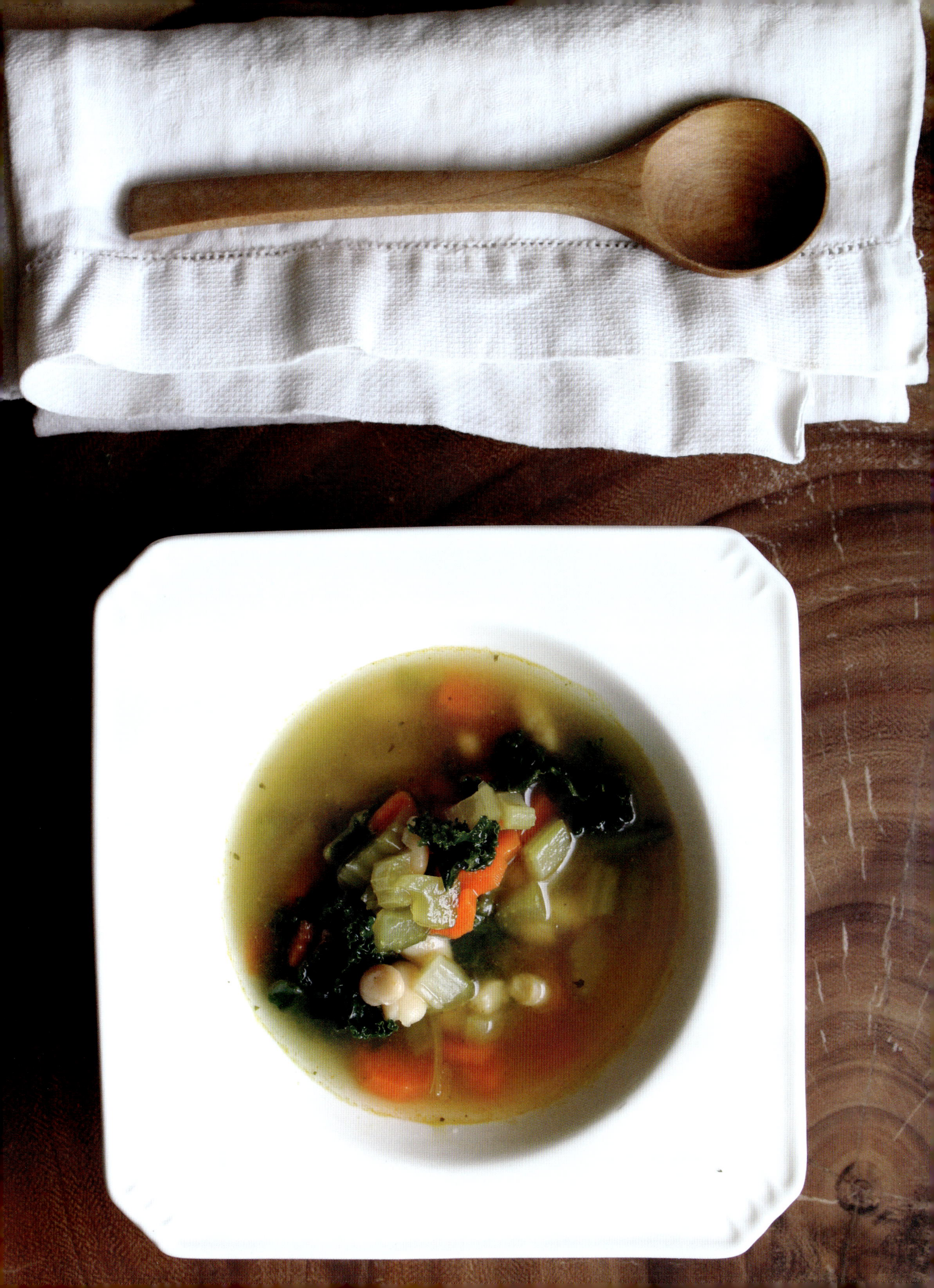

Tomato Soup

serves 2

4 Roma tomatoes
1 red bell pepper - halved and seeded
1 tsp crushed red pepper
salt + pepper

olive oil
+ fresh chopped basil
+ chopped hazelnuts
+ crushed red pepper

Preheat the oven to 450F / 230C. Line a baking sheet with parchment paper.
Place the whole tomatoes and red bell pepper on the prepared baking sheet.
Drizzle about 1 tbsp olive oil and 1 tsp salt. Toss to coat.
Roast in the preheated oven for 30 minutes.
Pulse the roasted vegetables (and the cooking juice) in a food processor until smooth – 2 minutes.
Season to taste with salt and pepper.
Transfer to individual bowls.
Garnish with fresh chopped basil, chopped hazelnuts and crushed red pepper.

vegan | gluten-free

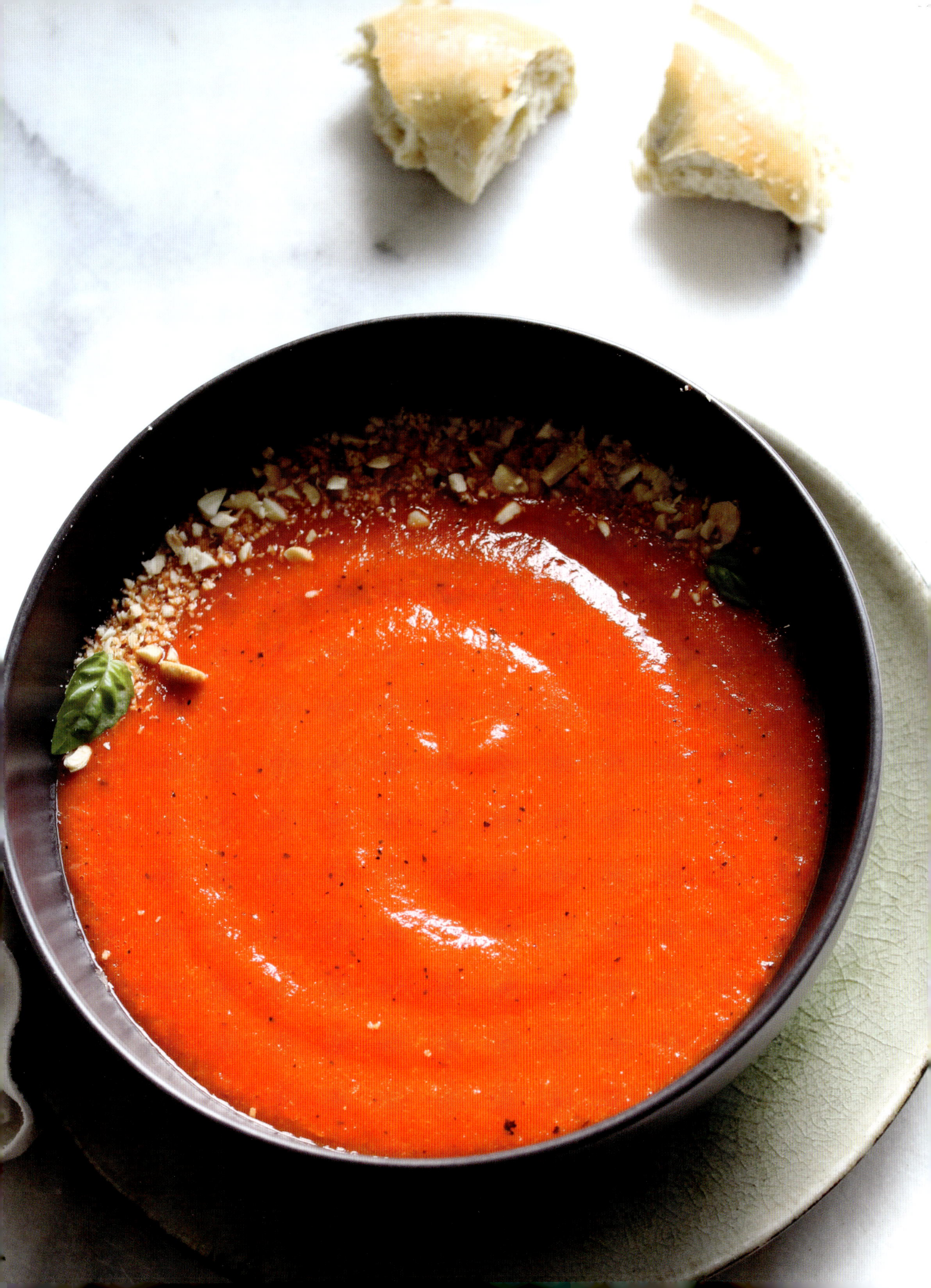

Creamy Tomato Pasta

serves 4

1 lbs. (454 gr) linguini pasta
1 cup (240 gr) roasted tomato soup - recipe p. 128
fresh basil leaves

½ tsp crushed red pepper
salt + pepper
+ roasted tomatoes - recipe p. 78

Bring a large pot of salted water to a boil. Add the pasta and cook as the label directs.
Drain and return to the pot with the roasted tomato soup.
Toss to coat using tongs. Thin with water if too thick.
Divide among 4 serving plates.
Scatter the roasted tomatoes over the pasta.
Garnish with fresh basil leaves, crushed red pepper and season to taste.
Serve immediately!

vegan | nut-free

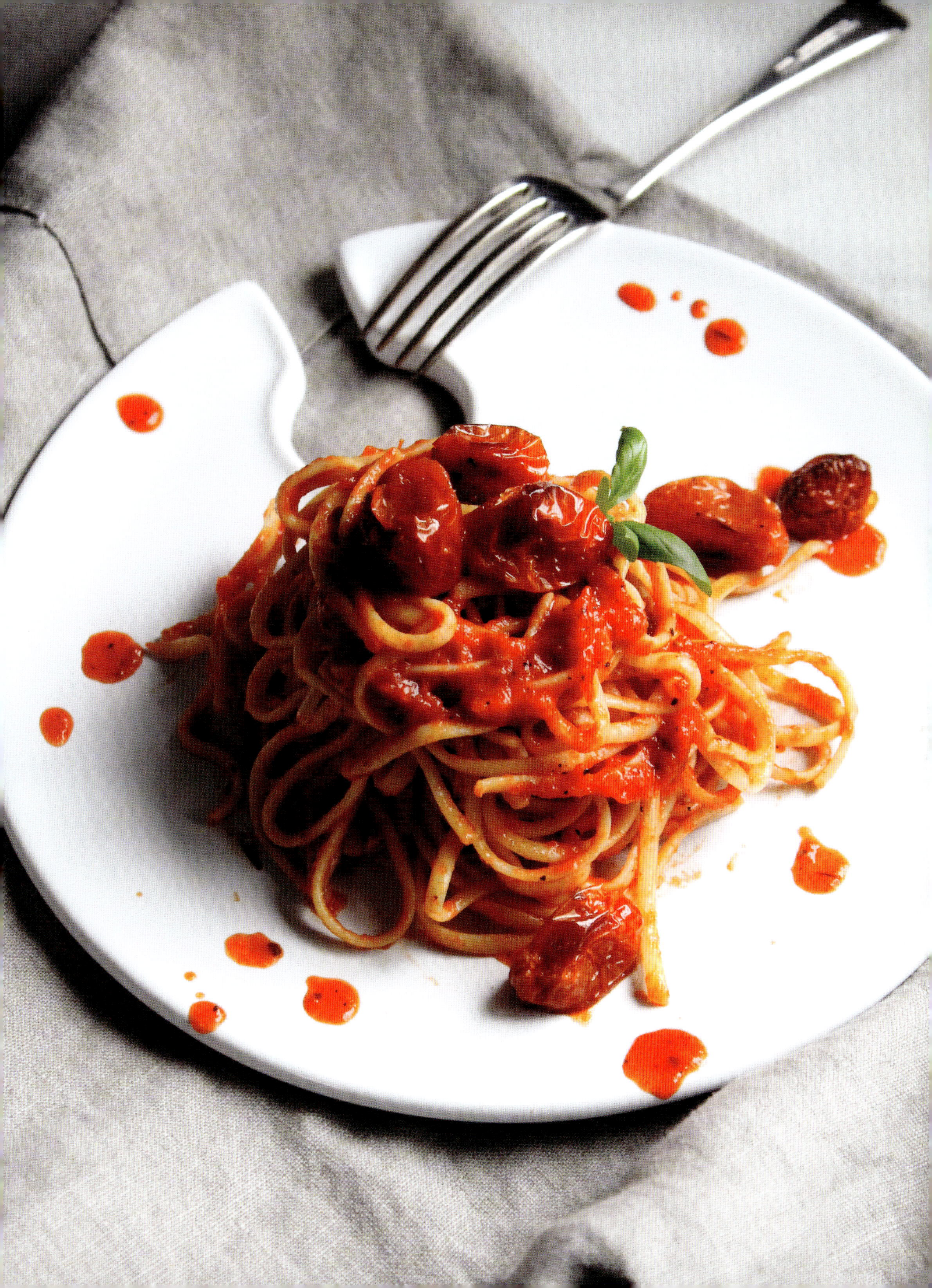

Shrimp Stir Fry
+ rice noodles

serves 4

16 wild caught shrimp
7 oz. (200 gr) stir-fry rice noodles
1 red bell pepper - halved and seeded
1 small bok choy - cleaned and chopped
2 rounded tbsp curry paste (Patak)
2 chives - chopped

1 tsp olive oil
½ cup (120 ml) vegetable broth - warm
10 fresh basil leaves
½ cup (75 gr) whole cashews
1 cup (240 ml) coconut cream
salt + pepper

Preheat the broiler. Place the red bell peppers face cut down on a baking sheet lined with parchment paper. Broil in the oven until the skins are charred - about 10 minutes.
Let cool completely. Remove the skins and chop the peppers.
Bring a large pot of salted water to a boil. Remove from the heat.
Add the noodles, cover and leave untouched until soft - about 8 minutes. Drain, rinse and reserve.
Place a large skillet over medium heat. Add the curry paste and the shrimp.
Cook for about 10 minutes, stirring occasionally and adding some of the warm broth if needed.
Add the olive oil, bok choy, chives, red bell pepper and the remaining broth, if any.
Stir in the noodles and coconut milk. Continue to cook for 3 minutes. Season to taste.
Transfer to a serving dish. Garnish with fresh basil and cashews.
Serve immediately!

dairy-free | gluten-free

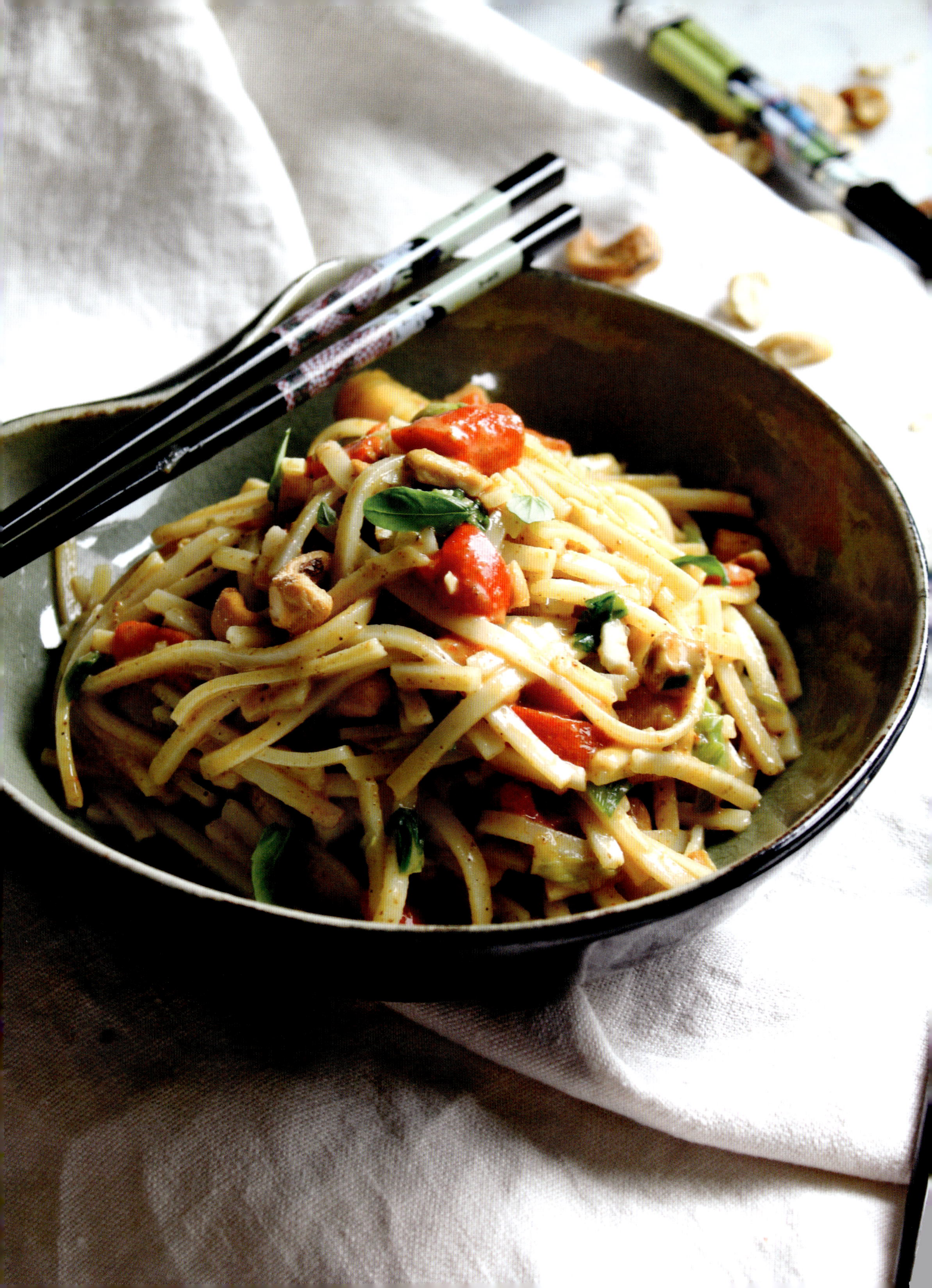

Vegan Curry & Lemon Quinoa

serves 4

1 carrot – peeled and halved
1 zucchini – halved
6 white mushrooms – cleaned and thinly sliced
1 cup (120 gr) frozen edamame
2 cups (500 ml) coconut cream + 5 tbsp
½ cup (120 ml) almond milk
1 tbsp curry powder

1 tbsp curry paste
1 cup (170 gr) quinoa
the zest of 1 lime
½ cup (60 gr) sliced almonds
¼ cup (10 gr) fresh coriander
olive oil
salt

Cut the carrot and zucchini in long strips of even size. Place in a saucepan, cover with salted water and cook until just tender – about 10 minutes. Drain and set aside in a mixing bowl.
Place the mushrooms and 1 tsp olive oil in a skillet over medium to low heat.
Cook for 5 minutes.
Stir in the edamame and cook 2 minutes more. Add to the mixing bowl with 2 cups of coconut cream, almond milk and curry powder. Season to taste. Cover and refrigerate overnight.
The next day, heat the curry paste in a large skillet over low heat.
Slowly add the 5 tbsp coconut cream, whisking constantly. Bring to a gentle simmer, about 2 minutes. Add the precooked vegetable curry.
Cook for 3 minutes more – do not bring to a boil.
Bring 2 cups of water to a boil. Add 1 tsp of salt and the quinoa.
Cook for 15 minutes or until all the water is absorbed.
Stir in the lime zest and about 4 tbsp of the curry sauce.
Divide the quinoa among 4 serving bowls.
Top with the vegetable curry. Garnish with sliced almonds and fresh coriander.

vegan | gluten-free

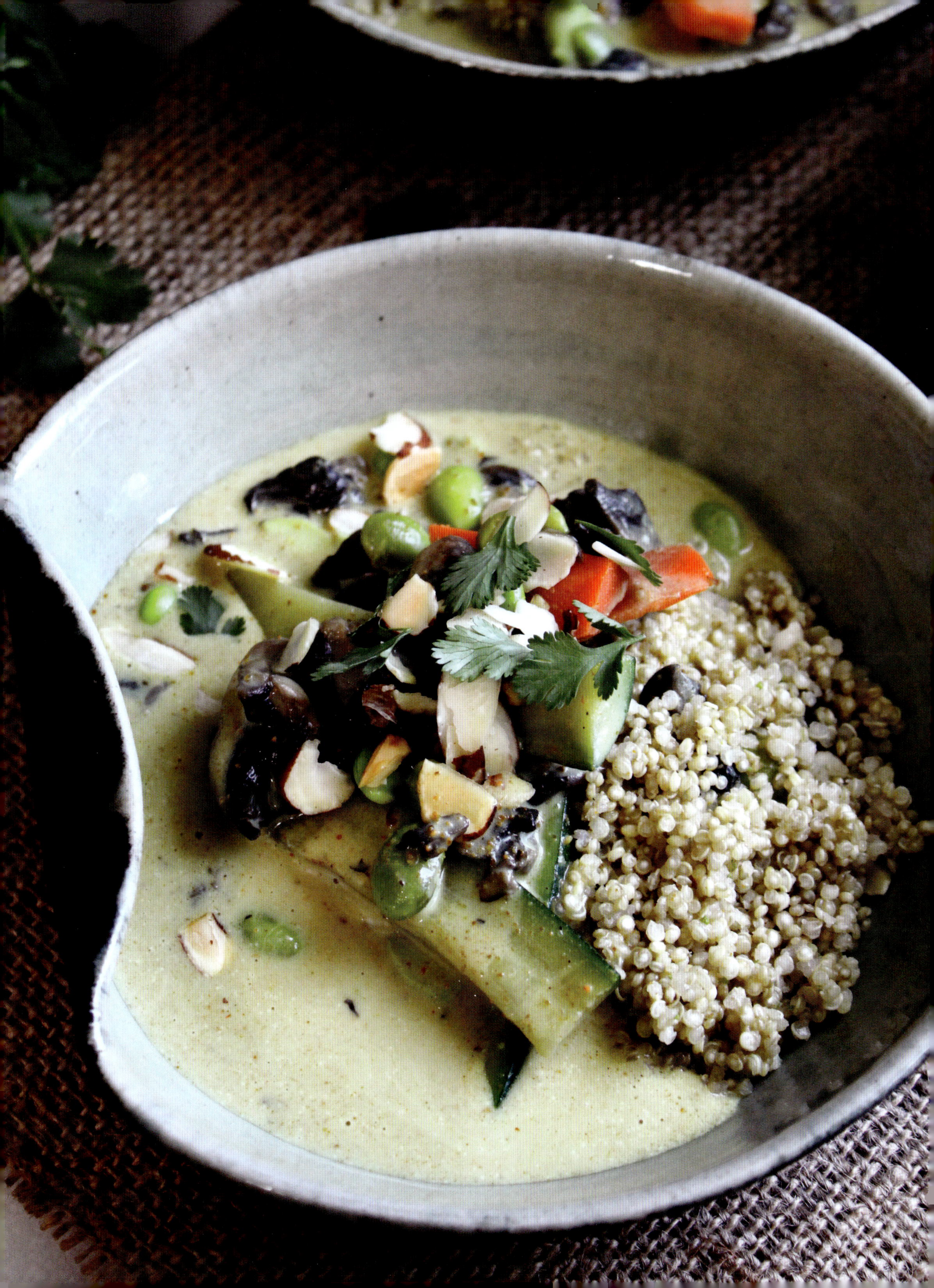

Zucchini Shooters

serves 4

3 medium zucchini (400 gr) – roughly chopped
2 cups (500 ml) vegetable broth
1 oz. (30 gr) cream cheese

a few leaves of fresh arugula
toasted hazelnut – chopped
1 cup (170 gr) quinoa

Place the zucchini and broth in a saucepan. Bring to a boil and cook until tender – 15 minutes.
Scoop out the zucchini with a slotted spoon reserving the broth. Place in a food processor.
Add the cream cheese. Puree until smooth adding some of the reserved broth if needed.
Place the quinoa and 2 cups of water in a saucepan over medium heat.
Cook until tender, about 15 minutes.
Divide among 4 serving ramekins.
Top with the zucchini puree. Garnish with arugula leaves and chopped hazelnut.
Serve immediately.

vegetarian | gluten-free

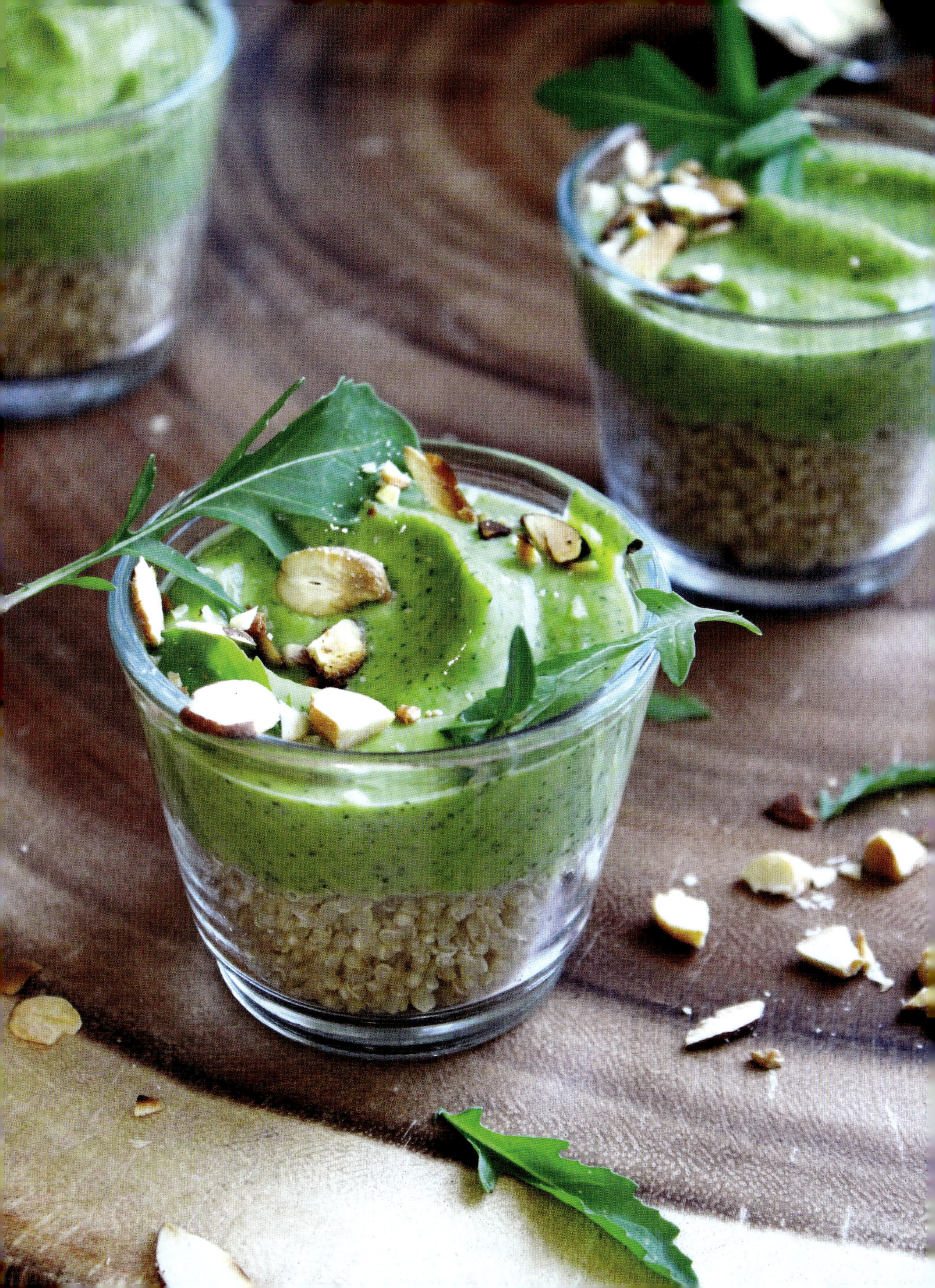

Vegan Fajitas
black bean puree + guacamole

serves 4

1 oz. (30 gr) chopped red onion
1 medium carrot – chopped
1 celery stalk – chopped
1 x 15 oz. (425 gr) can of black beans – rinsed and drained

2 cups vegetable broth
1 tsp olive oil
+ guacamole – recipe p. 72
+ Mexican rice – cooked
+ large flour tortillas

Heat the olive oil in a large pot over medium heat – 1 minute. Add the onions, carrots and celery. Cook for 2 minutes stirring occasionally. Add the beans and broth. Cook 15 minutes more. Place in the bowl of a food processor and pulse until smooth.
Serve with guacamole, Mexican rice and flour tortilla!

vegan | nut-free

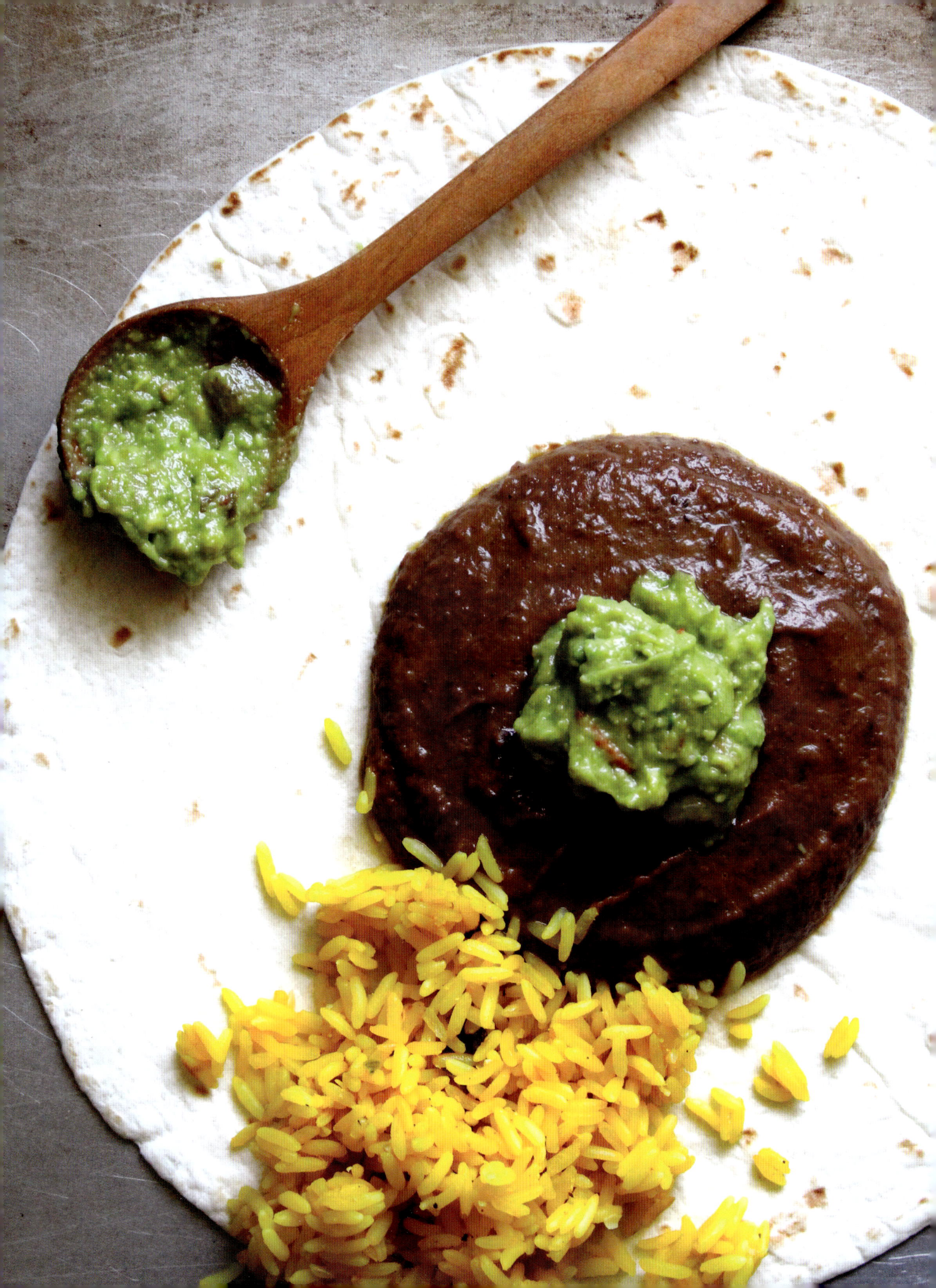

Roasted Brussel Sprouts

serves 4

1 lbs. (454 gr) Brussel sprouts – cleaned and halved
2 oz. (60 gr) red onion – thinly sliced
2 tbsp olive oil

½ tsp salt
1 tbsp balsamic vinegar
1 tsp balsamic glaze

Preheat the oven to 430F / 220C. Line a baking sheet with parchment paper.
Mix the Brussel sprouts, red onions, olive oil and salt in a large bowl.
Spread on the prepared pan in a single layer.
Roast in the preheated oven until browned and crispy – about 25 minutes. Toss every 10 minutes.
Add the balsamic vinegar and balsamic glaze right out of the oven. Toss to coat.
Serve immediately!

vegan | gluten-free | nut-free

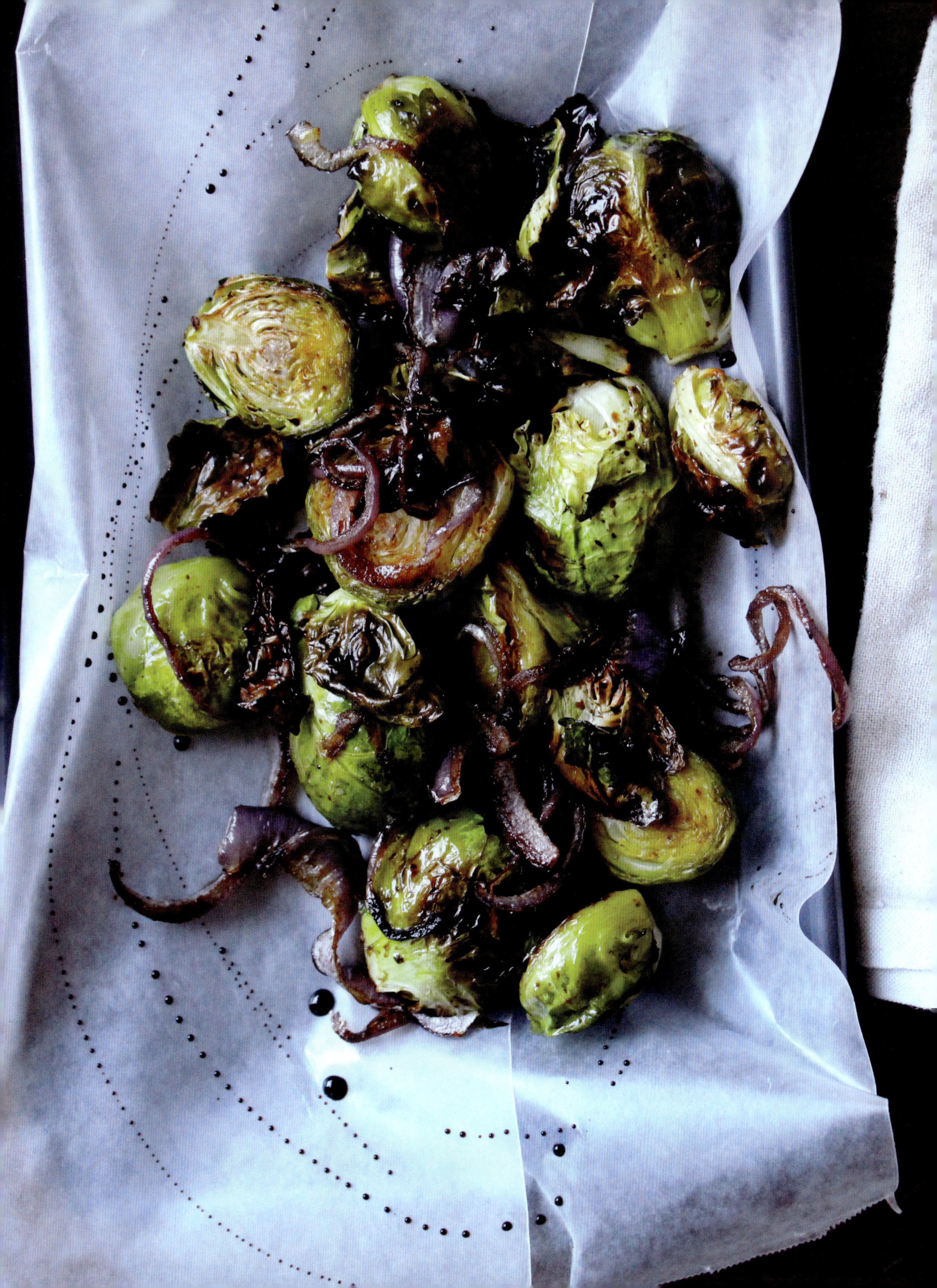

Avocado & Kale Pasta

serves 2

20 cherry tomatoes
8 oz. (230 gr) linguini pasta
1 ripe avocado
the juice of ½ lemon
20 fresh basil leaves + more to serve

⅓ cup (10 gr) chopped kale
1 tbsp curry powder
salt + pepper
olive oil
+ crushed red pepper

Preheat the oven to 450F / 230C. Line a baking sheet with parchment paper or silicone baking mat.
Add the tomatoes, drizzle with 1 tbsp olive oil and a pinch of salt.
Roast in the preheated oven for 20 minutes.
Bring a large pot of salted water to a boil. Add the pasta and cook as the label directs.
Drain reserving ¼ cup of the cooking water. Return to the pot.
Pulse the avocado, lemon juice, basil leaves, kale, curry powder and ½ tsp of salt in a food processor.
Add to the pasta. Stir to blend. Thin with some of the reserved pasta water if it's too thick.
Transfer to a serving bowl.
Garnish with roasted tomatoes, a few fresh basil leaves and crushed red pepper to spice it up!

vegan | nut-free

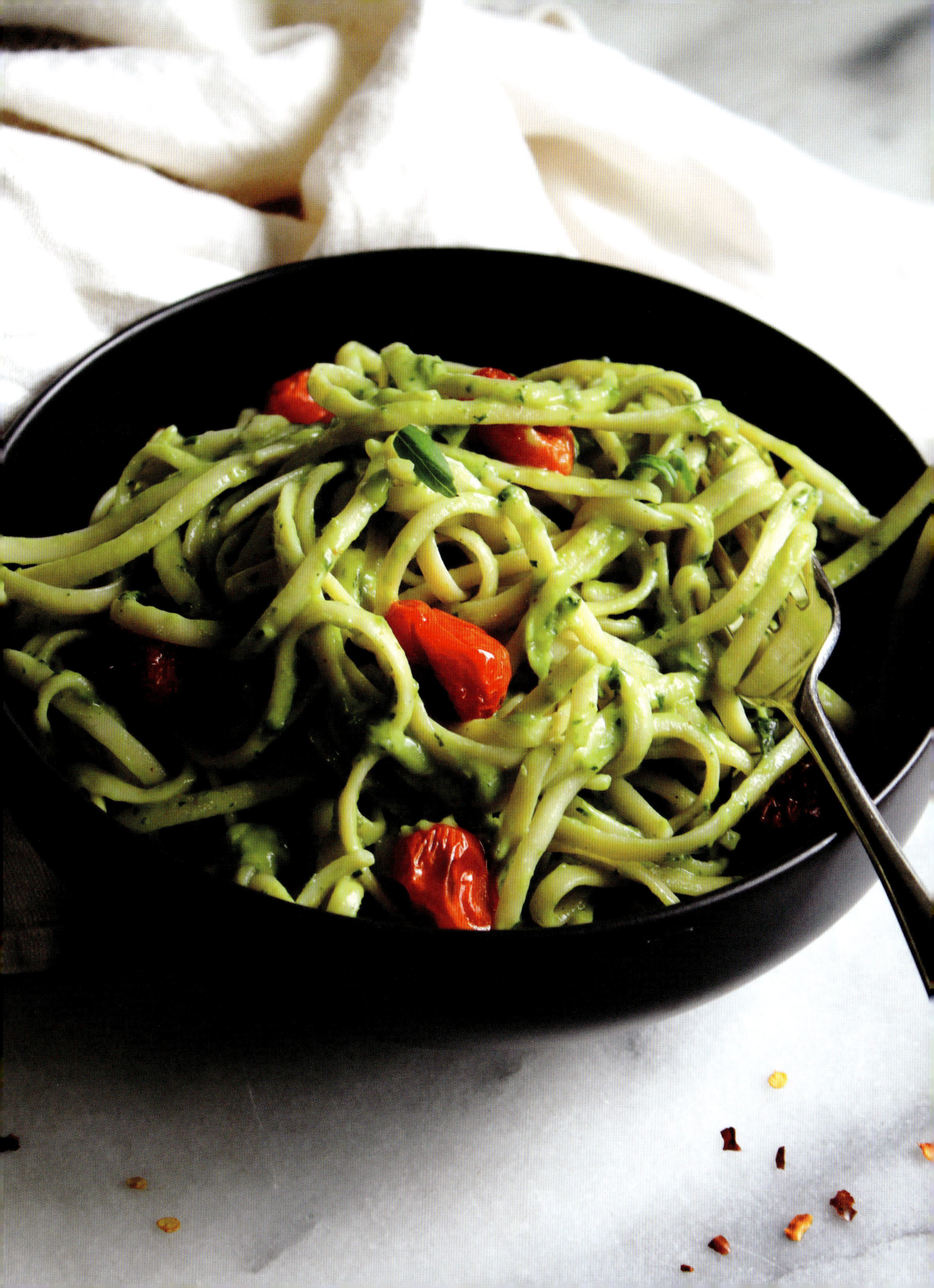

Lemon Pasta
+ burrata cheese

serves 4

1 lbs. (454 gr) linguini pasta
lemon oil or olive oil
1 lime
3 garlic cloves – thinly sliced
1 bundle of fresh spinach - washed and dried

1 cup (150 gr) frozen green peas
burrata cheese – 1 ball
salt + pepper
+ parmesan shavings

Bring a large pot of salted water to a boil. Add the pasta and cook as the label directs.
Drain reserving ¼ cup of the pasta water.
Mix 1 tbsp lemon oil, the juice and zest of the lime in a bowl. Set aside.
Heat the oil in a large pan over medium heat and fry the garlic – 2 minutes.
Add the spinach, cooked pasta, green peas and lemon mixture. Toss to coat – 1 minute.
Add some of the reserved pasta water if needed. Season to taste.
Divide among 4 serving plates. Tear the burrata cheese and sprinkle over the pasta.
Top with parmesan cheese and a drizzle of lemon oil.

vegetarian | nut-free

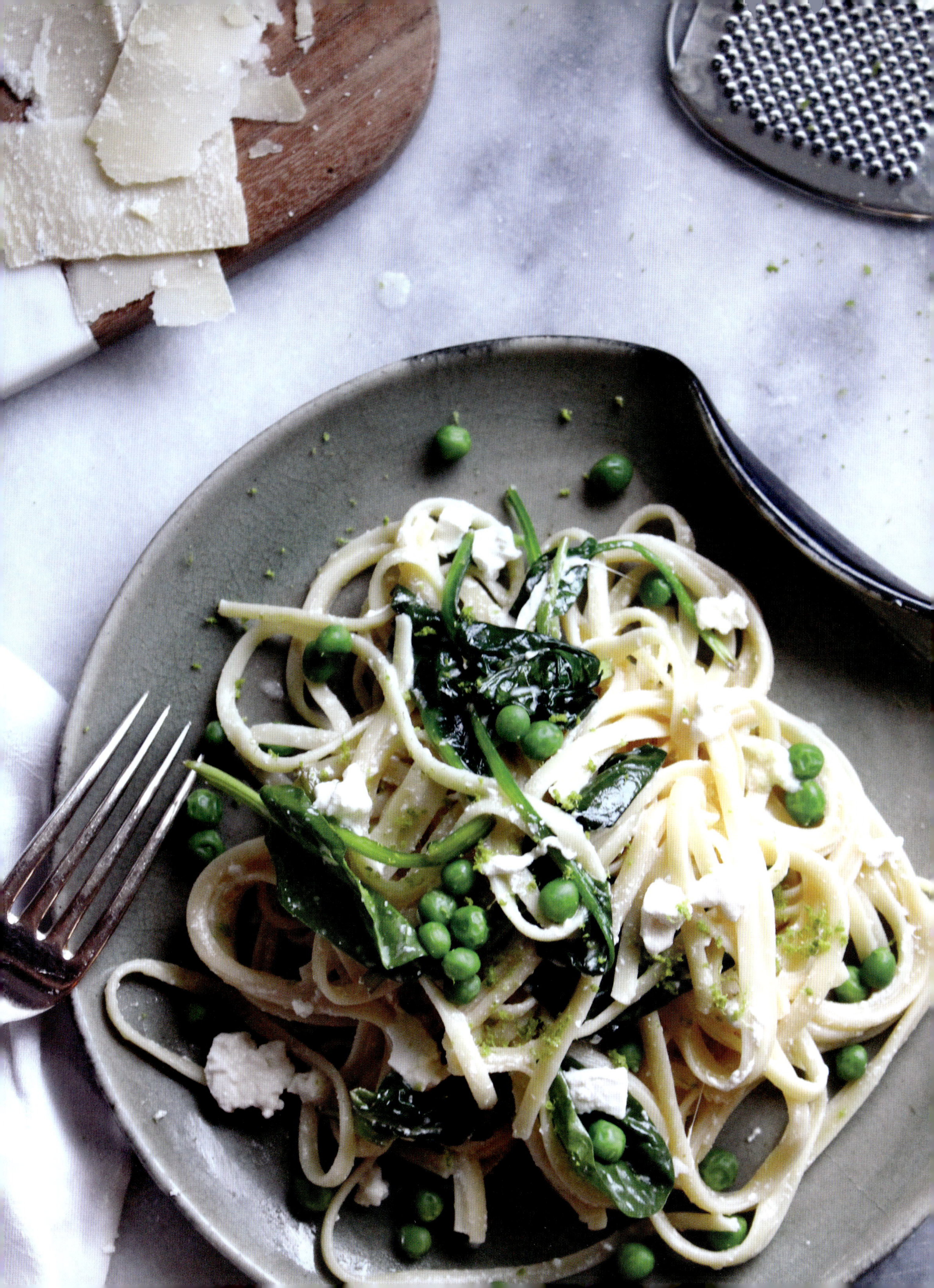

Pesto Pasta
+ parmesan tuiles

serves 4

20 cherry tomatoes – quartered
olive oil
1 frozen basil cube
1 lbs. (454 gr) rigatoni pasta
⅓ cup (90 gr) pesto – recipe p. 74
salt + pepper

parmesan tuiles:
¼ cup (25 gr) grated parmesan cheese
¼ tsp crushed red pepper
+ 1 tbsp toasted pine nuts
+ fresh basil

Make the Parmesan Tuiles: preheat the oven to 430F / 220C.
Line a baking sheet with parchment paper or silicone baking mat.
Combine parmesan cheese and crushed red pepper in a small bowl.
Drop tablespoons of this mixture on the prepared baking sheet. Flatten with the back of the spoon.
Bake in the preheated oven until golden – 4 minutes. Let cool completely before removing.
Combine the tomatoes, 1 tbsp olive oil and frozen basil cube in a small bowl. Season to taste.
Bring a large pot of salted water to a boil. Add the pasta and cook as the label directs.
Scoop out and reserve ½ cup of the pasta water before draining the pasta.
Return to the pot with the prepared tomatoes, pesto and reserved cooking water.
Cook over medium heat stirring constantly – 2 minutes.
Divide among 4 serving plates.
Garnish with fresh basil, toasted pine nuts and Parmesan Tuiles!

vegetarian

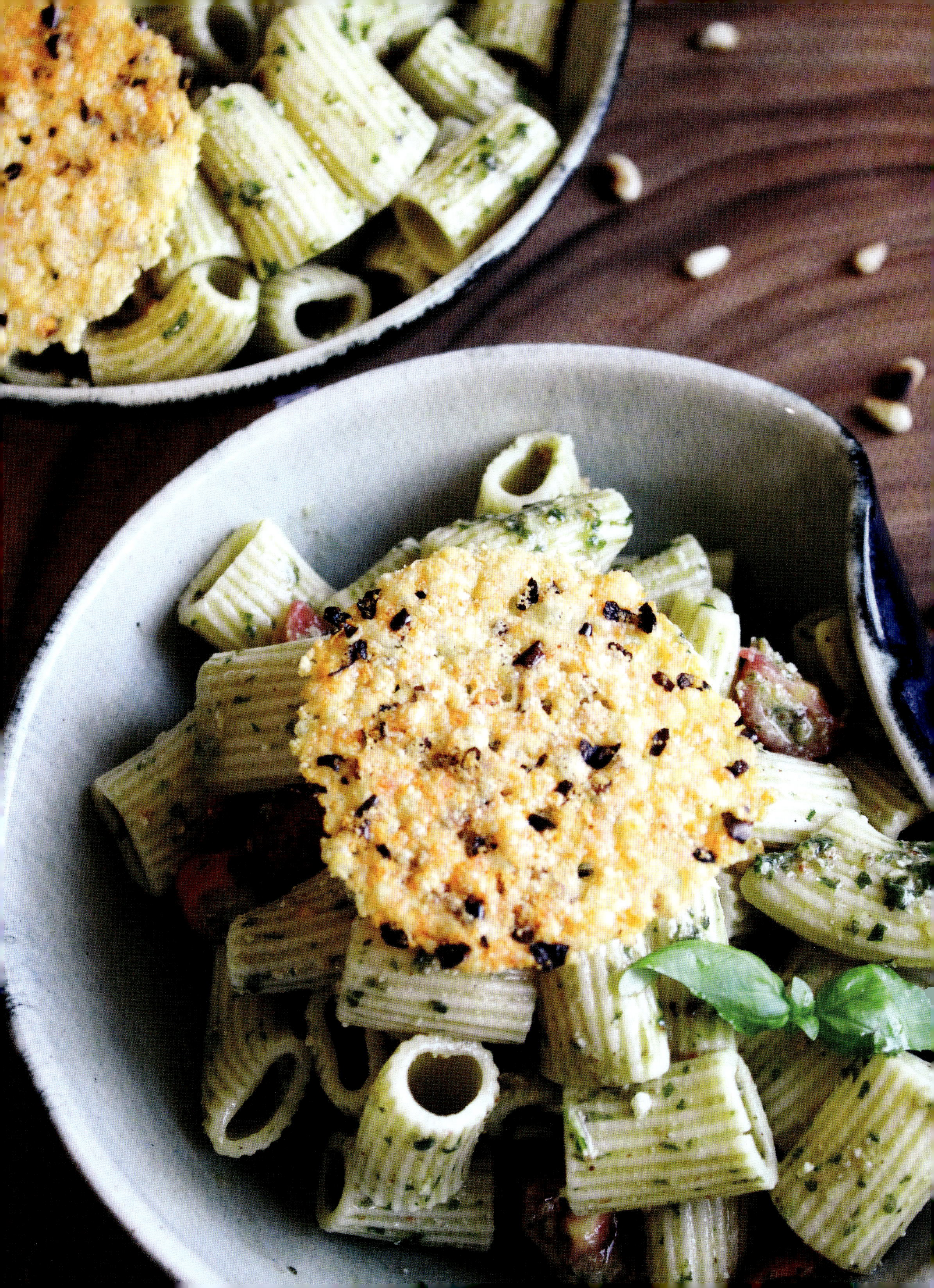

Coconut Poached Fish
+ mushroom risotto & truffle oil

serves 4

poached fish:
4 swordfish fillets
2 cups (500 ml) coconut cream
mushroom risotto:
10 oyster mushrooms – cleaned and chopped
a small bundle of enoki mushrooms – cleaned
4 cups (1 L) vegetable broth
2 tbsp salted butter

2 oz. (60 gr) red onion – chopped
1 cup (200 gr) Arborio rice
⅓ cup (80 ml) white wine
1 tbsp truffle oil
a few fresh thyme leaves
olive oil
¼ tsp salt

Place the coconut cream and a pinch of salt in a large skillet over medium heat.
Bring to a boil and reduce to a simmer. Add the fish fillets, cover and cook for 6 minutes.
Transfer to a bowl. Set aside.
To make the risotto, place 1 tbsp olive oil in a skillet over high heat. Add the mushrooms.
Cook for 2 minutes, flicking the pan every 10 seconds. Set aside.
Bring the broth to a boil in a small saucepan. Reduce the heat to low to keep it warm.
Melt the butter in a large pan over medium heat. Add the chopped onion.
Cook until tender and browned, stirring occasionally – about 2 minutes.
Stir in the rice, cook 1 minute.
Add the wine and cook until all the liquid is absorbed – about 3 minutes.
Add one cup of broth at a time and cook until all the liquid is absorbed each time.
Continue to cook until creamy and fully cooked.
The entire cooking time should be around 25 minutes.
Mix in the truffle oil and sautéed mushrooms. Season to taste.
Divide among 4 serving plates. Drizzle with truffle oil. Garnish with fresh thyme leaves.
Serve immediately with the poached fish and coconut cream.

gluten-free | nut-free

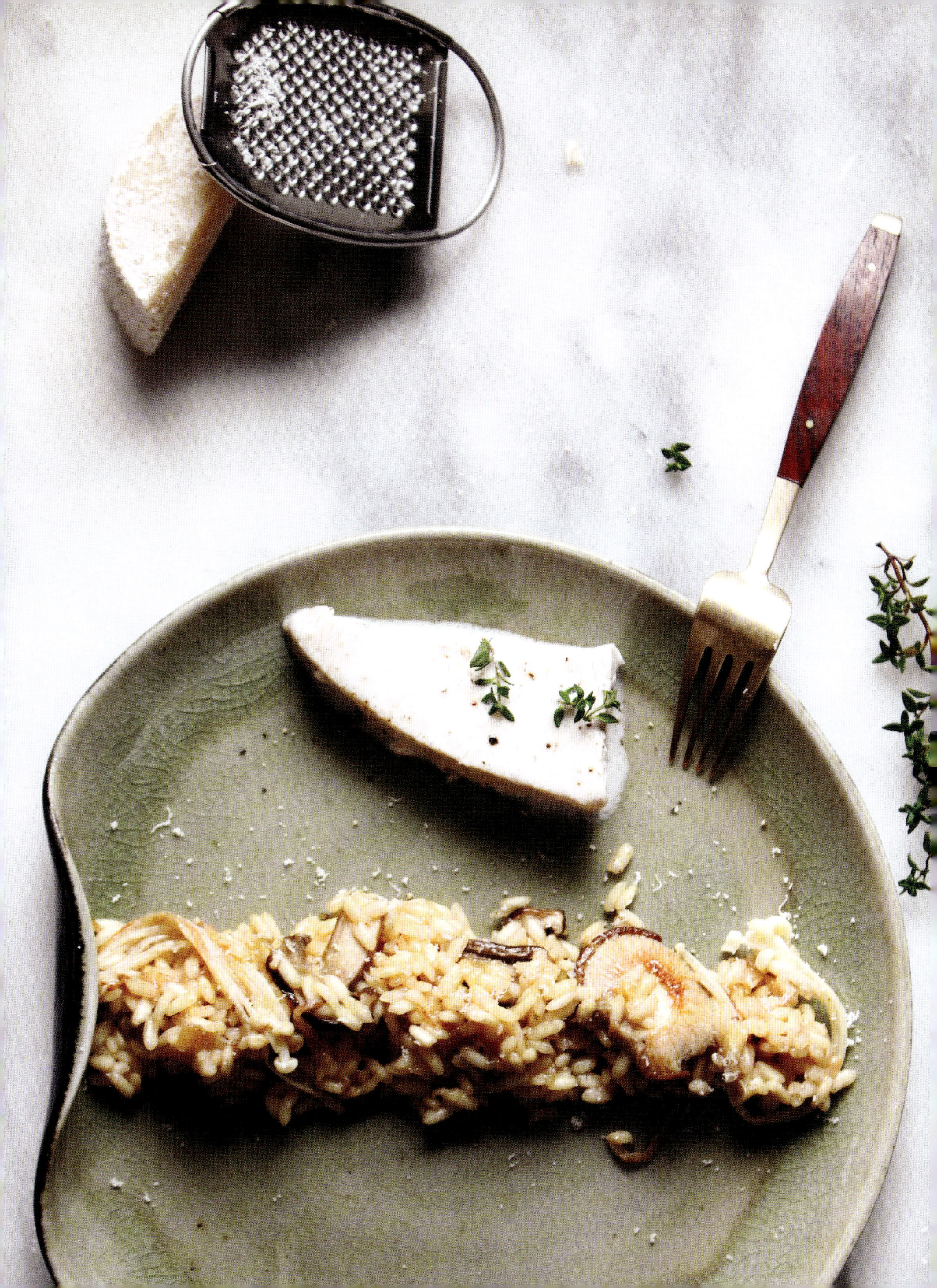

Dill Salmon
+ almond quinoa

serves 2

2 tbsp sliced almonds
½ cup (85 gr) quinoa
2 tbsp fresh chopped dill
2 wild Atlantic salmon fillets
a few leaves of fresh arugula

salt + pepper
almond oil
olive oil
pea & mint soup – recipe p. 118

Preheat the oven to 460F / 240C. Line a baking sheet with parchment paper or silicone baking mat.
Spread the sliced almonds in a single layer. Toast in the oven for 4 minutes.
Bring 1 ½ cups (300 ml) of water to a boil in a saucepan. Add ½ tsp of salt and the quinoa.
Cook over medium heat until all the water is absorbed and the quinoa is tender – 15 minutes.
Season with 1 tbsp almond oil and sprinkle with sliced almonds. Set aside.
Make the pea and mint soup. Set aside.
Mix together 1 tbsp olive oil and the dill in a small bowl. Season to taste.
Spread this mixture on the salmon using a brush. Transfer to the prepared pan.
Bake for 12 minutes in the preheated oven.
Place the salmon on serving plates. Garnish with a few leaves of fresh arugula.
Serve with a side of pea & mint soup and almond quinoa.

dairy-free | gluten-free

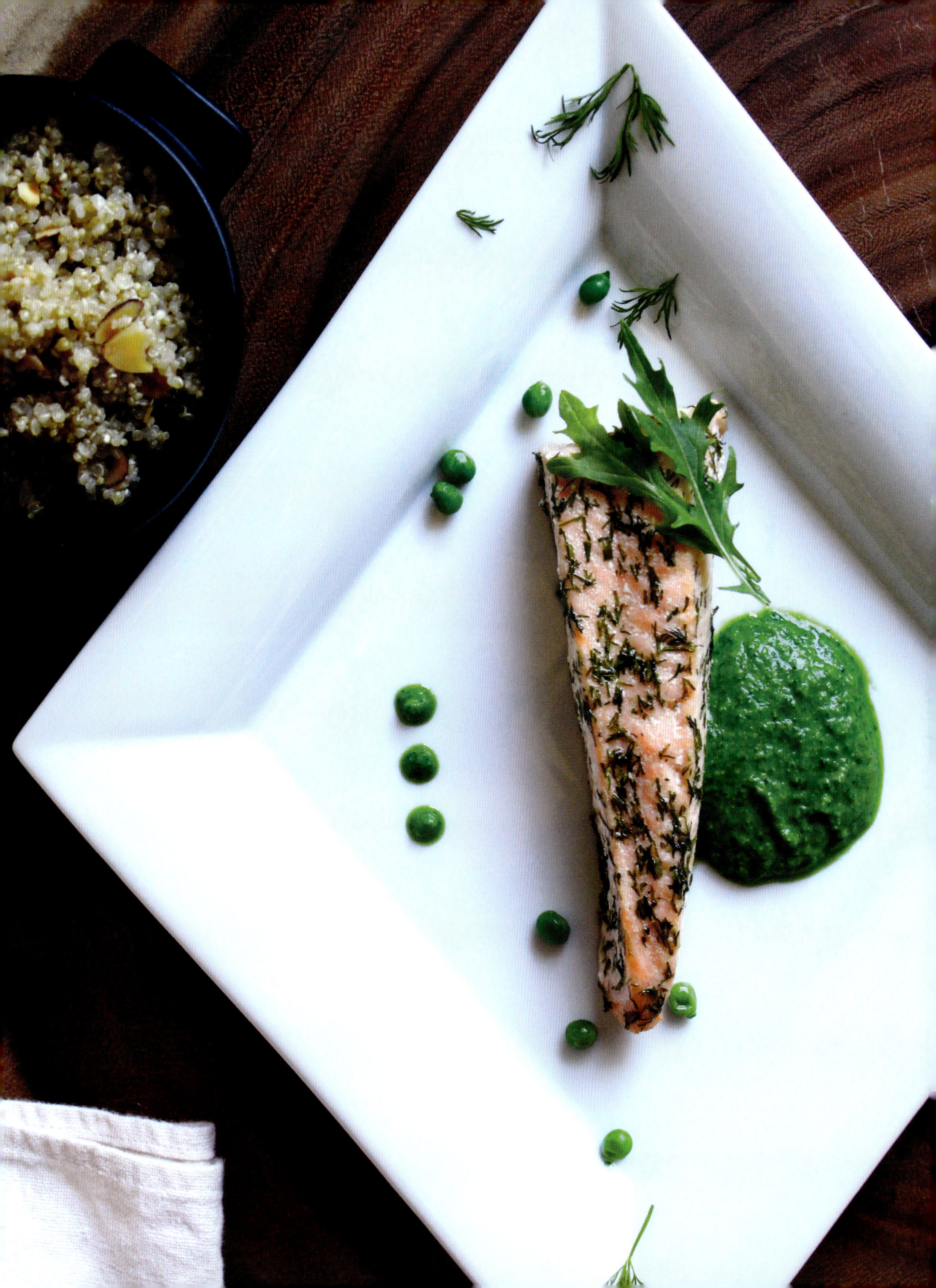

Lemon Butter Trout
+ mashed potatoes

serves 4

4 trout fillets – or salmon
4 large white potatoes – peeled and diced
½ cup (120 ml) whole milk
2 tbsp heavy cream
1 bundle of fresh spinach
2 garlic cloves – finely chopped
olive oil

salt + pepper
lemon butter sauce:
3 tbsp salted butter
1 tbsp fresh parsley
1 tsp lemon zest
1 tbsp lemon juice
+ ⅓ cup (50 gr) whole hazelnuts

Preheat the oven to 390F / 200C. Place the hazelnuts in a baking pan.
Roast in the preheated oven for 10 minutes. Remove from the oven, let cool and chop.
Bring a large pot of salted water to a boil. Add the potatoes and cook until soft – 20 minutes.
Meanwhile, place the trout fillets in a colander in a single layer. Season with salt and pepper.
Cover with aluminum foil and place over the pot of potatoes. Cook for about 15 minutes.
Melt the butter in a small saucepan.
Remove from the heat and stir in the parsley, lemon zest and lemon juice. Set aside.
Rinse the spinach under cold water and spin it dry in a salad spinner.
Heat 1 tbsp olive oil with the garlic in a large skillet – 1 minute. Cook the spinach for about 3 minutes.
Drain and mash the potatoes. Stir in the milk and heavy cream. Season to taste.
Spoon the mashed potatoes on individual plates using a cooking ring.
Top with the trout fillets and lemon butter sauce.
Serve with a side of sautéed spinach sprinkled with chopped hazelnuts.

gluten-free

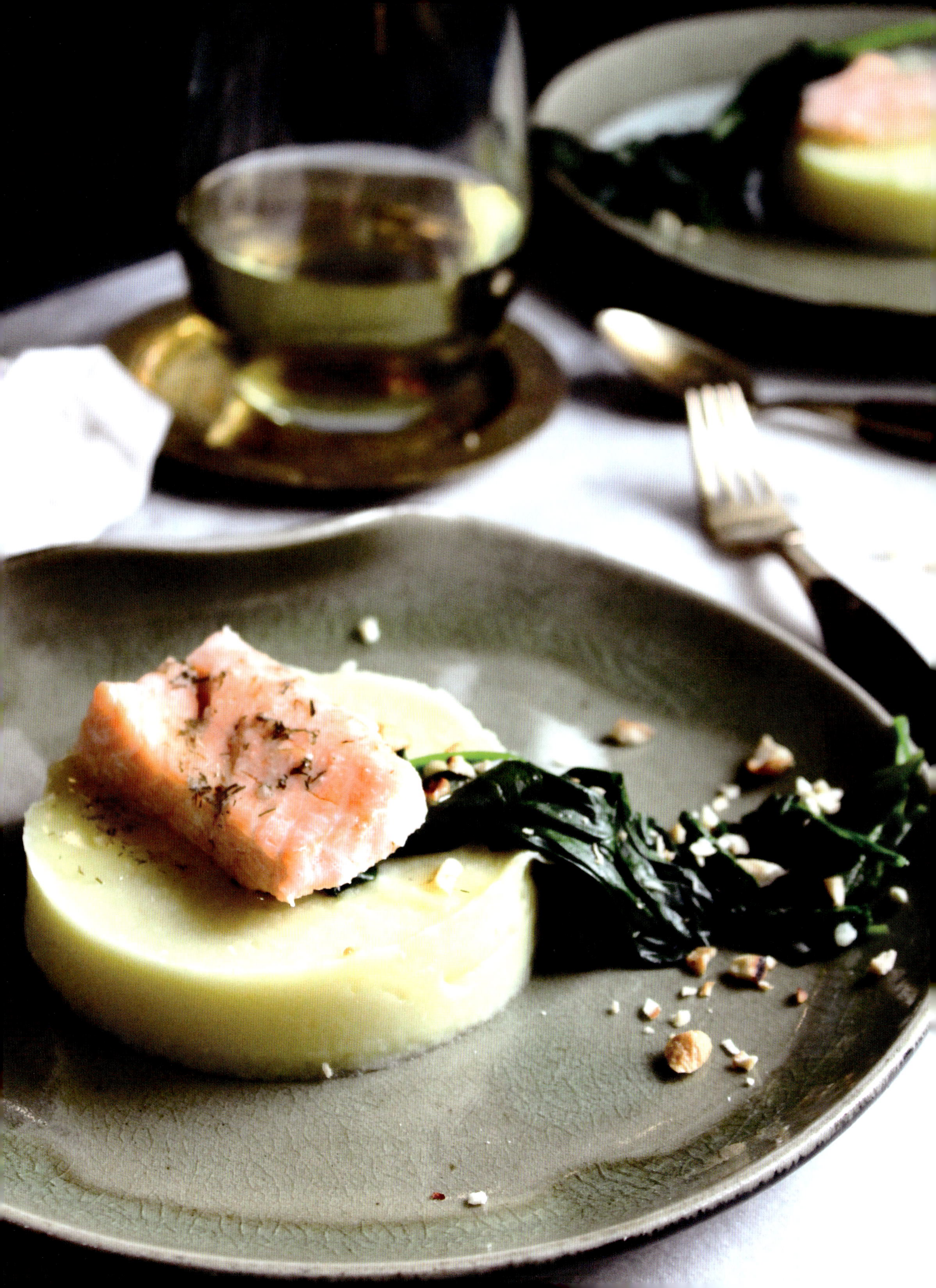

Oven Baked Halibut
+ coconut rice

serves 2

2 halibut fillets
1 tbsp olive oil
1 garlic clove
1 tsp lemon pepper
¼ tsp salt
1 tsp fresh chopped thyme
½ tsp fresh chopped sage

1 tsp mustard seeds
½ lime
¼ cup (40 gr) frozen lima beans
2 tbsp coconut cream
½ cup (100 gr) coconut rice
+ pesto - recipe p. 74

Cook the rice as the label directs. Drain and set aside in a bowl.
Preheat the oven to 460F / 240C. Line a baking sheet with parchment paper or silicone baking mat.
Combine olive oil, garlic, lemon pepper, salt, thyme, sage and mustard seeds in a small bowl.
Add the zest and juice of half a lime. Rub the halibut fillets with this mixture - use a brush!
Bake in the preheated oven for 12 minutes.
Place the lima beans in a small saucepan over medium heat. Cover with water.
Bring to a boil and cook for 4 minutes. Drain and place in the mixing bowl with the rice.
Stir in the coconut cream. Season to taste with salt and pepper.
To serve, spread a thin layer of pesto on the plates using a brush. Add the halibut fillets.
Garnish with a few leaves of fresh thyme and sage. Serve immediately with a side of coconut rice.

dairy-free | gluten-free

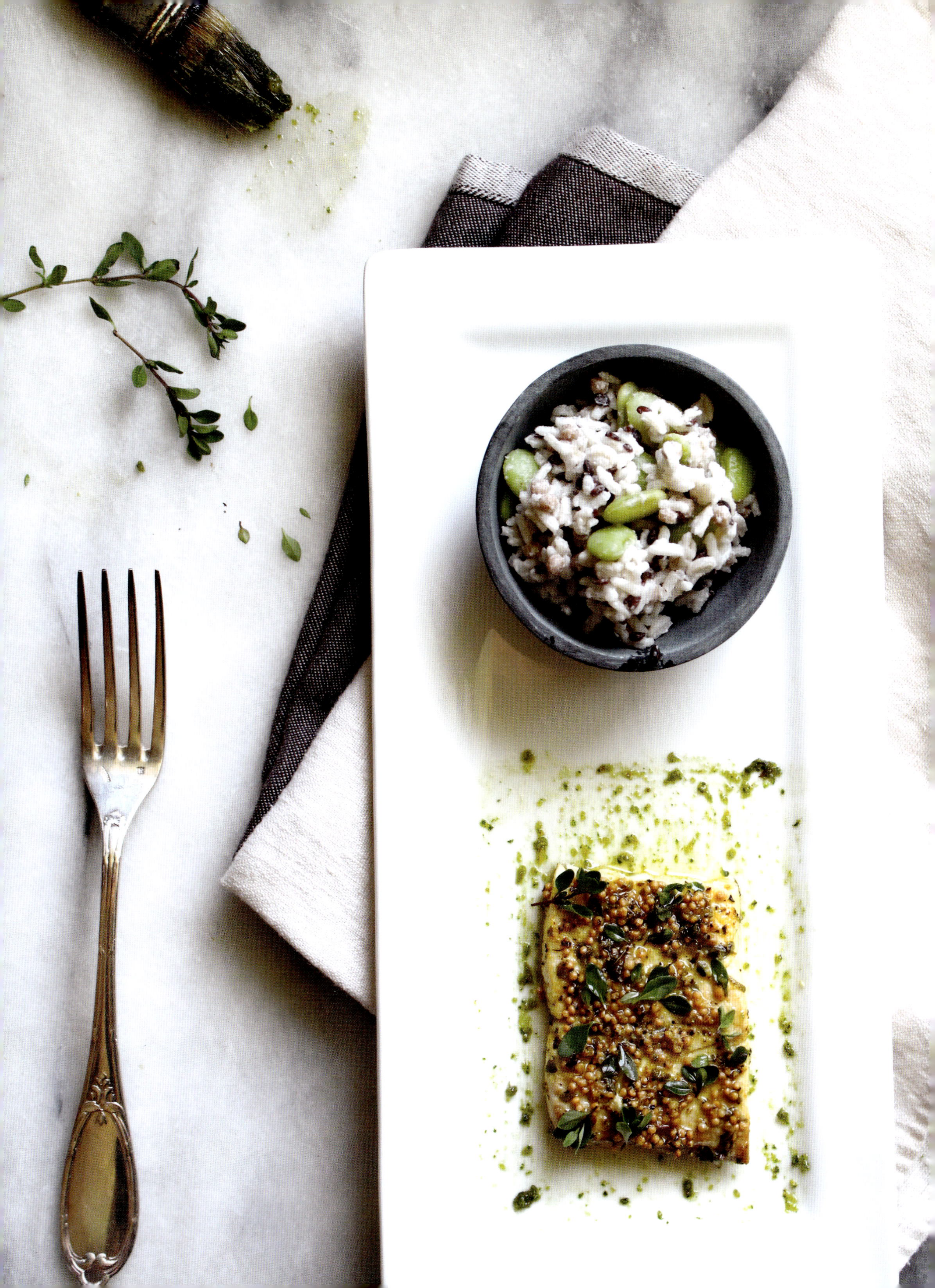

Grilled Shrimp
+ red bell pepper dip

serves 2

2 red bell peppers – halved and seeded
2 tbsp vegetable broth
12 large shrimps – cooked and peeled
1 lime

1 tbsp olive oil
1 cup (30 gr) fresh dill
salt + pepper

Line a baking sheet with silicone baking mat.
Place the red bell peppers face cut down under a high broiler in the oven
~10 minutes or until the shins are charred.
Let cool completely. Remove the skins.
Place in the bowl of a food processor with the broth. Blend until smooth – 2 minutes.
Place the shrimp, lime juice, olive oil and dill in a large mixing bowl. Toss to coat.
Spread the mixture evenly on a baking sheet lined with parchment paper.
Place under a low broiler in the oven for 6 minutes.
Serve with the red bell pepper dip and a side of arugula salad!

gluten-free | dairy-free | nut-free

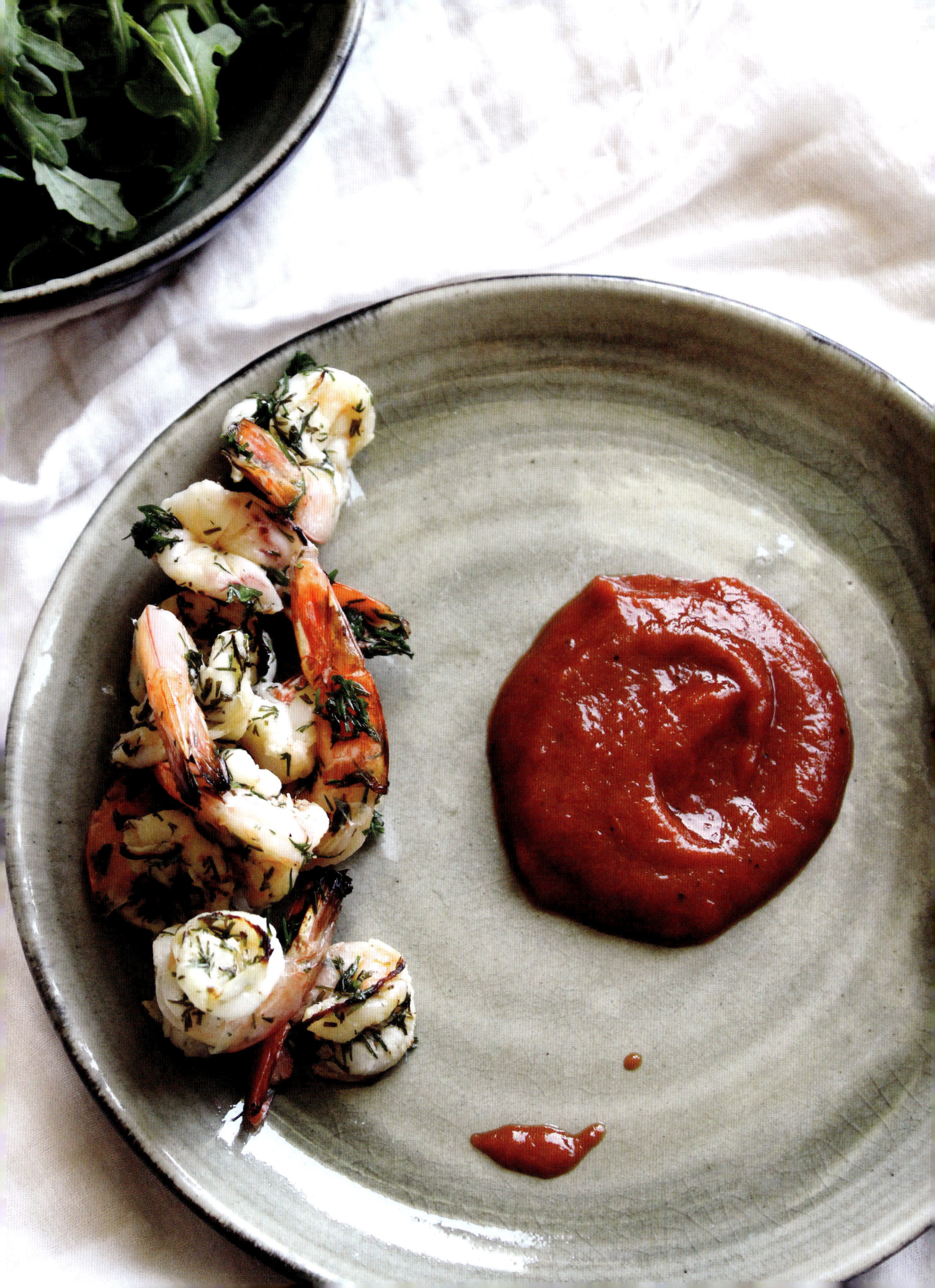

Chicken Fajitas
+ guacamole

serves 4

2 chicken breasts – free-range organic
2 tbsp cumin powder
the juice of 2 limes
1 tbsp olive oil
½ tsp salt

2 red bell peppers – halved and seeded
fresh cilantro
8 flour tortillas
guacamole – recipe p. 72

Cut the chicken breasts in long thin strips.
Place in a bowl with the cumin powder, lime juice, olive oil and salt. Toss to coat.
Cover and refrigerate for 1 hour or overnight.
Preheat the oven to 450F / 230C. Line a baking sheet with parchment paper or silicone baking mat.
Place the red bell peppers cut side down on the prepared sheet.
Roast 25 minutes or until the skins are wrinkled and charred. Remove from the oven.
Let cool completely and peel off the skins. Cut in long strips. Add to the chicken mixture.
Coat a large grill pan with non-stick cooking spray. Place over medium heat.
Add the chicken mixture and cook thoroughly – about 10 minutes.
Place two tortillas on each plate. Spoon some of the guacamole.
Top with chicken and garnish with fresh cilantro.
Serve immediately!

dairy-free | nut-free

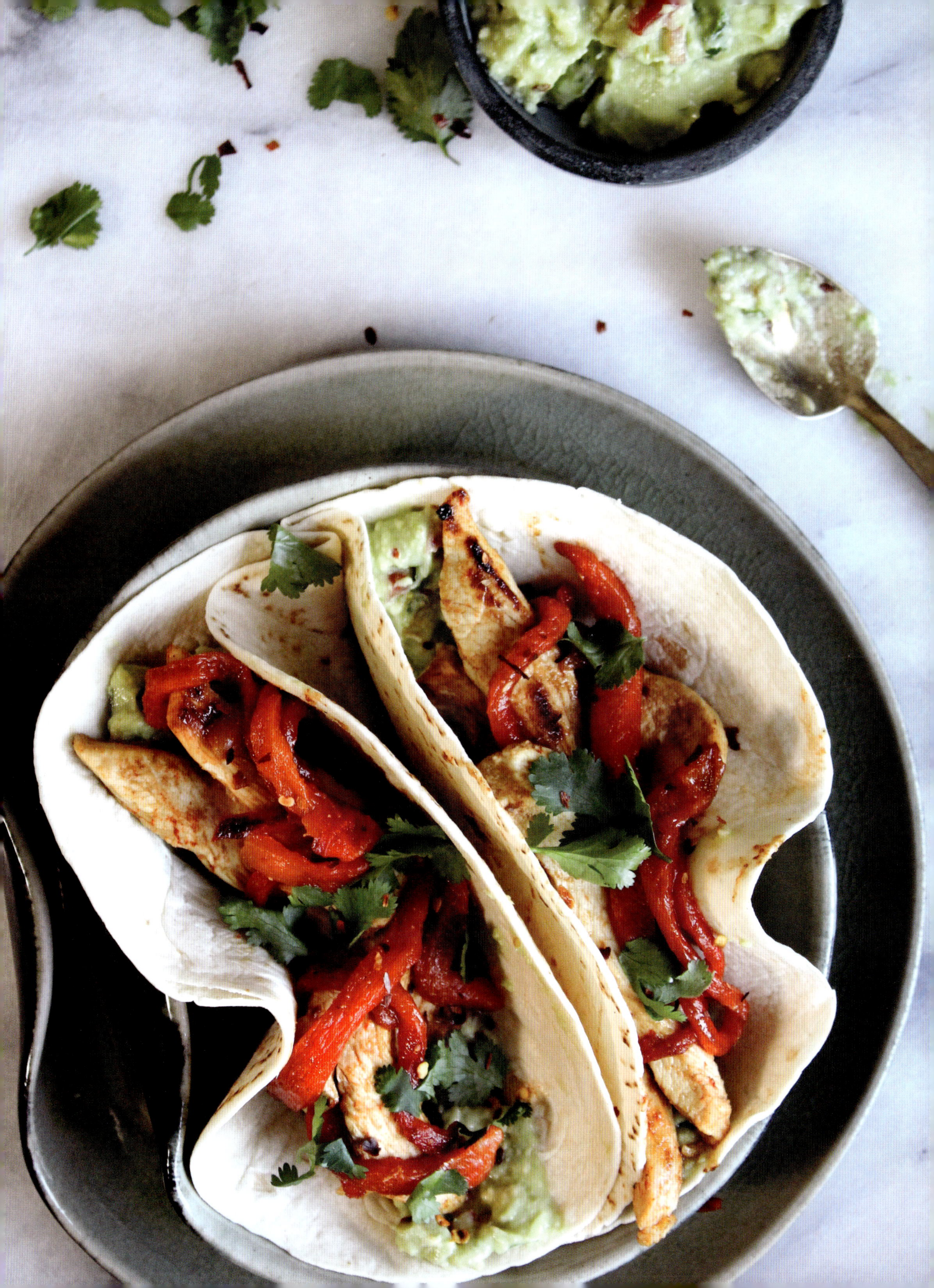

Chicken Tikka Masala

serves 4

1 eggplant - diced
2 chicken breasts - free-range organic
1 tbsp masala powder
1 tbsp olive oil
1 tbsp curry paste (Patak's)
⅓ cup (160 ml) coconut cream

1 x 15 oz. (410 gr) can of organic roasted tomatoes - diced
3 tbsp fresh chopped coriander
½ cup (60 gr) sliced almonds
1 cup (200 gr) brown rice
salt + pepper

Preheat the oven to 450F / 230C. Line a baking sheet with parchment paper or silicone baking mat.
Spread the eggplant in a single layer.
Sprinkle with 1 tsp of salt and bake in the preheated oven for 20 minutes.
Place the chicken breasts in a mixing bowl with the masala powder, olive oil and a pinch of salt.
Stir to coat.
Line another baking sheet with parchment paper.
Add the chicken and bake for 20 minutes at 430F / 220 C.
Remove from the oven. Cut in strips.
Cook the rice as the label directs. Rinse, drain and set aside.
Heat the curry paste in a large skillet over medium heat for 1 minute.
Slowly whisk in the coconut cream. Add the tomatoes, roasted eggplants, chicken strips and 1 cup of water. Cook for 15 minutes, stirring occasionally. Season to taste with salt and pepper.
Transfer to a serving bowl. Garnish with sliced almonds and fresh cilantro.
Serve with a side of brown rice.

dairy-free | gluten-free

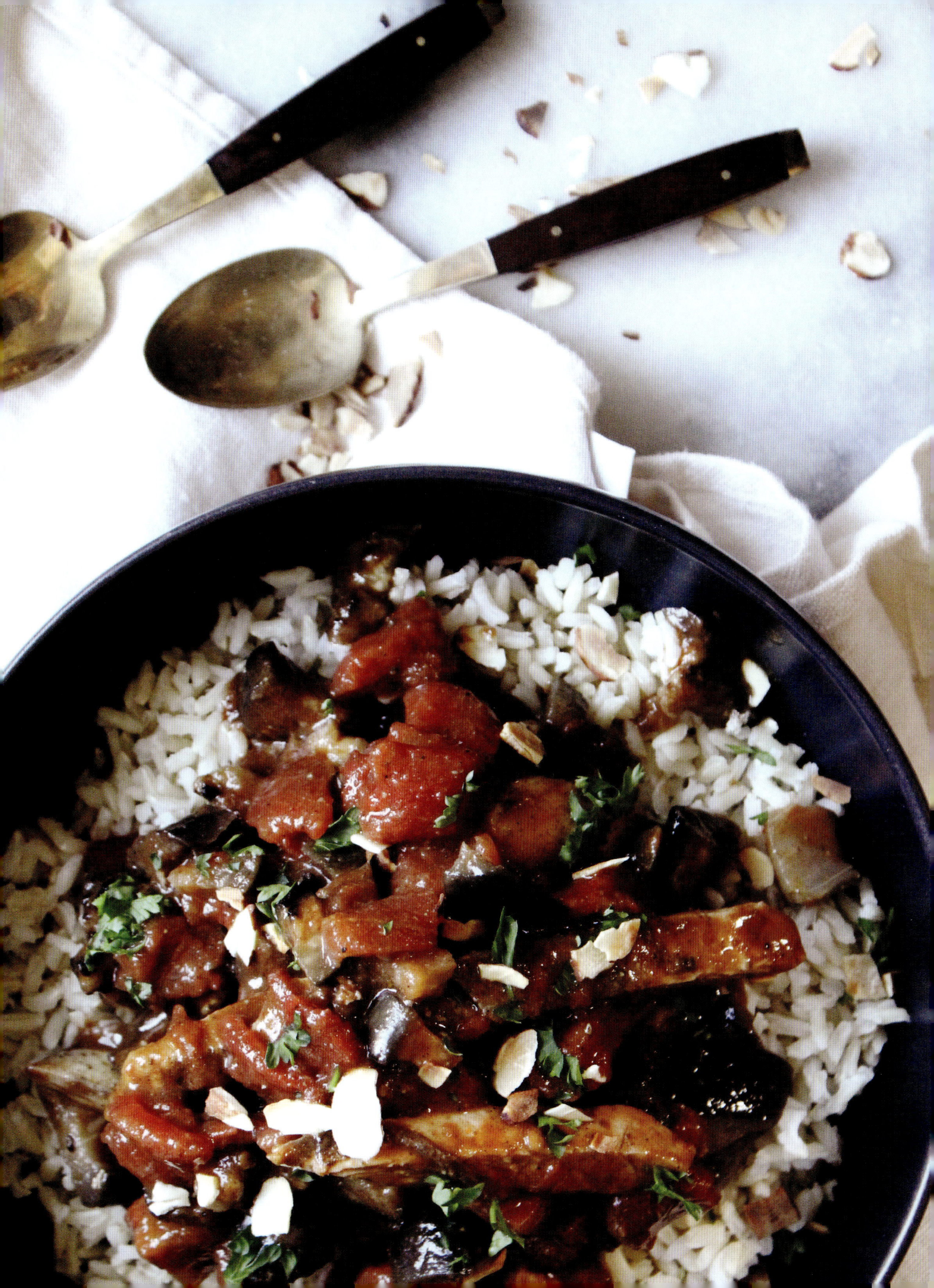

Simple Breaded Chicken
+ ratatouille

serves 4

2 large zucchini – diced large
2 red bell peppers – halved and seeded
2 Roma tomatoes – peeled and diced large
1 tbsp olive oil
2 frozen basil cubes
1 cup (240 ml) vegetable broth

1 lbs. (454 gr) chicken breast - free-range organic
½ cup (45 gr) breadcrumbs
1 tsp fresh chopped thyme
3 tbsp Dijon mustard
salt

To make the ratatouille, place the zucchini in a colander.
Add 1 tbsp salt and leave untouched for 30 minutes.
Arrange the red bell peppers cut side down on a baking sheet lined with parchment paper.
Place under a high broiler in the oven for 10 minutes or until the skins are charred.
Remove from the oven. Let cool completely. Remove the skins and cut into large pieces.
Heat the olive oil in a large skillet over medium heat. Rinse the zucchini under cold water and add to the pan with the basil cubes. Cook for 5 minutes, stirring occasionally. Stir in the peppers, tomatoes and broth. Continue to cook for 15 minutes. Season to taste with salt and pepper.
To make the breaded chicken, preheat the oven to 450F / 230C.
Line a baking sheet with parchment paper or silicone baking mat.
Combine breadcrumbs, thyme, salt and Dijon mustard in a large bowl.
Spread the chicken with this mixture, coating both sides. Transfer to the prepared baking pan.
Cook in the preheated oven for 18 minutes or until golden and crispy.
Serve immediately with a side of ratatouille.

dairy-free

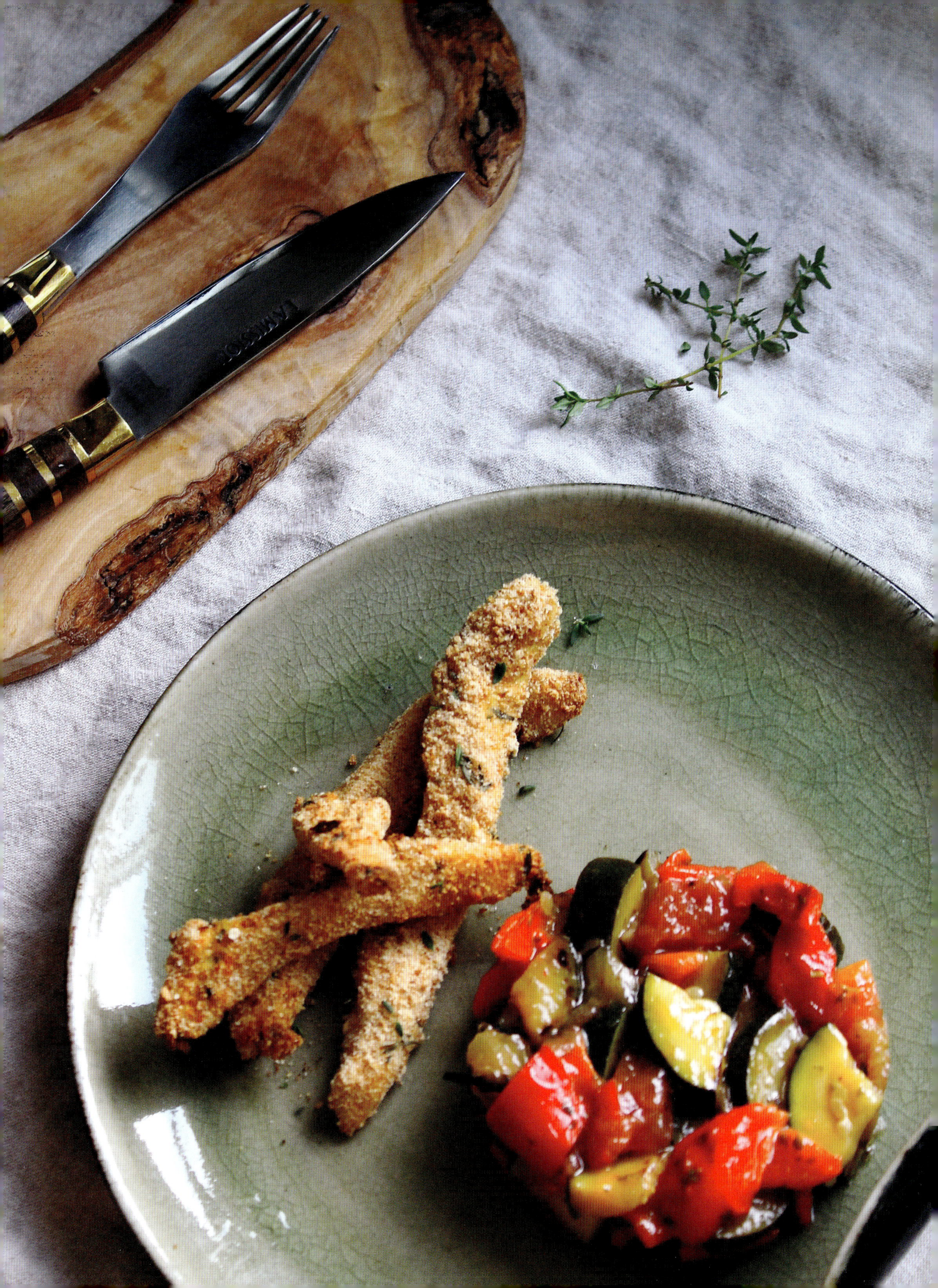

gourmandise. *noun.*

a mouth-watering delicacy.

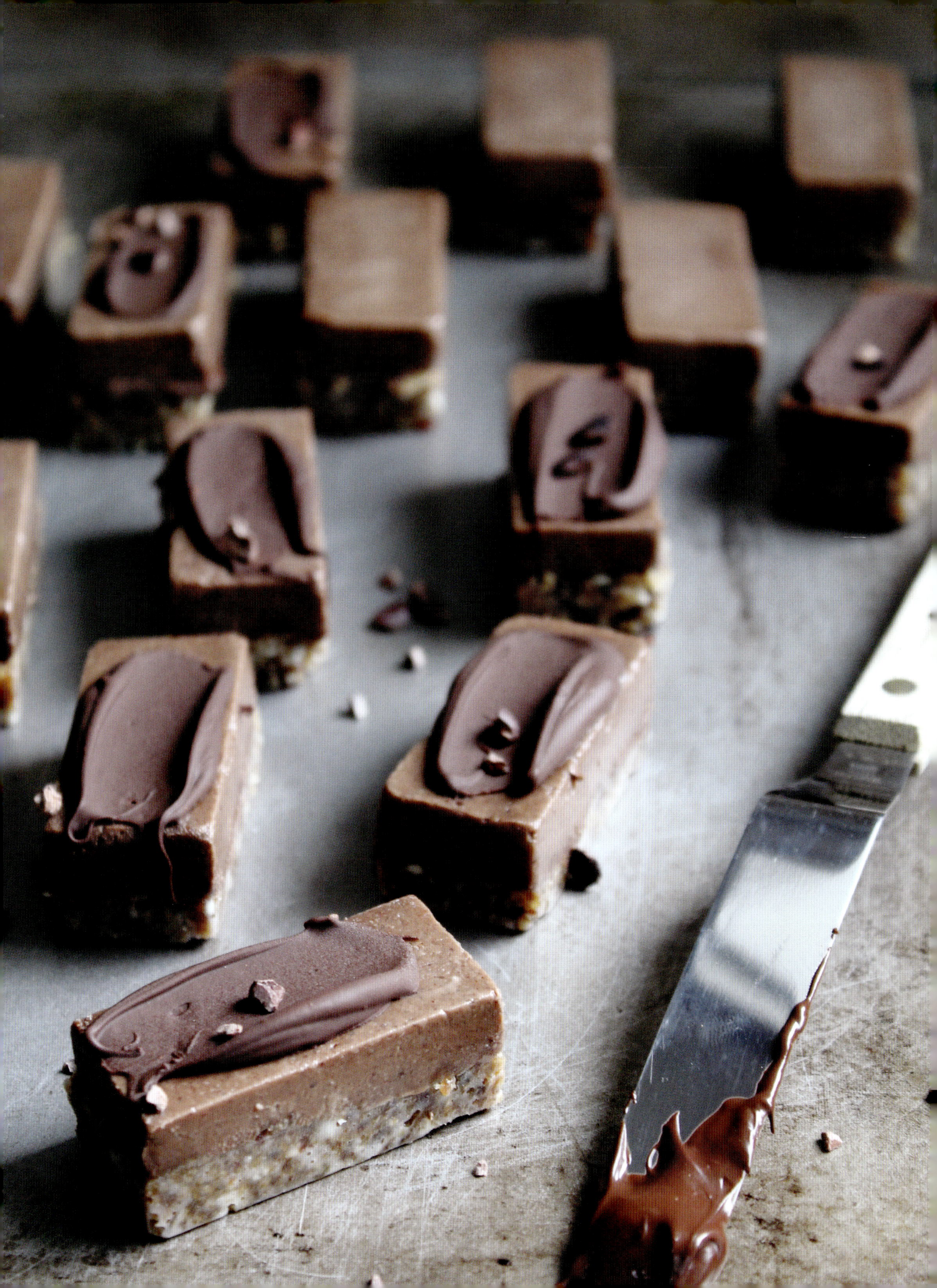

Just Almond Butter

makes 1 jar

3 cups (420 gr) whole almonds

Preheat the oven to 284F / 140C.
Place the almonds in a baking pan. Roast in the preheated oven for 10 minutes.
Pulse the warm almonds in a food processor until smooth – about 20 minutes.
The almonds will go from whole to chopped and transform into a fine powder. Only then, after about 15 minutes will they start turning into a paste and then a smooth almond butter.
You can stop and scrape down the sides of the bowl at any time so it all blends evenly.
Transfer to a glass jar and store in the fridge for months!

For a longer shelf life, keep the almond butter plain.
Flavor it to your taste when needed with coconut oil, cocoa powder, cinnamon or any other sweeteners.

raw | vegan | gluten-free

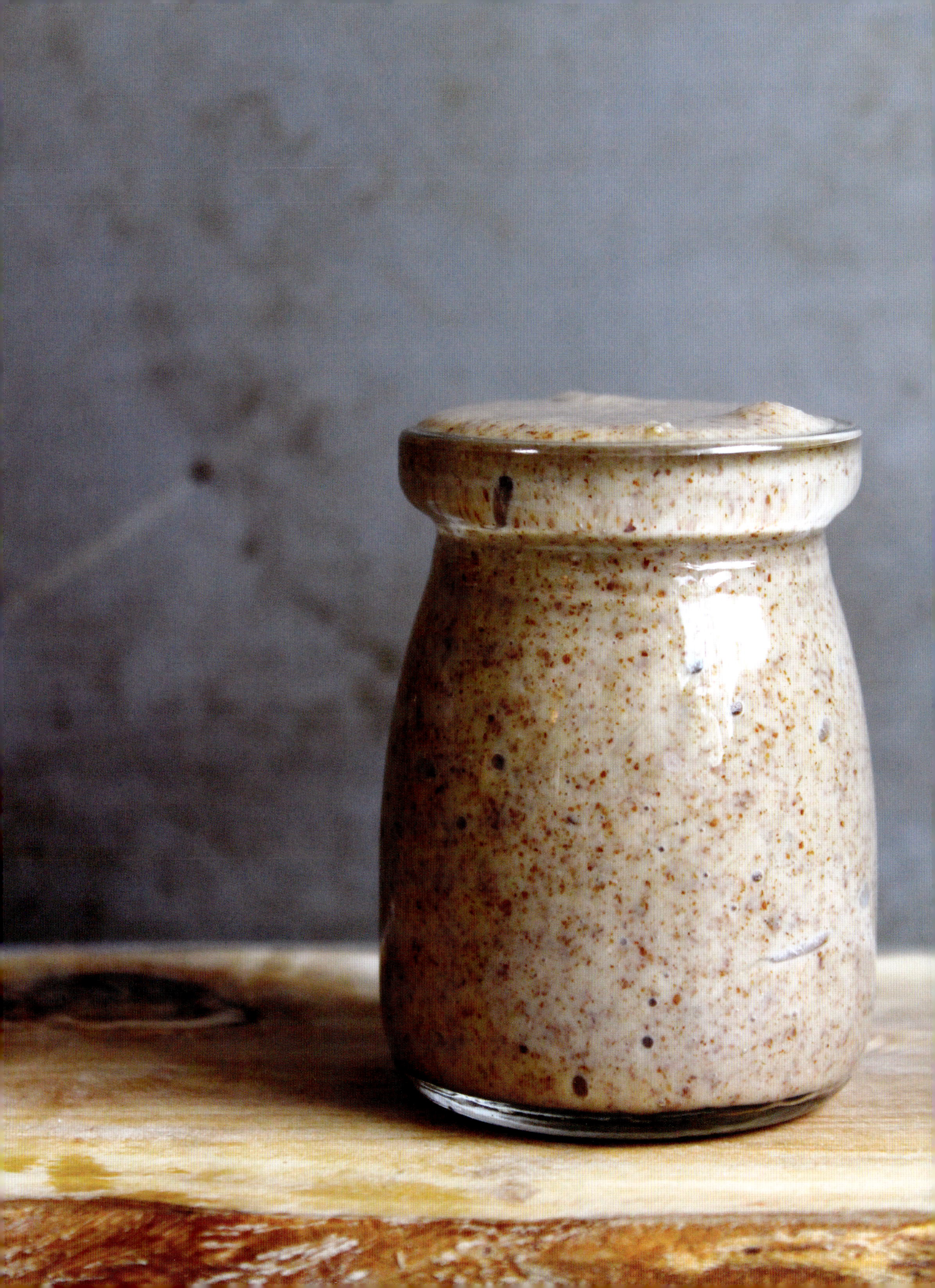

Magic Bliss

So nutritious, the magic bliss balls are highly addictive!

Raw, vegan, gluten-free, low-calorie and loaded with superfoods.

Quick and easy to make these bites of heaven will sure become your favorite snack or breakfast topping!

Store the magic bliss balls in an air-tight container in the freezer for months.

Just allow a few minutes to thaw before eating!

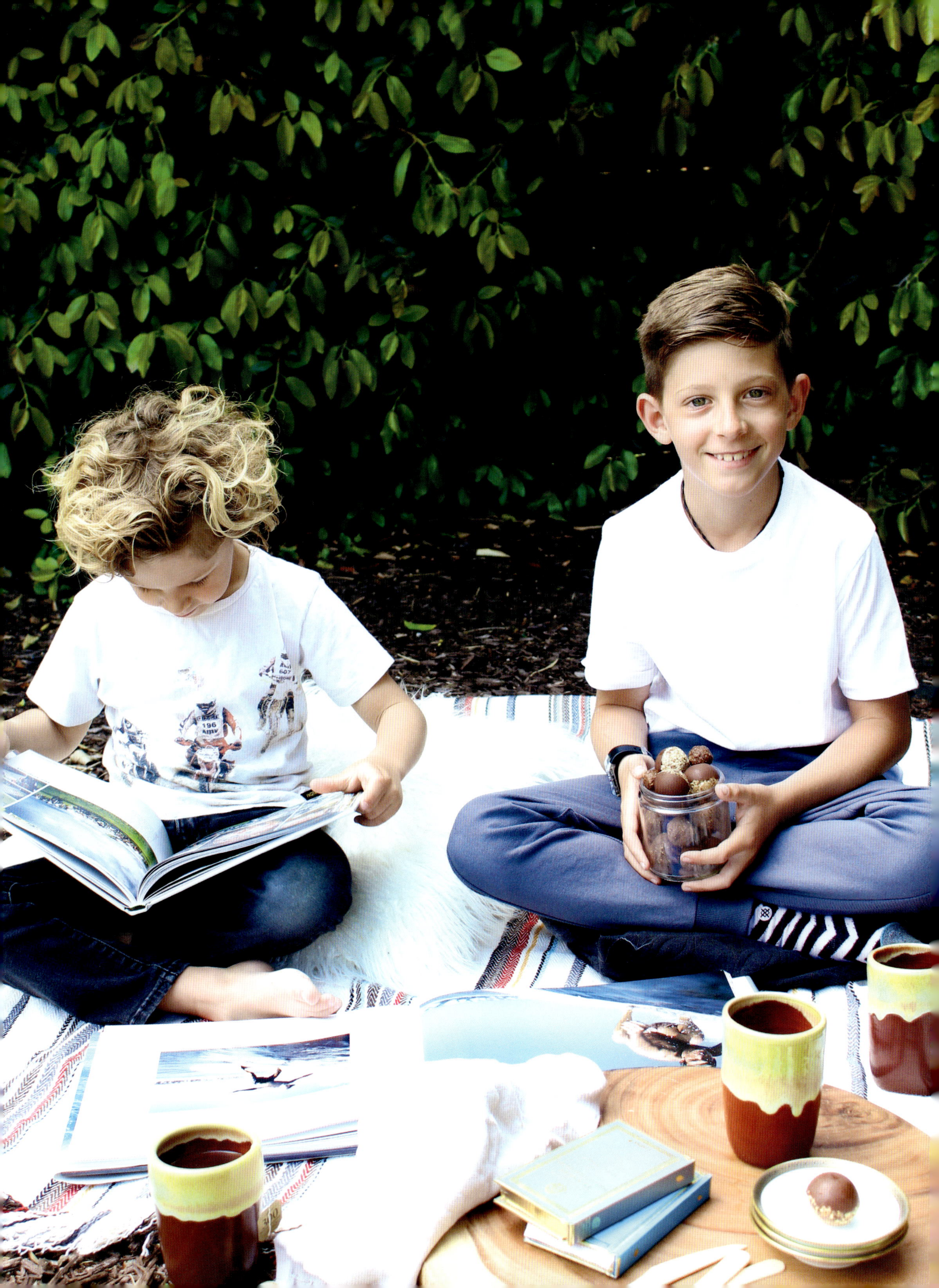

Dark Chocolate
+ granola

makes 10 pieces

nut sphere:
¼ cup (30 gr) sliced almonds
¼ cup (30 gr) chopped cashews
½ cup (45 gr) rolled oats
8 whole pitted dates
1 tbsp coconut oil
1 tbsp almond butter – recipe p. 166
1 tbsp quinoa
1 tsp vanilla extract
1 tbsp coconut flakes

chocolate sphere:
⅔ cup (115 gr) dark chocolate chips
½ cup (125 gr) almond butter – recipe p. 166
+ half sphere silicone mold

Nut ½ sphere: pulse all the ingredients in a food processor until combined –2 minutes.
Press this mixture into the cavities of a half sphere silicone mold.
Place in the freezer for at least 2 hours or until firm.
Save the leftovers in an airtight container and use as a topping in your morning bowls!

Chocolate ½ sphere: melt the chocolate and almond butter in the microwave.
Pour into the cavities of the same half sphere silicone mold.
Place the nut half spheres on top and return to the freezer for at least 2 hours or until set.

Store in the freezer for a few months.

raw | vegan | gluten-free

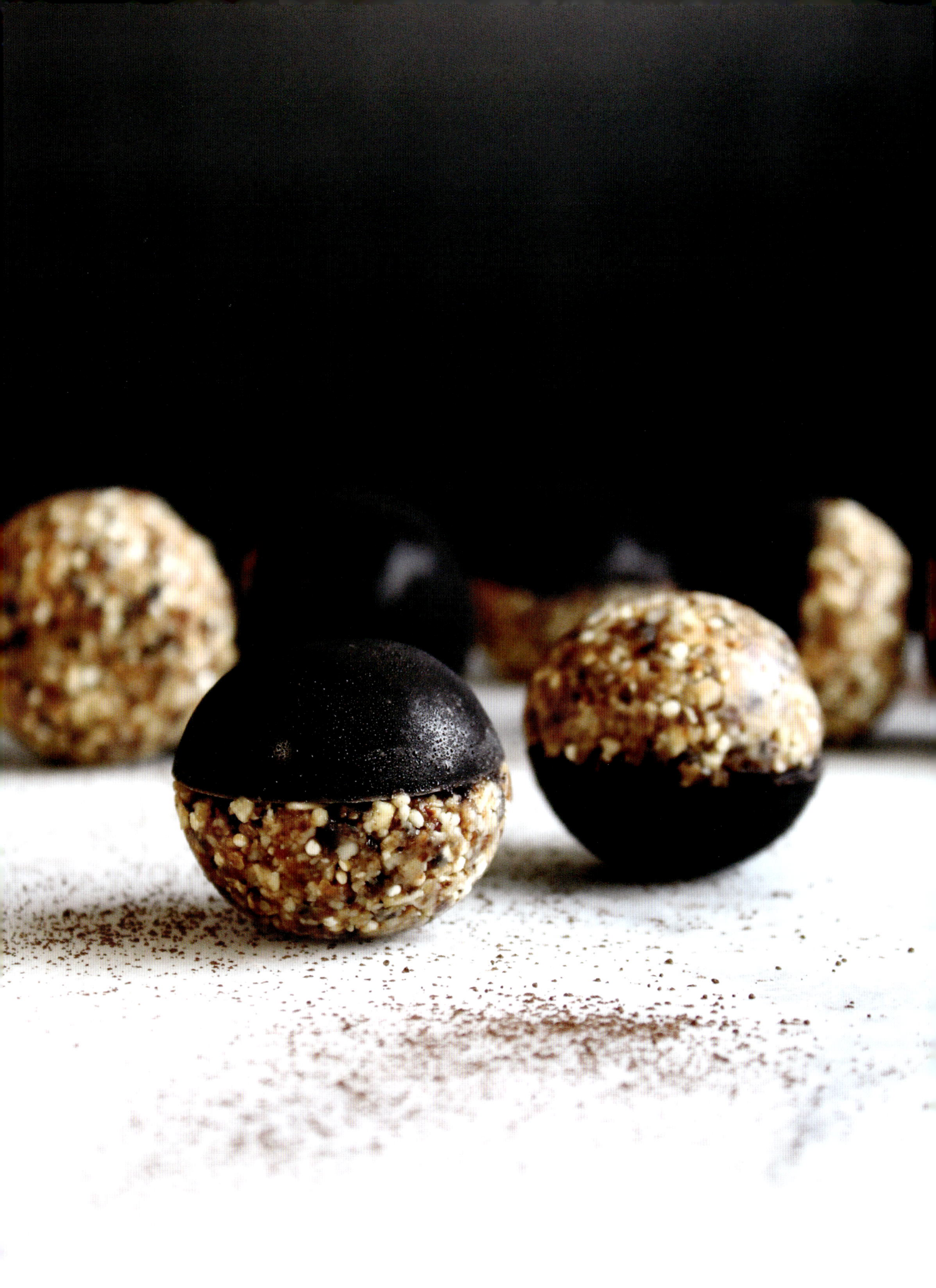

Sesame Bliss Balls

makes 6 balls

½ cup (125 gr) almond butter – recipe p. 166
1 tbsp maple syrup
1 tbsp unsweetened cocoa powder

1 tbsp almond flour
1 cup (140 gr) sesame seeds

Combine almond butter, maple syrup, cocoa powder and almond flour in a bowl.
Roll the paste in the palm of your hands to form bite-size balls.
Place in the freezer for 15 minutes.
Place the sesame seeds in a small skillet over low heat.
Toast for about 3 minutes, stirring constantly.
Remove from the heat and place in a small shallow bowl.
Roll each bliss ball in the seeds to coat.
Store in an airtight container in the freezer for a few months!

vegan | gluten-free

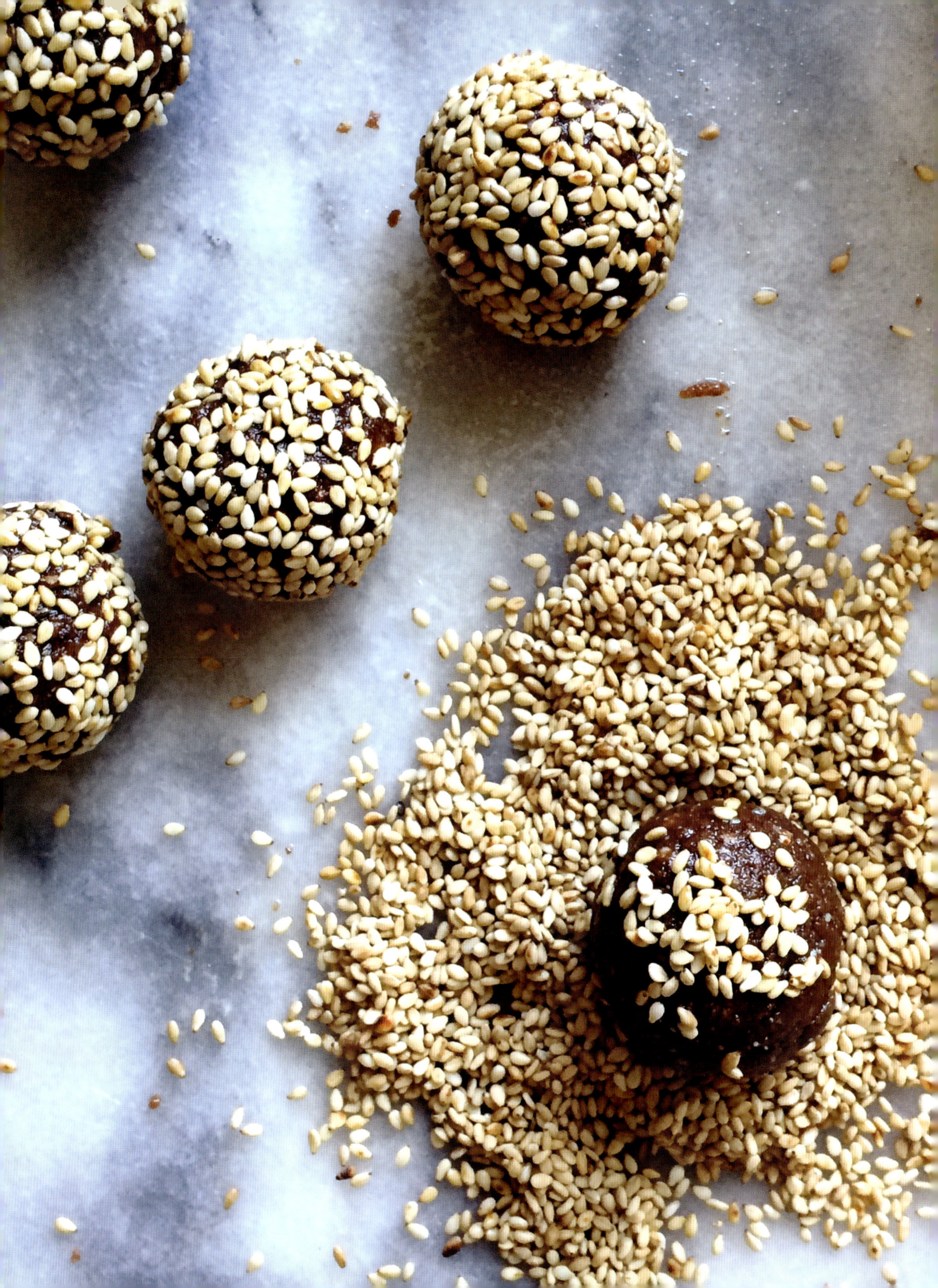

Power Bliss Balls
matcha + pistachio

makes 18 pieces

¼ cup (40 gr) whole macadamia nuts
¼ cup (40 gr) whole cashews
⅓ cup (50 gr) whole pistachios + extra to coat
1 tbsp quinoa
3 tbsp almond butter – recipe p. 166

1 tsp matcha powder
1 tbsp old fashioned oats
2 tbsp maple syrup
half of ¼ tsp salt
5 whole figs

Pulse the macadamia nuts, cashews and pistachios in a food processor until finely chopped.
Add the rest of the ingredients and blend until combined.
Roll the paste in the palm of your hands to form bite-size balls.
Place in the freezer for 15 minutes.
Finely chop the extra pistachios and roll each bliss ball to coat.
Store in the freezer for a few months and enjoy straight from the freezer!

vegan | gluten-free

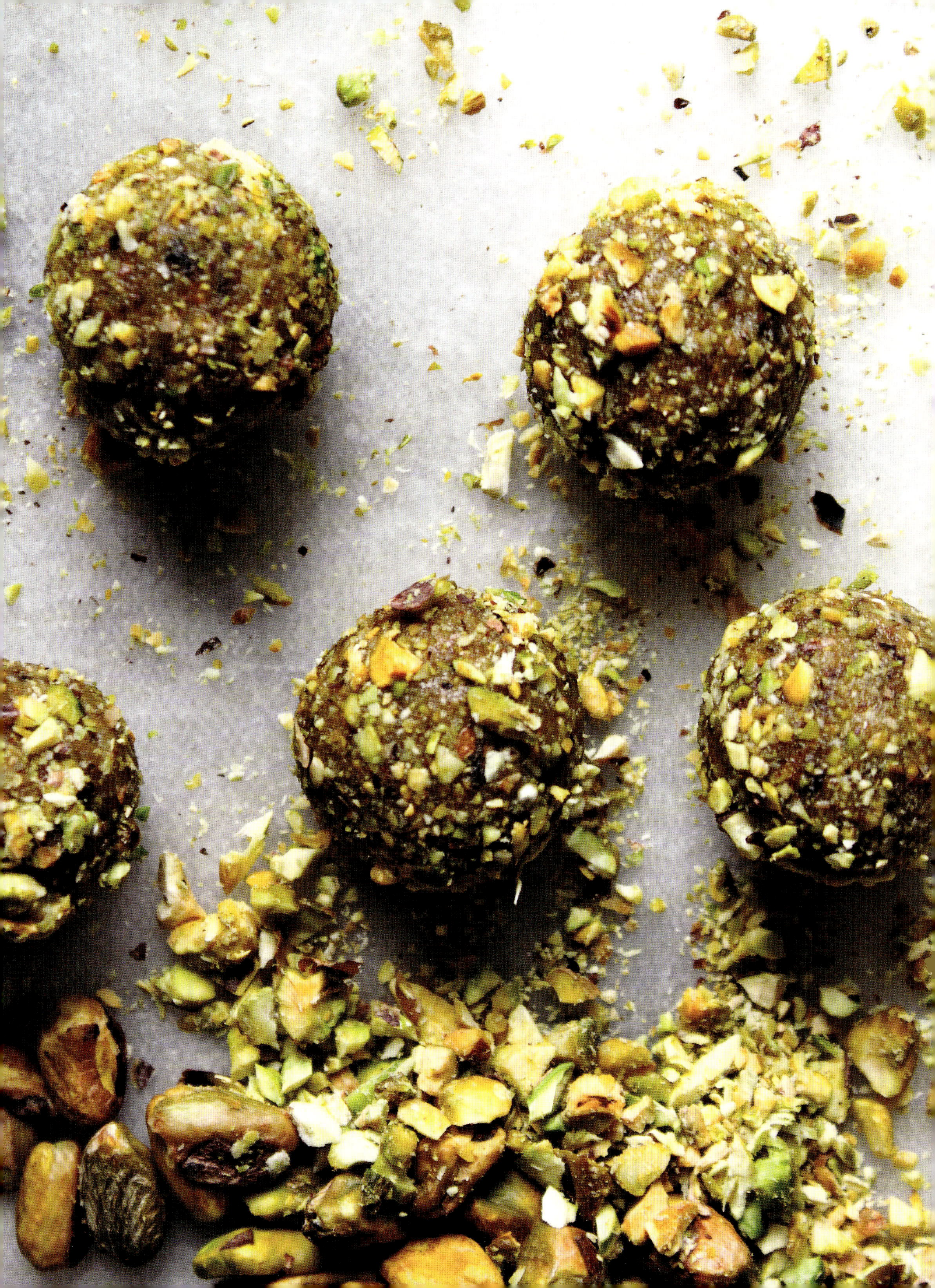

Shiny Chocolate

Chocolate is easy to melt but very sensitive to temperature and humidity.
The right technique for coating is called Chocolate Tempering:
low heat, constant stirring and no water.
One drop of water causes damage to the texture and makes the chocolate unusable.
Make sure the bowl and spatula are perfectly clean and dry.
Choose a high-quality chocolate also known as "couverture chocolate".

Temperature plays an important role as well.
The right temperature for dark chocolate is 90F / 32C.
The chocolate must be melted slowly to avoid overheating and to get a nice glossy texture.
Check the temperature with a candy thermometer for accuracy.

For best results, finely chop the chocolate so it melts evenly.
The whole process should take no longer than 5 minutes.

The two easiest ways to melt chocolate are "au bain-marie" or in the microwave.

"Au bain-marie" (double-boiler):
It is a slow cooking technique used to respect and preserve the nutritional benefits of the food.
It provides controlled, even heating and prevents over cooked or burned food.
Place a large saucepan on the stove. Add 1 inch (2.5 cm) of water and bring to a boil.
Reduce the heat to keep a low simmer. Place the chopped chocolate in a metal bowl that fits snugly over the saucepan. Make sure there is a lot of space between the water and the top bowl so the water does not touch the upper bowl. Stir at all times until the chocolate is melted and smooth.

Microwave:
Place the chocolate in a bowl and melt in 10 seconds intervals. Stir well between each interval using a rubber spatula. Stir until no lumps are found and the chocolate is smooth and glossy.

Imagination is more important than knowledge.

— ALBERT EINSTEIN

For knowledge is limited,
whereas imagination embraces the entire world,
stimulating progress, giving birth to evolution.

Pure Coconut
+ chocolate

makes 18 pieces

1 cup (75 gr) coconut flakes
2 tbsp coconut oil
⅓ cup (80 ml) coconut cream
½ tsp vanilla powder

1 tsp maple syrup
1 tsp coconut sugar
2 cups (350 gr) dark chocolate chips

Pulse all the ingredients (except the chocolate) in a food processor until combined.
Form bite-size balls by rolling the mixture in the palm of your hands.
Melt the chocolate in the microwave, stirring well every 10 seconds until smooth and shiny.
Dip each coconut ball in the melted chocolate.
Place on a silicone baking mat. Refrigerate until set – about 1 hour.
Store in the freezer for a few months and enjoy straight from the freezer!

vegan | gluten-free | nut-free

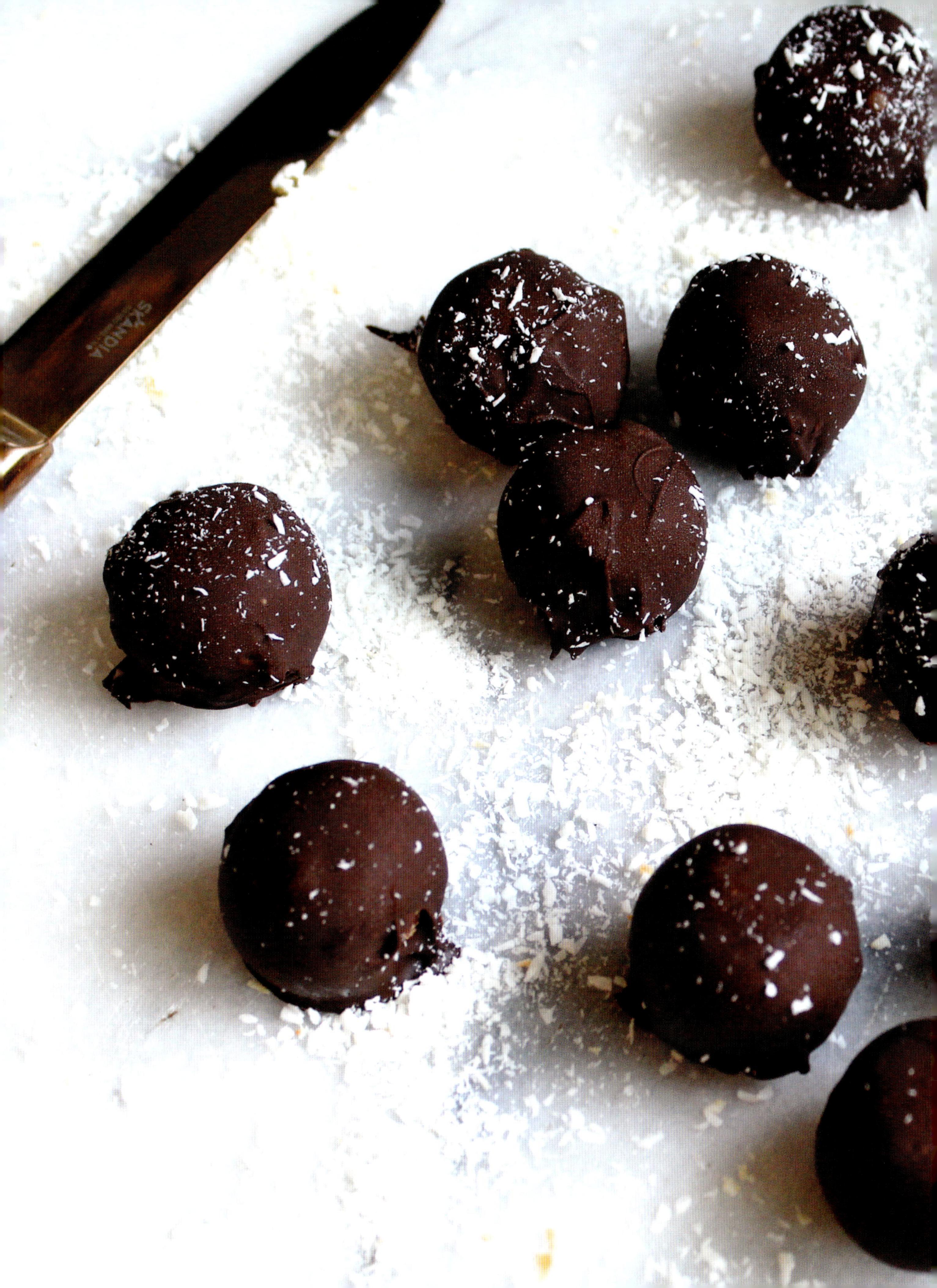
SKANDIA

Coconut Magic Bliss

makes 15

nut half sphere:
8 whole pitted dates
1 tsp almond butter - recipe p. 166
1 tbsp coconut oil
¼ cup (20 gr) coconut flakes
½ cup (45 gr) rolled oats
¼ cup (30 gr) sliced almonds
1 tsp maple syrup
1 tbsp quinoa

coconut half sphere:
1 cup (235 ml) heavy whipping cream - cold
½ cup (120 ml) coconut cream – cold and full fat content
4 tbsp coconut sugar
1 vanilla bean
¼ cup (20 gr) coconut flakes
+ half sphere silicone mold

To make the nut half sphere, pulse all the ingredients in a food processor until blended. Press this mixture firmly into each cavity of a half sphere silicone mold. Place in the freezer for 3 hours.
To make the coconut half sphere, place the coconut flakes on a baking sheet in a single layer. Quickly toast in the oven under a low broiler - 1 minute.
Cut the vanilla bean lengthwise with a small curved knife. Scrape the seeds out and place in the bowl of an electric mixer with the whip attachment. Add the heavy whipping cream, coconut cream and coconut sugar. Mix on high speed until stiff peaks form. It takes a few minutes to reach the desired consistency. Transfer to a piping bag with an open end (no tip).
Sprinkle the toasted coconut in the cavities of a half sphere silicone mold and pipe out the coconut cream. Place the frozen nut half sphere on top. Put back in the freezer for 24 hours or until set.
Store these treats in the freezer for a few weeks - allow 10 minutes to thaw.

gluten-free

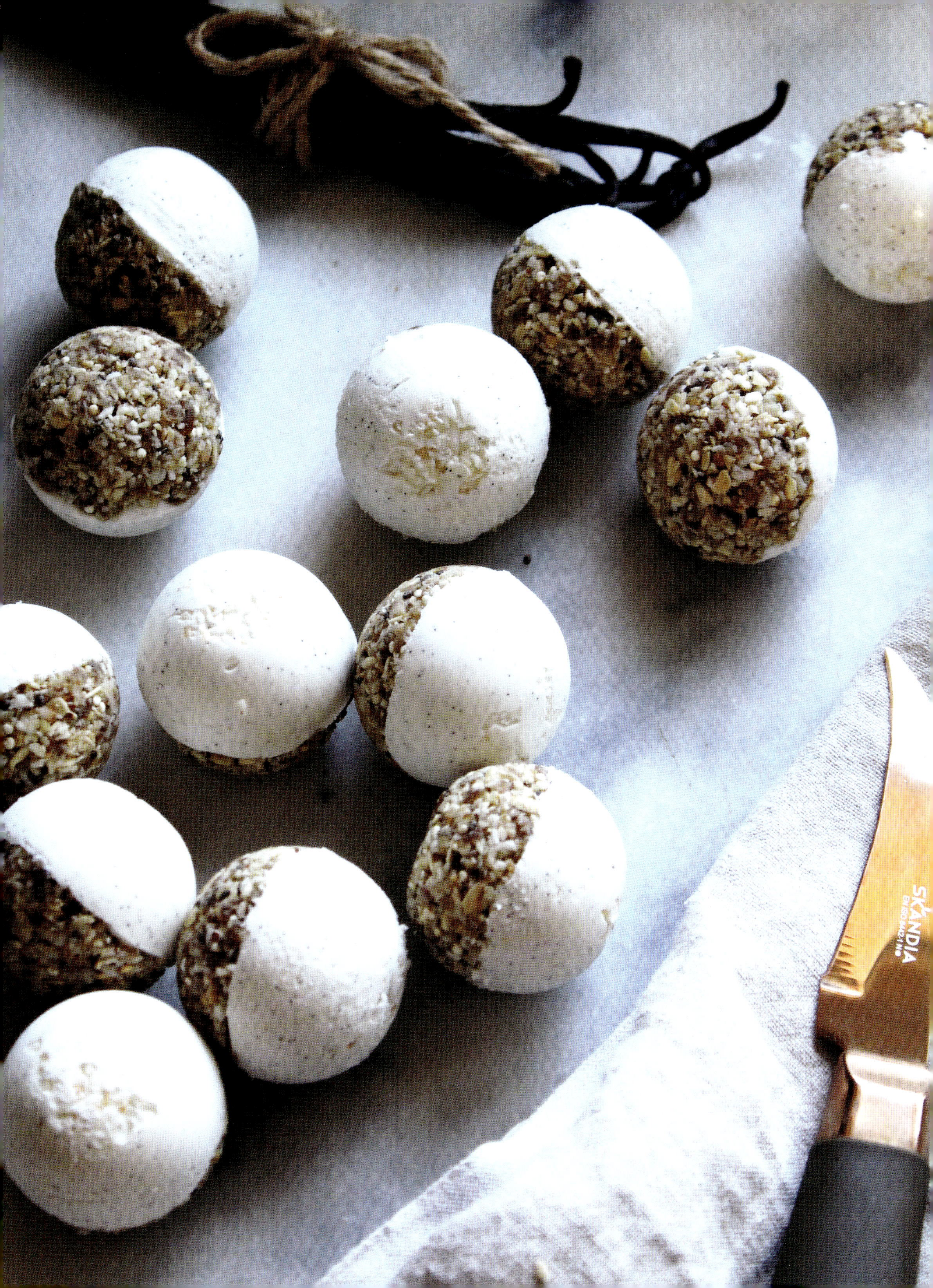
SKANDIA

Raw Granola Bar

makes 24 mini bars

15 whole pitted dates
1 cup (90 gr) rolled oats
¼ cup (60 ml) coconut oil
1 tsp vanilla extract
¼ cup (30 gr) cranberries

¼ cup (25 gr) goji berries
1 tbsp pumpkin seeds
1 tbsp quinoa
1 tbsp flax seeds

Chop the dates in a food processor. Add the oats, coconut oil, vanilla extract, cranberries and goji berries. Pulse until combined – 1 minute. Fold in the pumpkin seeds, quinoa, flax seeds.
Make a ball with the dough and wrap in plastic wrap. Refrigerate 20 minutes.
Place the dough in between two sheets of wax paper.
Flatten using a rolling pin – about ½ inch / 1.2 cm.
Freeze until it hardens and becomes sliceable – 2 hours.
Place the bars in an airtight container.
Keep in the fridge for 2 weeks or in the freezer for a few months!

raw | vegan | gluten-free

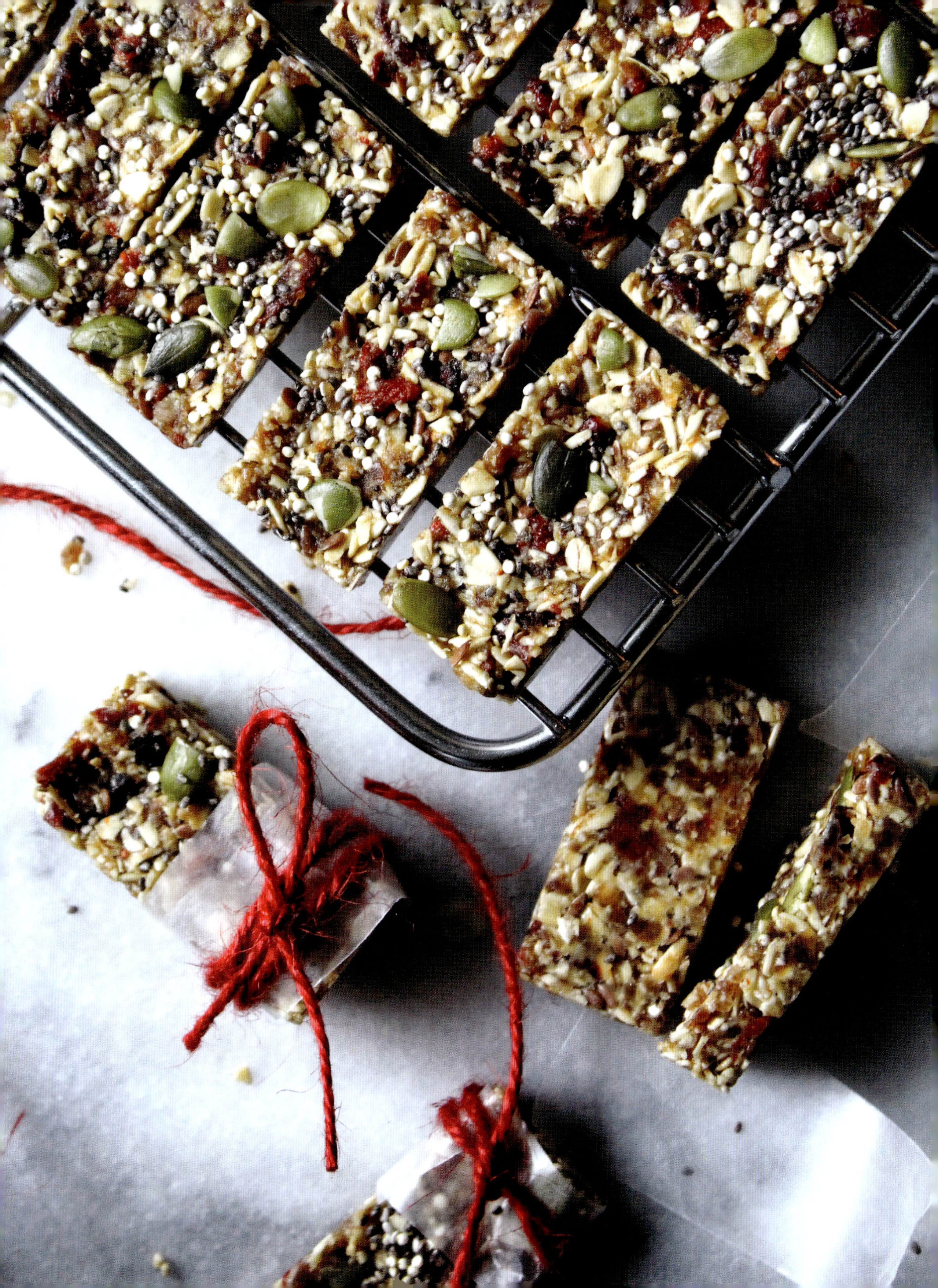

Vegan Cookies
raw or baked

makes 20

¾ cup (120 gr) brown rice flour
1 cup (90 gr) rolled oats
1 tsp baking soda
1 tsp baking powder
1 tsp unsweetened cocoa powder

½ cup (110 gr) margarine (Earth Balance)
or 2 tbsp coconut oil
1 tsp vanilla extract
½ cup (130 ml) maple syrup
1 ¼ cup (220 gr) dark chocolate chips

Raw cookies: pulse all the ingredients in a food processor until combined. Refrigerate for 20 minutes. Form bite-size balls by rolling tablespoons of the batter in the palm of your hands.
Place in an airtight container.
Store in the freezer for a few months – allow 10 minutes to thaw before eating.

Baked cookies: preheat the oven to 350F / 180C. Line a baking sheet with parchment paper or silicone baking mat. Place the balls on the prepared baking pan. Flatten with your fingers to 0.2 inch (5 mm). Bake for 17 minutes in the preheated oven.
Keep the baked cookies in an airtight container at room temperature for a few days!
Let the leftovers dry at room temperature for a few hours. It will crumble into a fine powder that can be used to sprinkle on top of your cakes or breakfast bowls!

vegan | gluten-free | nut-free

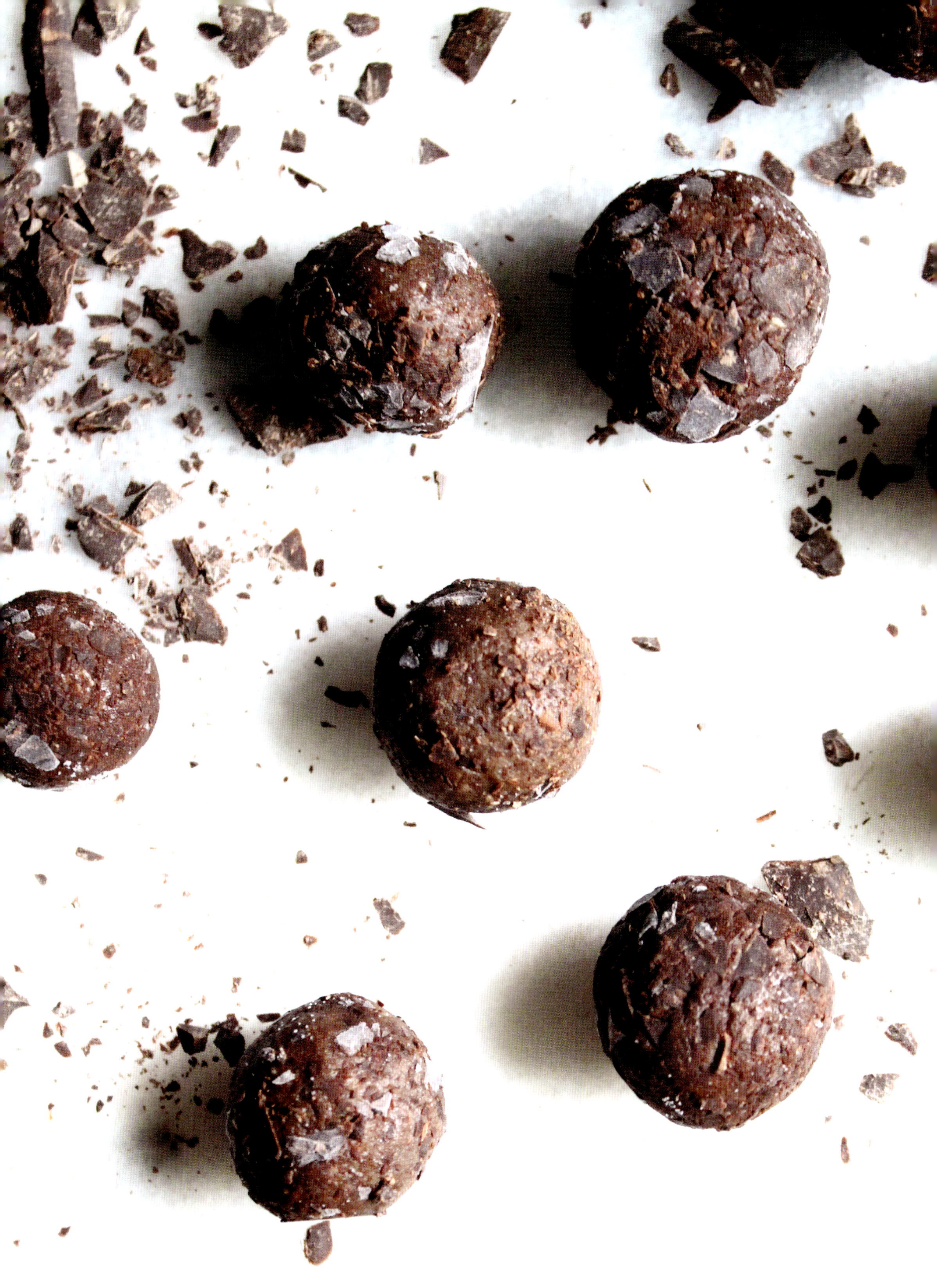

Vegan Cake
coconut + chocolate

makes 1 x 8" cake

cashew plate:
1 ¼ cup (200 gr) whole cashews
3 tbsp maple syrup
6 whole pitted dates
1 tsp flax seeds
½ cup (45 gr) rolled oats

dark chocolate ganache:
1 ¼ cup (220 gr) dark chocolate chips
4 tbsp coconut oil
4 tbsp maple syrup

coconut mousse:
2 cups (480 ml) coconut cream - cold and full fat content
3 tbsp maple syrup
2 tbsp coconut oil
⅔ cup (115 gr) dark chocolate chips
+ dark chocolate to decorate the sides
+ vegan cookies - recipe p. 184
+ 6" and 8" cake rings

To make the cashew plate, pulse all the ingredients in a food processor until combined. Place the mixture in between 2 sheets of wax paper and roll flat using a rolling pin (about 1 cm / 0.4 in). Cut out the bottom of your cake using an 8" cake ring. Keep in the freezer until needed.

The chocolate ganache will be used as the centerpiece of the cake and to decorate the cake. Prepare a 6" cake ring: place the ring on a baking tray. Cover with plastic wrap.

Melt the chocolate chips, coconut oil and maple syrup over a double boiler (saucepan with simmering water). Pour ½ of the dark chocolate ganache into the prepared ring. Place in the freezer at least 2 hours or until set. Reserve the remaining chocolate ganache in a bowl at room temperature. You will need it to decorate the cake.

To make the coconut mousse, place the ingredients in a bowl (except for the chocolate chips). Cover and refrigerate 2 hours. Place the cold mixture in the bowl of an electric mixer with the whip attachment. Whip until stiff – about 3 minutes. Stir in the dark chocolate chips using a spatula. Spread ¾ of that mousse on the cashew plate.

Remove the plastic wrap from the frozen chocolate ganache and place in the center of the coconut mousse. Gently press and fill with the remaining coconut mousse. Level the surface with a palette knife. Put the cake in the freezer until completely frozen.

Warm the frame with a cooking torch or hair dryer. Carefully remove the ring. Place on a serving plate. To decorate, quickly reheat the remaining chocolate ganache in the microwave if needed - 10 seconds. Transfer to a piping bag fitted with a Wilton tip #104. Pipe the ganache on the cake.

Garnish with vegan cookies and drizzle with melted dark chocolate on the sides.

Let the cake completely defrost in the fridge - about 5 hours.

vegan | gluten-free

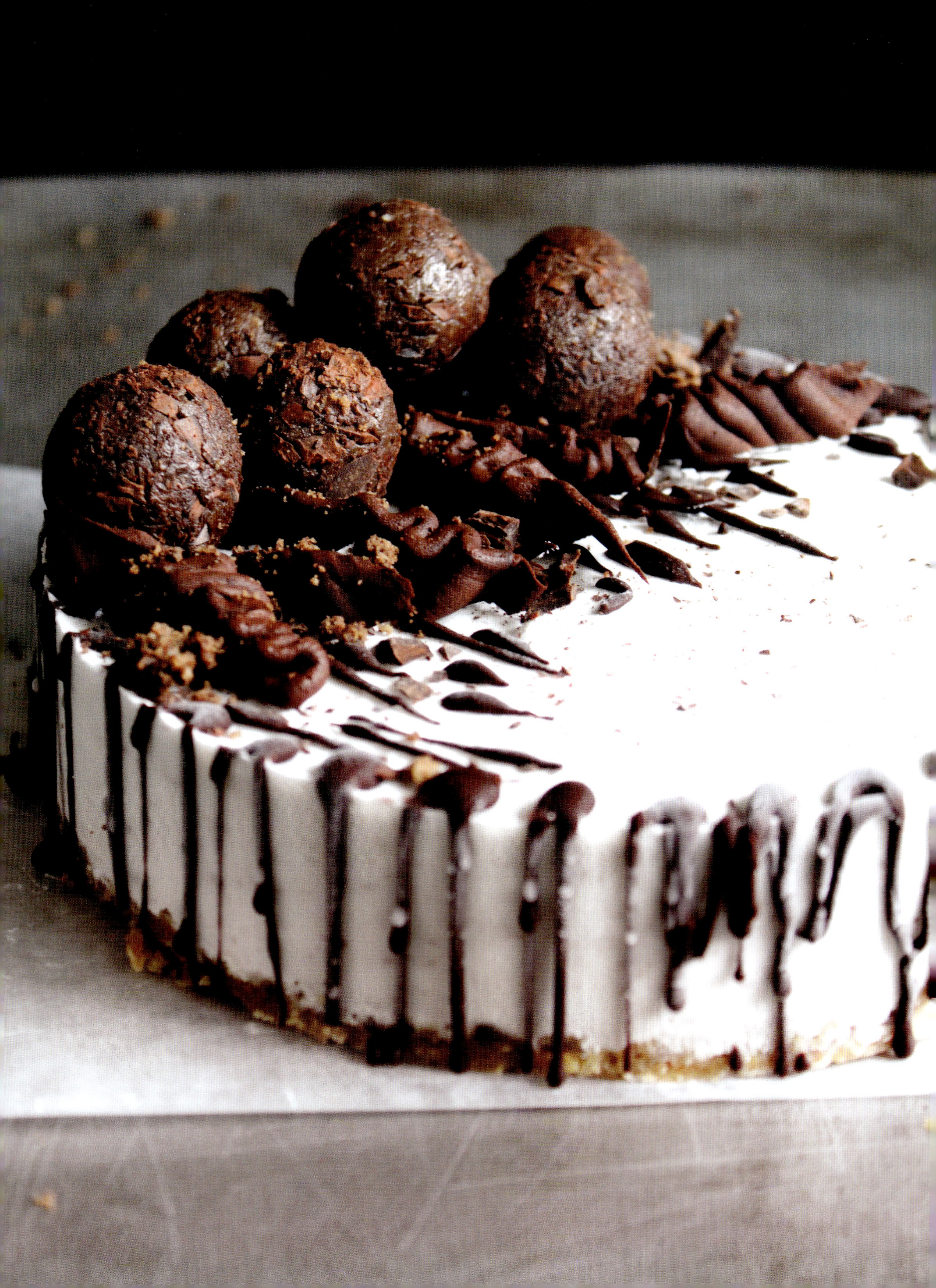

Chocolate Cups

makes 18 cups

1 cup (175 gr) dark chocolate chips
chocolate ganache:
1 ½ cups (260 gr) dark chocolate chips
1 cup (235 ml) heavy cream
1 tbsp granulated sugar

2 tbsp (30 gr) butter - diced
+ baked vegan cookies - recipe p. 184
+ silicone baking cups
+ small paint brush

Start by tempering 1 cup of chocolate following the instructions p. 176.
Paint a thin layer of chocolate onto the inside of each silicone baking cups.
Refrigerate until set - about 20 minutes.
Paint a second layer of chocolate. Set aside in the fridge.
Carefully pop the chocolate cups out.
To make the chocolate ganache, place the chocolate chips in a large bowl.
Heat the heavy cream and sugar in a small saucepan over medium heat.
Bring just to a boil and pour over the chocolate chips. Stir until smooth.
Add the butter, stir with a rubber spatula until incorporated.
Fill a piping bag with chocolate ganache. Cut the tip and pipe into the chocolate cups.
Sprinkle with some vegan cookie crumbs and serve.
Store in the fridge for up to a week.

vegetarian | gluten-free | nut-free

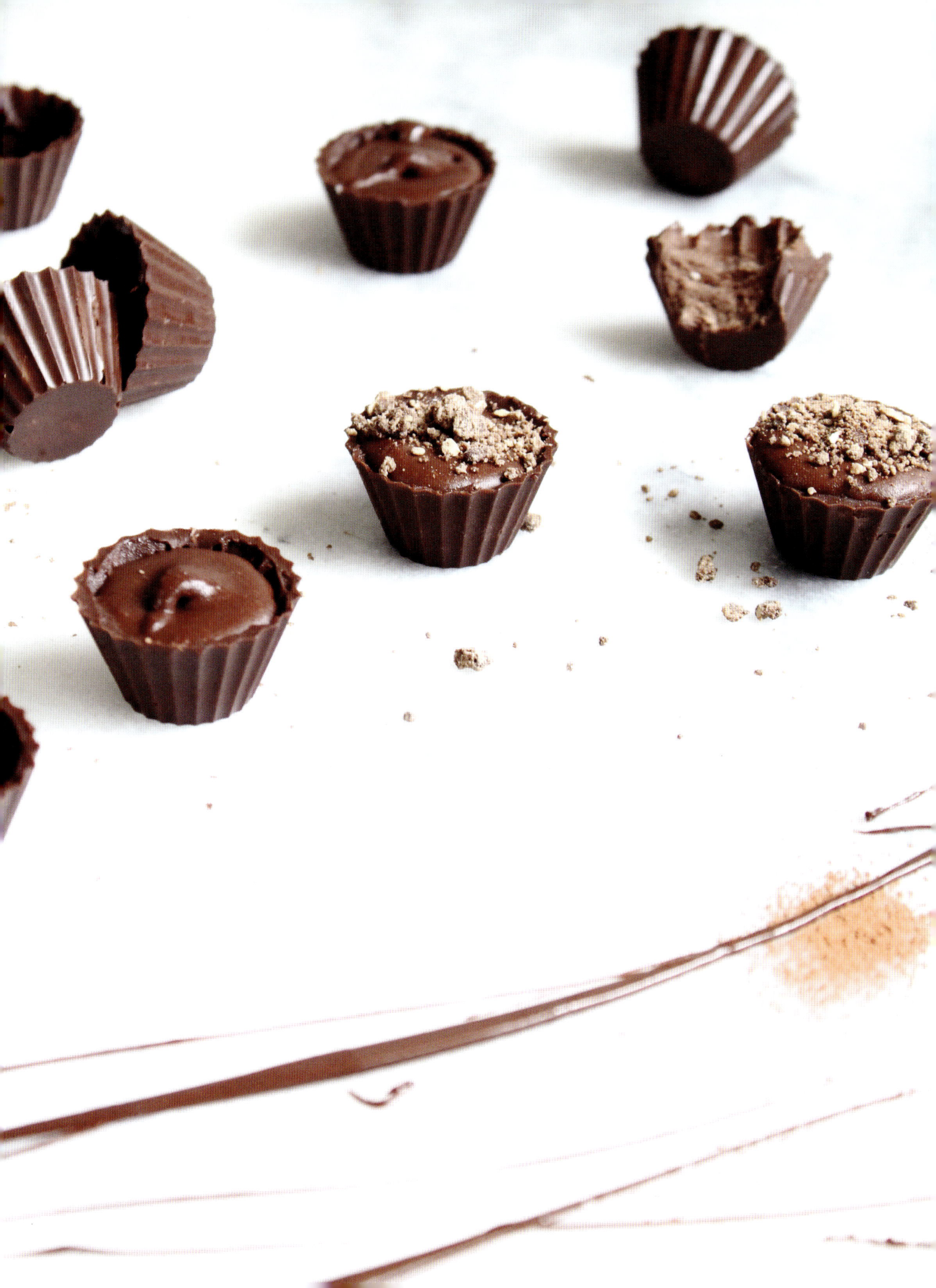

well-being . *noun.*

the state of being contented,
happy, healthy.

To live a positive life, live with no regrets.

Regrets are worthless and aggravate your own sense of well-being.

Know to appreciate food and sweets with no guilt.

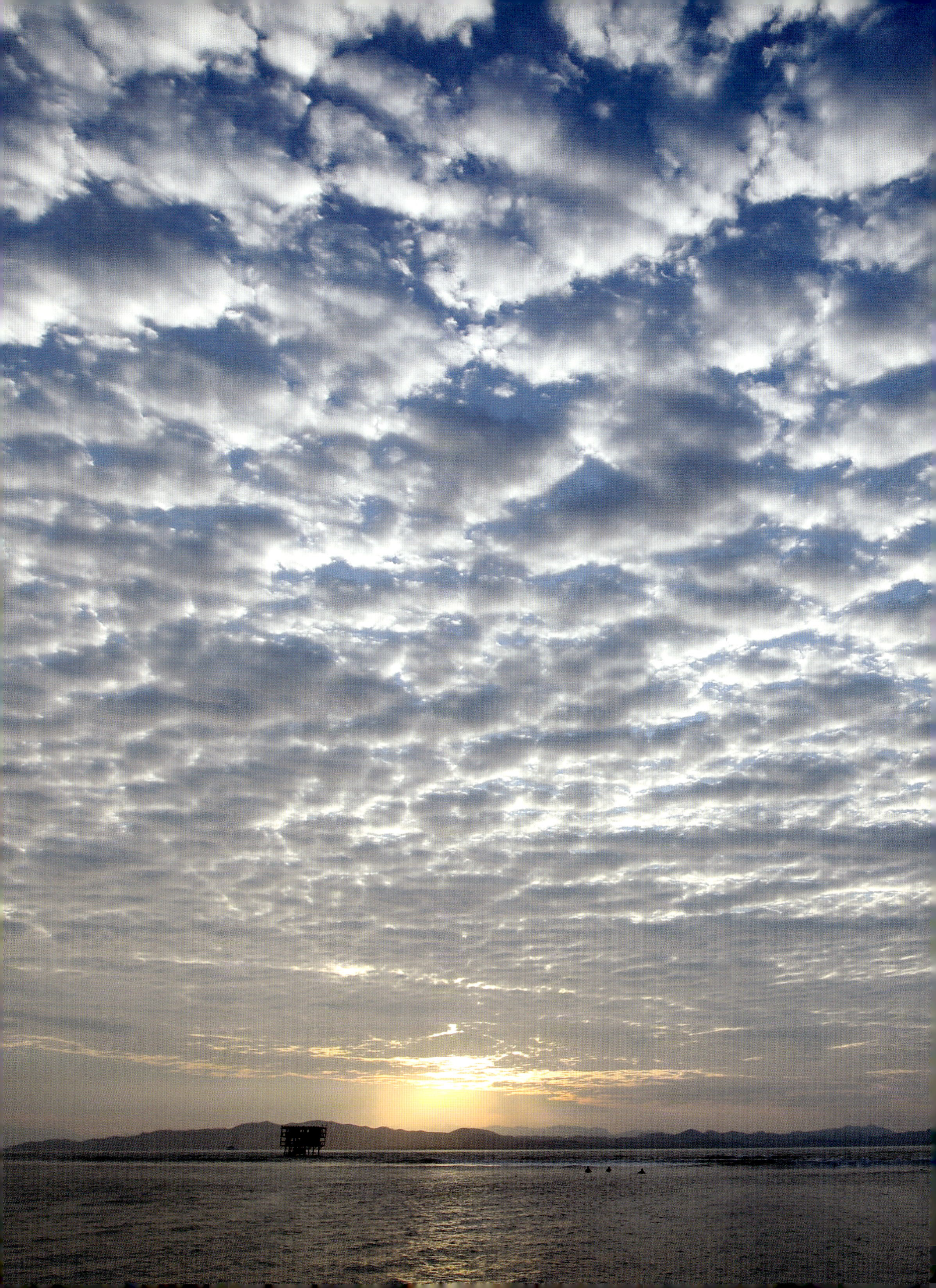

Moelleux au Chocolat

makes 6 cakes

¾ cup (130 gr) dark chocolate chips
⅓ cup (75 gr) butter
3 eggs – free-range organic
⅓ cup (60 gr) granulated sugar

¼ cup (35 gr) flour
+ cupcake pan
+ paper liners

Preheat the oven to 460F / 240C. Place the paper liners in the cupcake pan.
Place the chocolate chips and butter in a mixing bowl.
Melt over a double boiler (saucepan with simmering water).
Whisk together the eggs and sugar in a large mixing bowl until light in color and bubbly – 1 minute.
Whisk in the flour and finally the chocolate mixture. Stir to combine.
Pour the batter into the paper liners using a measuring cup for easy pour.
Refrigerate 20 minutes or until needed and up to 24hours.
Bake for 14 minutes in the preheated oven.
Serve immediately with vanilla ice cream and whipped cream!

vegetarian | nut-free

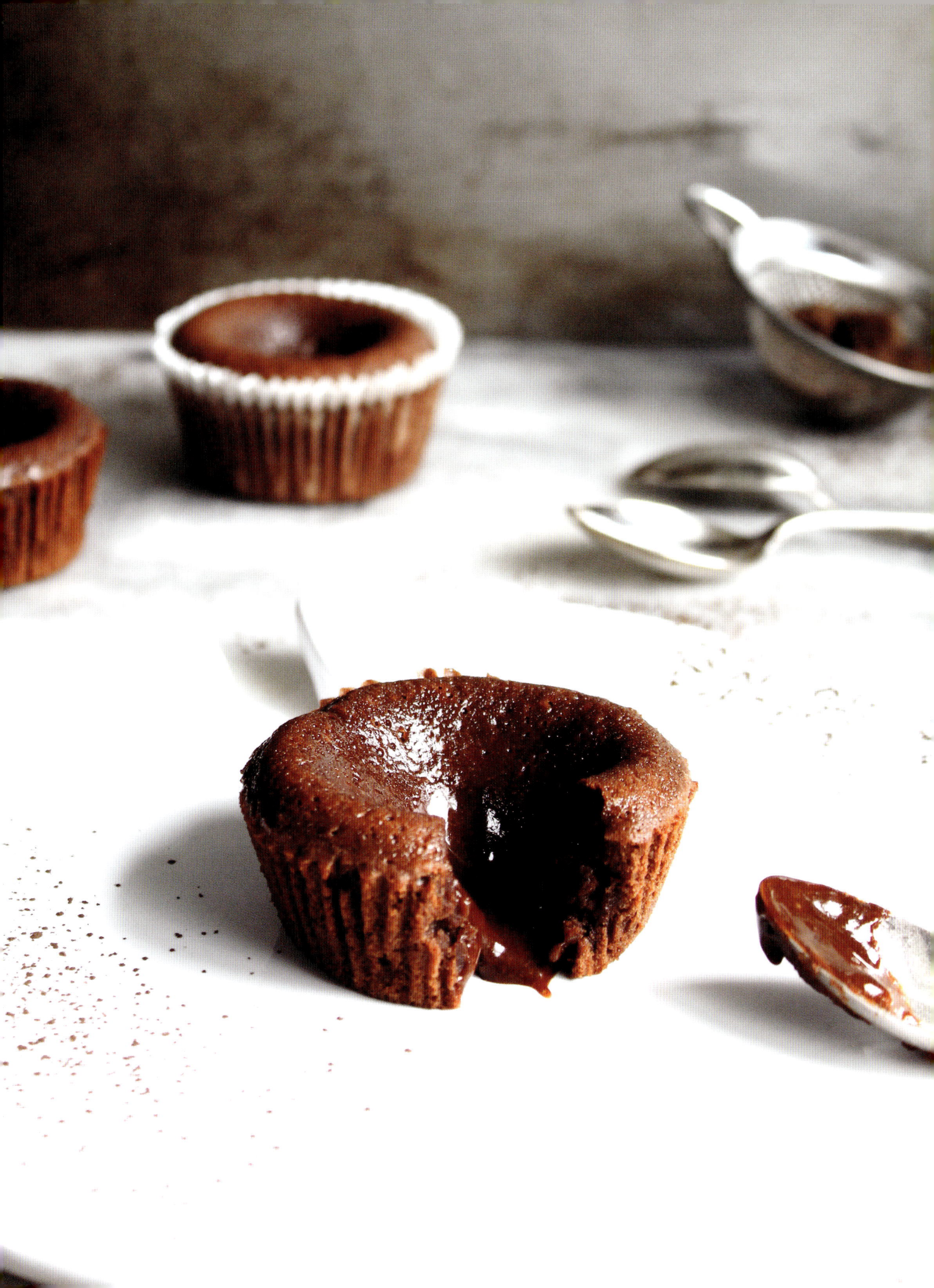

Caramelized Pear & Chocolate Crumble

serves 4

3 medium pears - diced
2 tbsp granulated sugar
1 vanilla bean
crust:
¾ cup (100 gr) flour

¼ cup (25 gr) hazelnut flour
¼ cup (50 gr) brown sugar
⅓ cup (75 gr) butter - cold and diced
⅔ cup (115 gr) dark chocolate chips

Preheat the oven to 430F / 220C.
Melt the granulated sugar with 1 tsp water in a large skillet over medium heat – 2 minutes.
Add the diced pears. Cook for about 5 minutes or until the pears have a nice brown color, stirring occasionally. Cut the vanilla bean lengthwise, scrape the seeds out and stir in the pear mixture.
Set aside.
Place the flour, hazelnut flour and brown sugar in a large bowl.
Cut the butter into the dry ingredients using your fingertips until crumbly.
Place a handful of chocolate chips in the bottom of a baking dish (or small individual ones).
Top with the fruit mixture. Sprinkle with the remaining chocolate chips.
Scatter the crumble mixture evenly on top.
Bake 10 minutes in the preheated oven or until the top is nicely browned.
Serve warm with a side of ice cream!

vegetarian

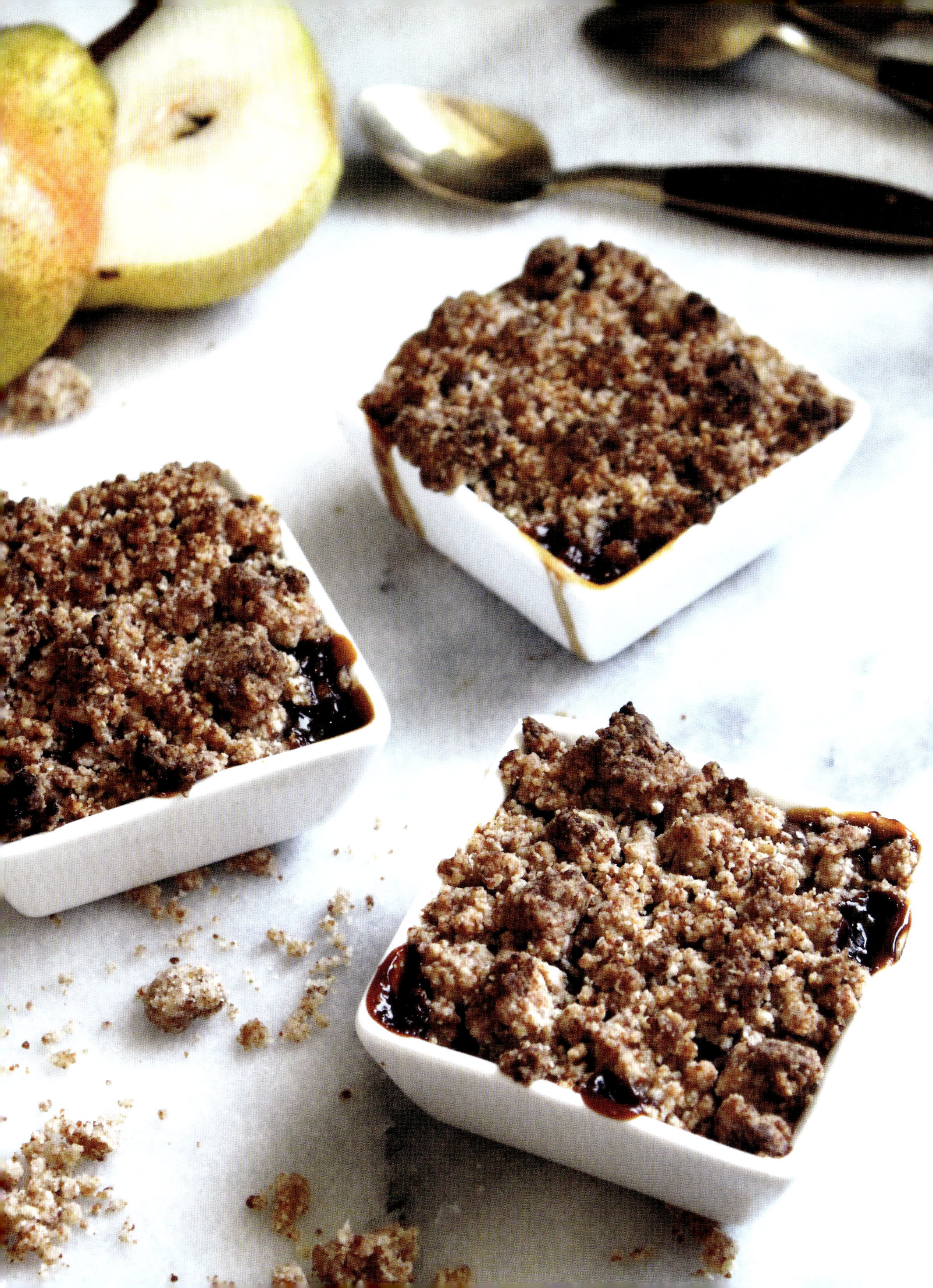

Creamy Vanilla Panna Cotta
+ wild berry compote

serves 6

panna cotta:
1 ¼ cup (300 ml) heavy cream
¾ cup + 2 tbsp (200 ml) whole milk
⅓ cup (65 gr) granulated sugar
2 ½ gelatin leaves
1 vanilla bean

berry compote:
1 cup (110 gr) frozen wild berries
2 tbsp granulated sugar

To make the berry compote, place the berries and sugar in a small saucepan over low heat.
Bring to a boil and cook 10 minutes or until thick and syrupy.
Remove from the heat. Let cool completely.
Soak the gelatin leaves in a bowl of cold water. Using a small curved knife, halve the vanilla bean lengthwise. Scrape the seeds out and place in a medium saucepan.
Add the heavy cream, milk and sugar. Bring to a simmer, stirring occasionally - do not bring to a boil!
Remove from the heat. Gently squeeze the gelatin and whisk into the saucepan.
Place a spoonful of the berry compote in the bottom of six serving ramekins.
Fill with the panna cotta mixture. Place in the fridge uncovered for 4 hours.
Gently spoon the rest of the wild berry compote on top of the panna cottas.
Refrigerate for 1 hour more and serve.
Keep in the fridge for up to 2 days.

gluten-free | nut-free

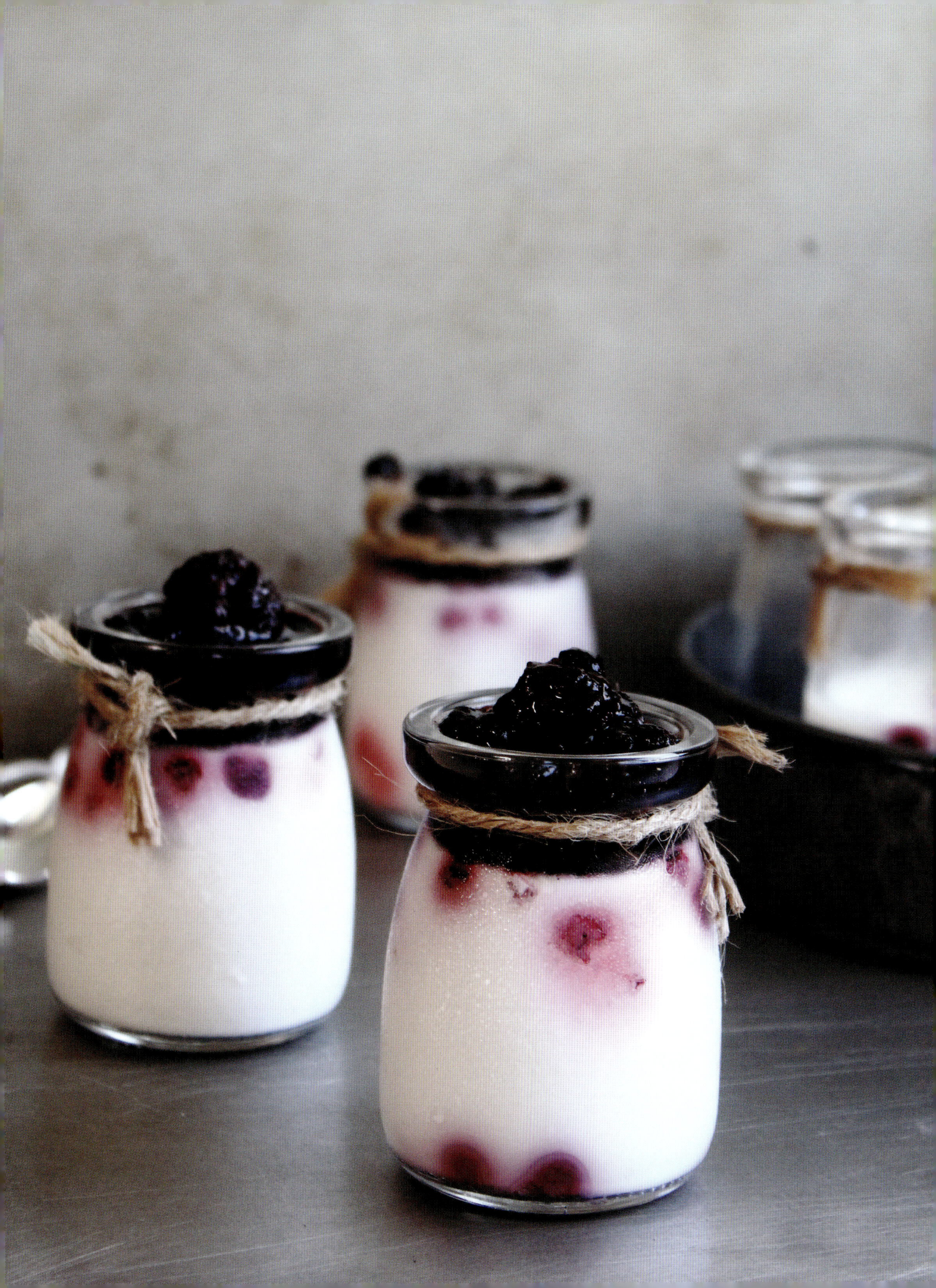

Nutella® Mousse

serves 6

1 cup (240 ml) heavy whipping cream - cold
½ cup (150 gr) Nutella®

Place the cold heavy whipping cream and Nutella® in the bowl of an electric mixer with the whip attachment. Beat on medium speed for 1 minute. Increase to high speed for 3 minutes or until soft peaks form. Quickly whip with a wire whisk to get a uniform consistency.
Spoon the mousse into serving glass dishes - use a piping bag!
Refrigerate for 4 hours and up to 3 days.
Serve chilled!

vegetarian | gluten-free

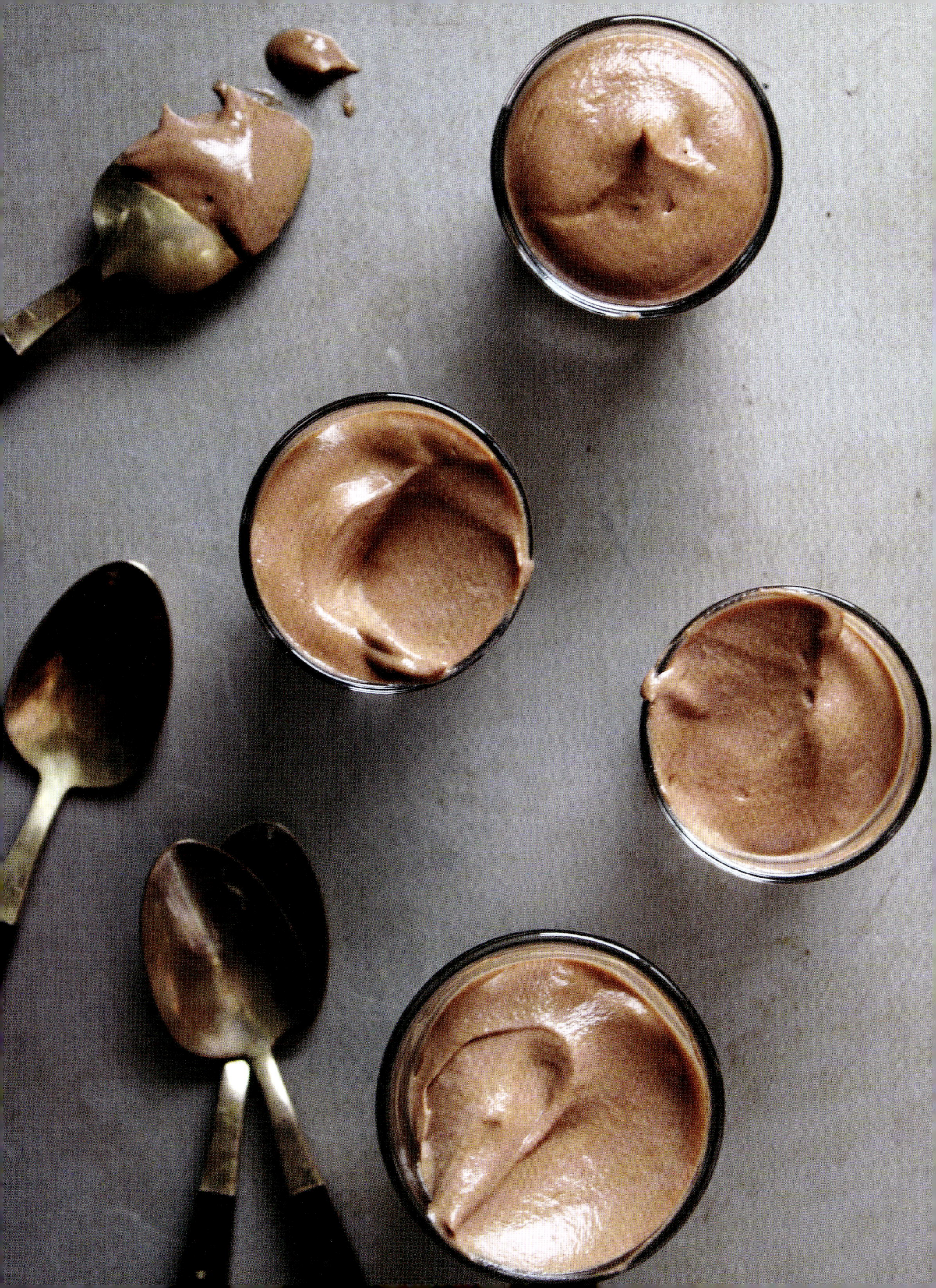

a r t s y . *adj.*

defining one's identity
by non-conformity
to the standards of others.

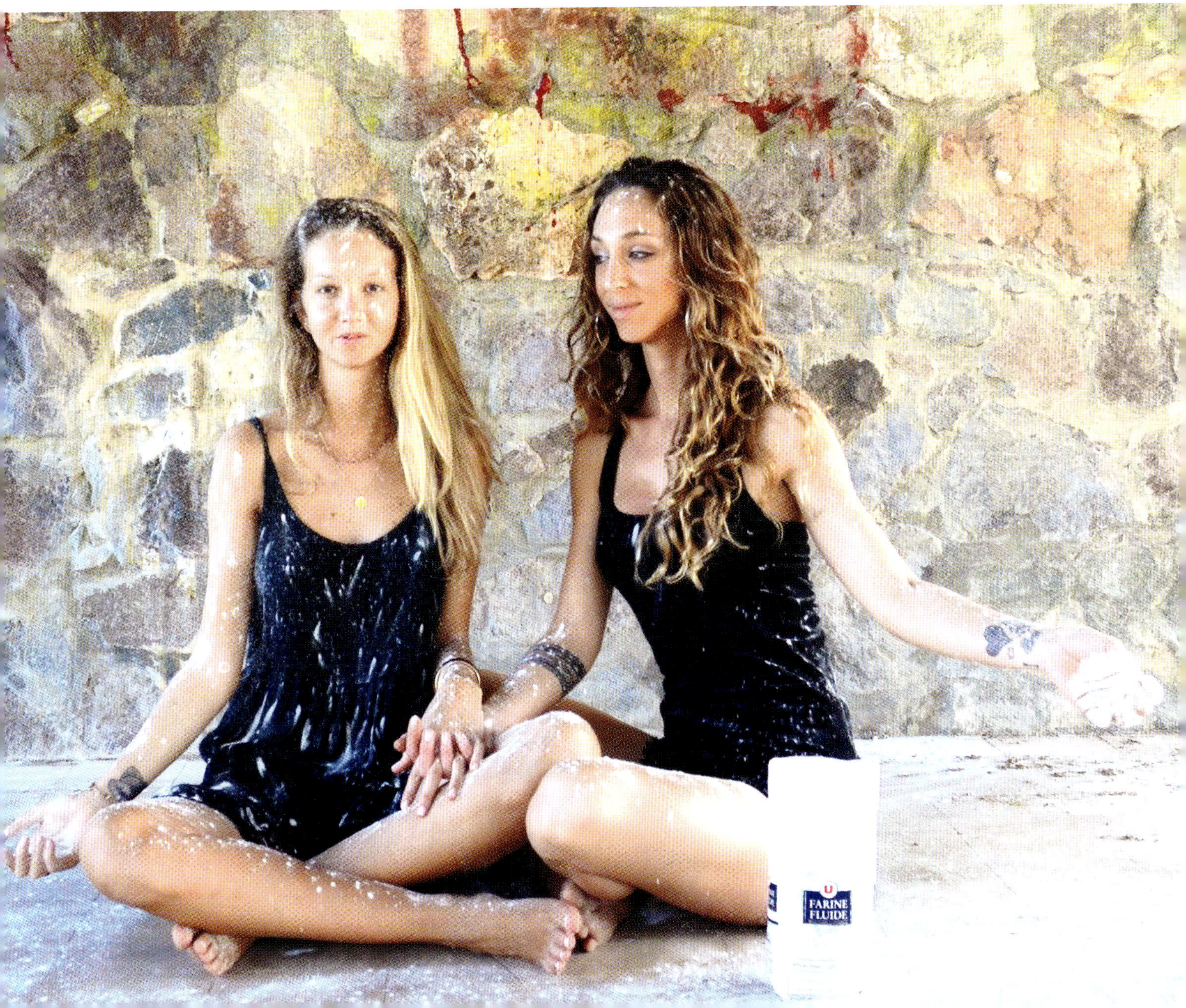
FARINE
FLUIDE

White & Dark Chocolate Bites

makes 12 mini cakes

dark chocolate layer:
1⅓ cups (230 gr) dark chocolate chips
¾ cup (180 gr) butter – diced
5 eggs – free-range organic
¾ cups (170 gr) granulated sugar
1 tbsp cornstarch
1 ½ tbsp unsweetened cocoa powder

white chocolate vanilla layer:
1 cup (230 gr) heavy whipping cream
1 vanilla bean
1 cup (175 gr) white chocolate chips
+ 1 date cake - recipe p. 62
+ dark chocolate chips to decorate

Start by making the date cake. Bake in an 8" (20 cm) square cake pan.
Let cool completely in the fridge. Remove from the pan. Set aside.
To make the dark chocolate layer, coat the same baking pan with non-stick cooking spray.
Preheat the oven to 300F / 150C.
Place the dark chocolate chips and butter in a mixing bowl.
Melt over a double boiler (saucepan with simmering water). Stir occasionally until melted. Set aside.
Place the eggs and sugar in another bowl over the double boiler. Whisk constantly until the sugar has fully dissolved and the mixture is warm to the touch – about 3 minutes. Stir in the chocolate mixture.
Add the cornstarch and cocoa powder, stir to combine. Pour this batter into the prepared pan.
Place into a larger pan in the oven. Fill the deeper pan with hot water - about ⅓ inches (1 cm).
Bake "au bain-marie" for 45 minutes or until set. Remove from the oven.
Let cool completely in the pan. Invert the pan on a parchment paper. Set aside in the fridge.
To make the white chocolate vanilla layer, halve the vanilla bean lengthwise using a small curved knife.
Scrape the seeds out and place in a saucepan. Add the heavy cream and bring to just a boil.
Turn off the heat, cover and let infuse 15 minutes.
Place the white chocolate chips in a mixing bowl. Melt over a double boiler, stirring occasionally until fully melted. Take off the heat. Quickly reheat the cream and combine with the melted white chocolate. Use a hand blender for a smooth consistency. Cover and refrigerate for 6 hours.
Place the white chocolate cream in the bowl of an electric mixer with the whip attachment.
Mix until soft peaks form – 1 minute. Transfer this mixture to a piping bag fitted with a Wilton tip #45.
To assemble the cake, place the dark chocolate layer on top of the date cake.
Cut into 12 squares of even size using a long sharp knife. Pipe some white chocolate cream on top.
To decorate, line a baking sheet with a silicone baking mat.
Melt 1 cup dark chocolate following the instructions p. 176
Fill in a piping bag fitted with a Wilton round tip #12.
Pipe small amounts of chocolate on the baking mat.
Gently tap the pan to flatten. Refrigerate until set – about 1 hour and place on the cakes.
Keep the cakes in the fridge for a few days!

vegetarian | gluten-free | nut-free

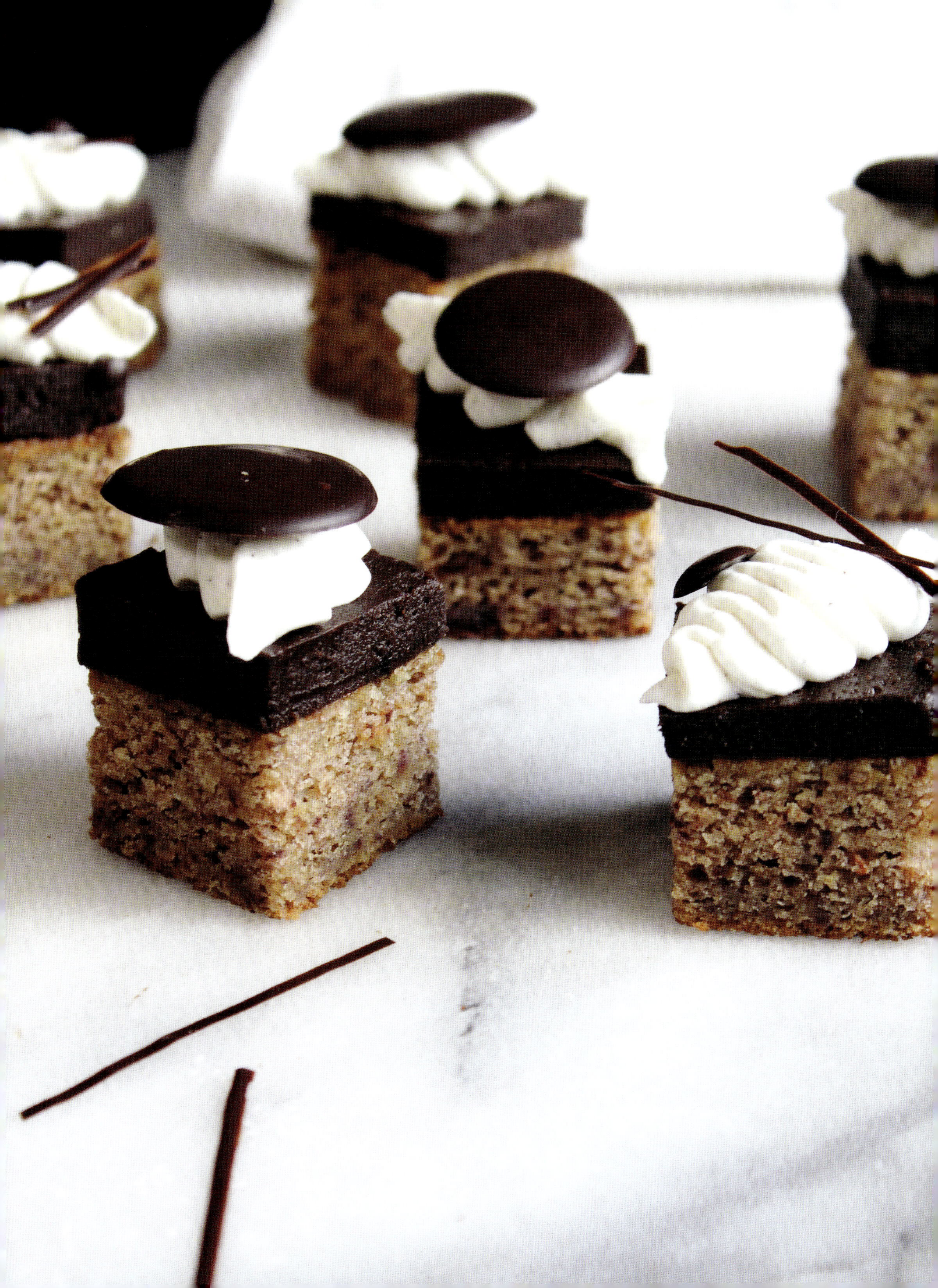

Italian Meringue

2 egg whites (55 gr) – at room temperature
¾ cup (150 gr) granulated sugar

2 ½ tbsp (37 gr) water
+ candy thermometer

Place the granulated sugar and water in a small saucepan over medium heat. Bring to a boil. Meanwhile, whip the egg whites in the bowl of an electric mixer on medium speed (speed 4) until foamy. When the sugar syrup reaches 230F / 110C, increase the speed to high (speed 10). Check the temperature with a candy thermometer for accuracy. Remove from the heat as soon as the thermometer shows 242F / 117C. Immediately pour the sugar syrup all at once over the egg whites in a thin stream with the mixer running on low (speed 1). Increase to high speed (speed 10) and beat until the egg whites are stiff and glossy - about 3 minutes. Check the temperature. The meringue should have cooled down to 100F / 38C.

vegetarian | gluten-free | nut-free

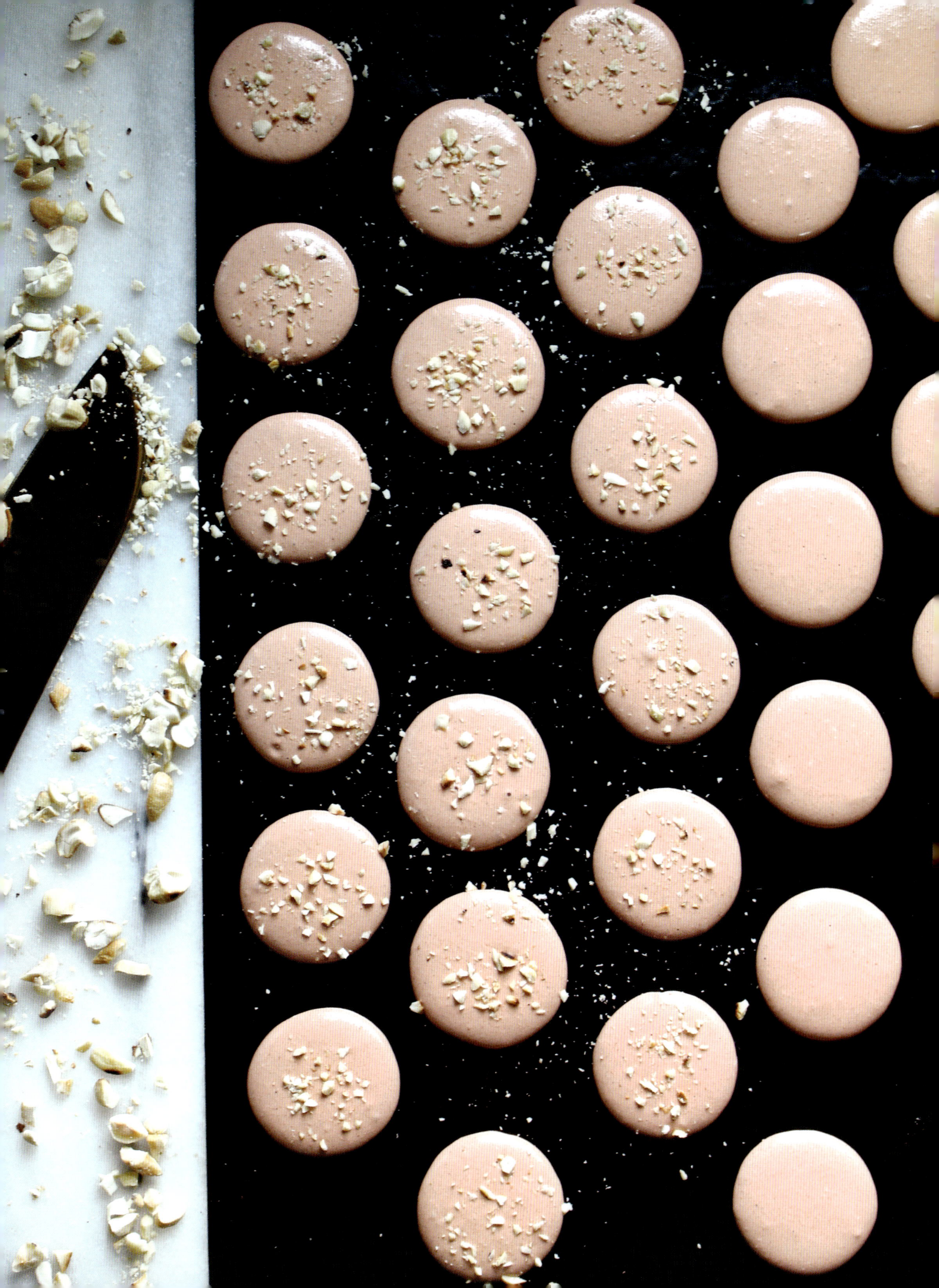

Unconventional Lemon Tart

serves 10

sweet tart dough:
1 stick (110 gr) butter - soft
1 ½ cups (210 gr) flour
½ cup (50 gr) almond flour
9 tbsp (70 gr) powdered sugar
1 egg – free-range organic
½ tsp vanilla powder

chocolate ganache:
¾ cup (180 ml) heavy whipping cream
1 ½ cups (260 gr) dark chocolate chips
2 tbsp (30 gr) butter- cold and diced

lime cream:
2 eggs – free-range organic
¾ cup (150 gr) granulated sugar
½ cup (120 ml) lime juice
the zest of 2 limes
2 gelatin leaves
½ stick (55 gr) butter
italian meringue - recipe p. 204
+ 1 cup (175 gr) milk chocolate chips to decorate
+ 8" square cake ring

To make the dough, place the butter in the bowl of an electric mixer with the whip attachment. Mix for 2 minutes on medium speed.
Stir in the rest of the ingredients. Whisk for 1 minute more or until combined on low speed.
Wrap the dough in plastic wrap and refrigerate for 1 hour. Preheat the oven to 350F / 180C.
Line a baking sheet with a silicone baking mat.
To roll out the dough, place it in between 2 sheets of wax paper. Sprinkle with some flour and roll flat from the center out using a rolling pin. Flip occasionally and add more flour to keep it from sticking. Place the dough on the prepared baking sheet. Cover with another silicone baking mat. Place a baking tray on top to bake nice and flat. Bake in the preheated oven for 20 minutes.
Remove the upper baking tray and silicone baking mat. Bake for 10 minutes more or until evenly browned. Remove from the oven and immediately cut out the base of the tart using the cake ring.
Place on a baking sheet and refrigerate.

To make the chocolate ganache, warm the cream in a small saucepan over medium heat.
Place the dark chocolate chips in a mixing bowl and add the warm cream.
Stir from the center out until combined. Mix in the butter.
Fill in the ring (on the sweet tart dough) and place in the freezer until set – about 30 minutes.

To make the lime cream, soak the gelatin leaves in cold water. Rub the lime zest in the sugar in a medium bowl until the sugar is moist and aromatic. Mix in the lime juice. Beat the egg and add to the mixture. Pour into a saucepan. Place over low heat and cook until the mixture thickens, stirring constantly. Take away from the heat.
Stir in the butter. Squeeze the gelatin leaves, mix into the lime cream.
Let cool and pour on the chocolate ganache. Place in the freezer until set.
Make the Italian meringue and spread on top of the lemon cream.
Level the surface with a palette knife. Put back in the freezer for 10 minutes.
Quickly warm the frame using a cooking torch or hair-dryer. Carefully push the cake out.
Refrigerate until needed.
To decorate, melt the milk chocolate chips using the instructions p. 176.
Drizzle all around on the sides of the cake using a spoon.
Serve immediately or keep in the fridge for up to a day.

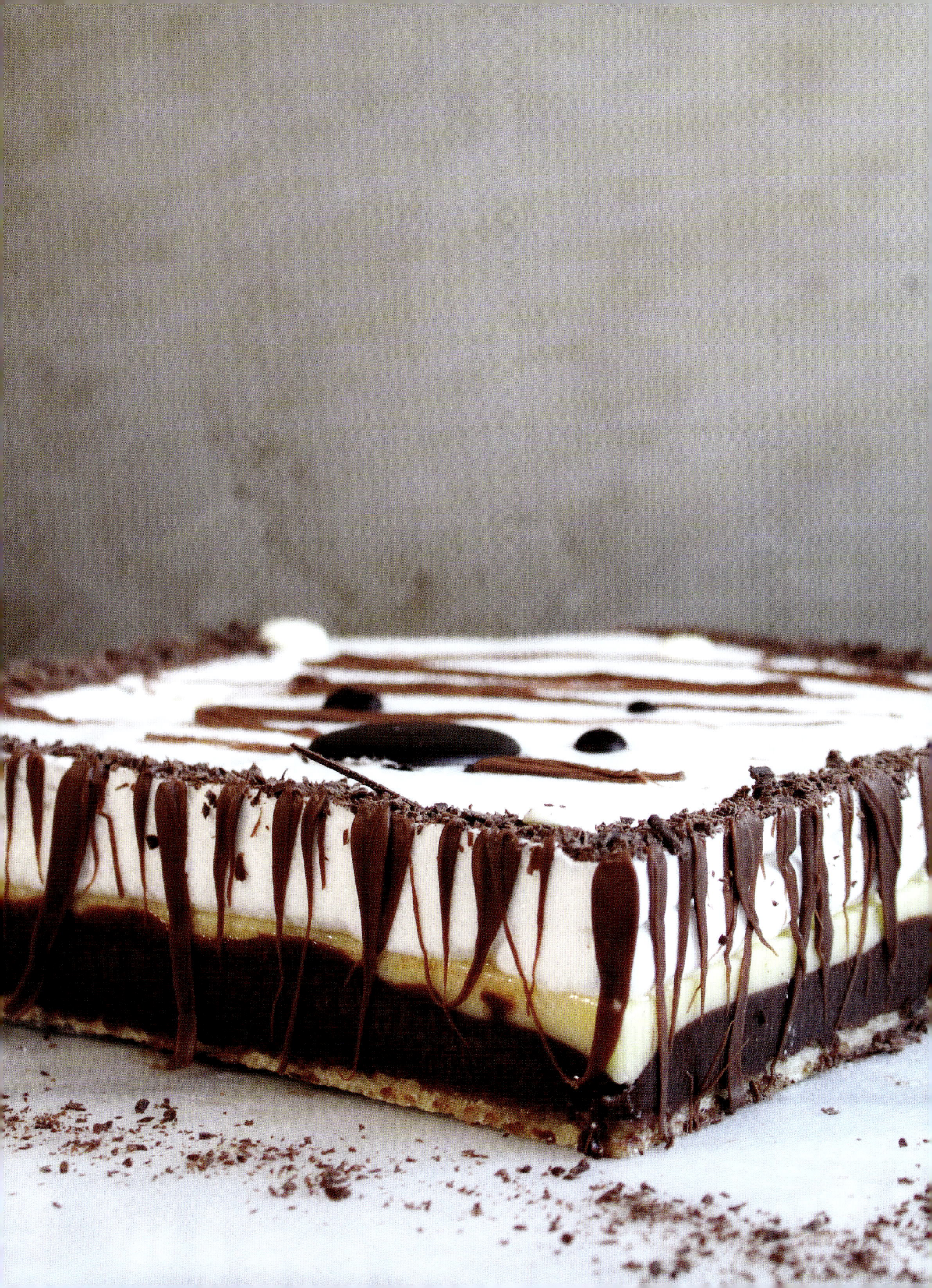

Wild Berry Tart
+ vanilla pastry cream

serves 10

sweet tart dough:
1 stick (110 gr) soft butter
1 ½ cups (210 gr) flour
½ cup (50 gr) almond flour
9 tbsp powdered sugar
1 egg – free-range organic
½ tsp vanilla powder
2 tbsp cocoa powder

vanilla pastry cream:
2 cups (500 ml) whole milk
2 vanilla beans
5 egg yolks
¾ cup (150 gr) granulated sugar
3 rounded tbsp. flour
⅓ cup (45 gr) cornstarch
½ stick of butter (60 gr) - diced
4 cups (400 gr) fresh wild berries

Preheat the oven to 356 F / 180 C. Place the butter in the bowl of an electric mixer with the whisk attachment. Whisk for 2 minutes. Stir in the rest of the ingredients. Continue to whisk for 1 minute or until combined. Wrap the dough in plastic wrap, refrigerate 1 hour.

To roll out the dough, sprinkle some flour and cocoa powder on a large sheet of wax paper. Place the dough in the center. Sprinkle some more flour and cocoa powder. Cover with a second piece of wax paper of equal size. This will prevent sticking. Flatten from the center out into the desired shape using a rolling pin. Flip the dough occasionally. Lightly dust the top with more flour as needed. Keep rolling until the dough is about 1/8 in (3 mm) thick. Disregard the wax paper sheets and transfer the dough to the tart pan. Gently press into place. Firmly roll the rolling pin off the top edge to remove the excess dough. Refrigerate for 20 minutes. When chilled, line with parchment paper and cover with pie weighs or dry beans. Bake in the preheated oven for about 25 minutes or until the edges are nicely brown. Take the crust out of the oven. Carefully remove the parchment paper and weighs.

Return to the oven. Bake a few more minutes until the center is light-brown as well.

To make the vanilla cream, halve the vanilla beans lengthwise using a small curved knife. Scrape the seeds out and place in a medium saucepan with 1 cup (250 ml) milk. Bring to a gentle boil.

Remove from the heat, cover and leave undisturbed for 20 minutes.

Disregard the vanilla beans and place the saucepan over medium heat. Bring to a boil. Meanwhile, whisk the egg yolks, sugar, flour and cornstarch in a large bowl. Whisk in the warm milk stirring constantly. Return the mixture to the saucepan and place over medium heat. Cook the cream stirring constantly until it comes to a gentle boil and thickens (count 1 minute per 2 cups / 500 ml from the simmering stage). Remove from the heat. Mix in half of the butter. Stir well until incorporated. Add the other half. Stir well.

Pour directly into the tart crust. Let cool completely in the fridge and arrange the berries on top. Remove the rim of the tart pan before serving! This tart keeps in the fridge for up to 24 hours.

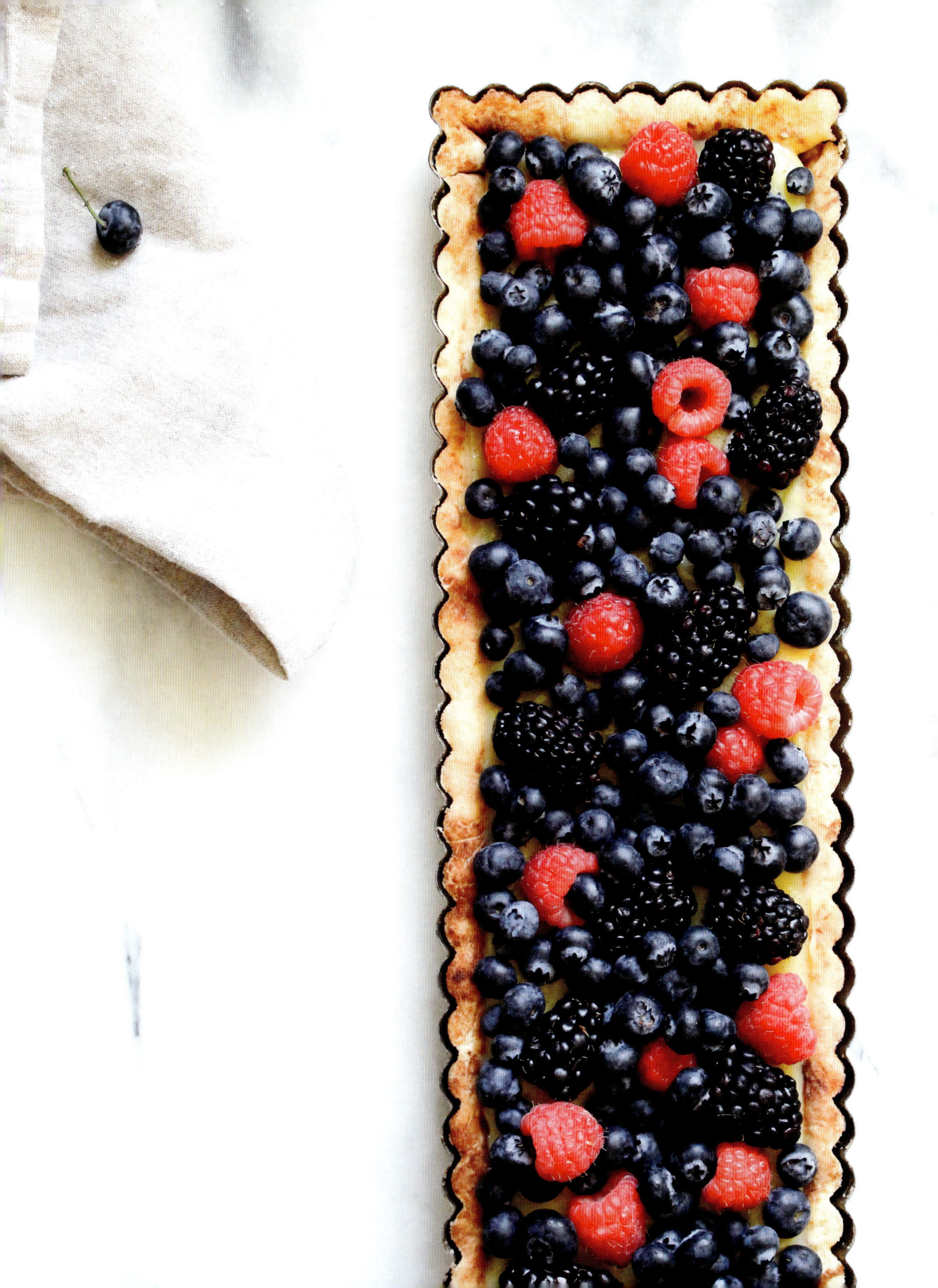

Macarons

Baking macarons is intimidating but they are not hard to make.

The following tips will help you in the process of baking the most amazing treats.

Egg whites at room temperature
Italian meringue for best consistency
Roasted almond flour to reduce humidity in the batter
Bake at low temperature to build the perfect "feet"
Bake on black silicone baking mats
Every step matters

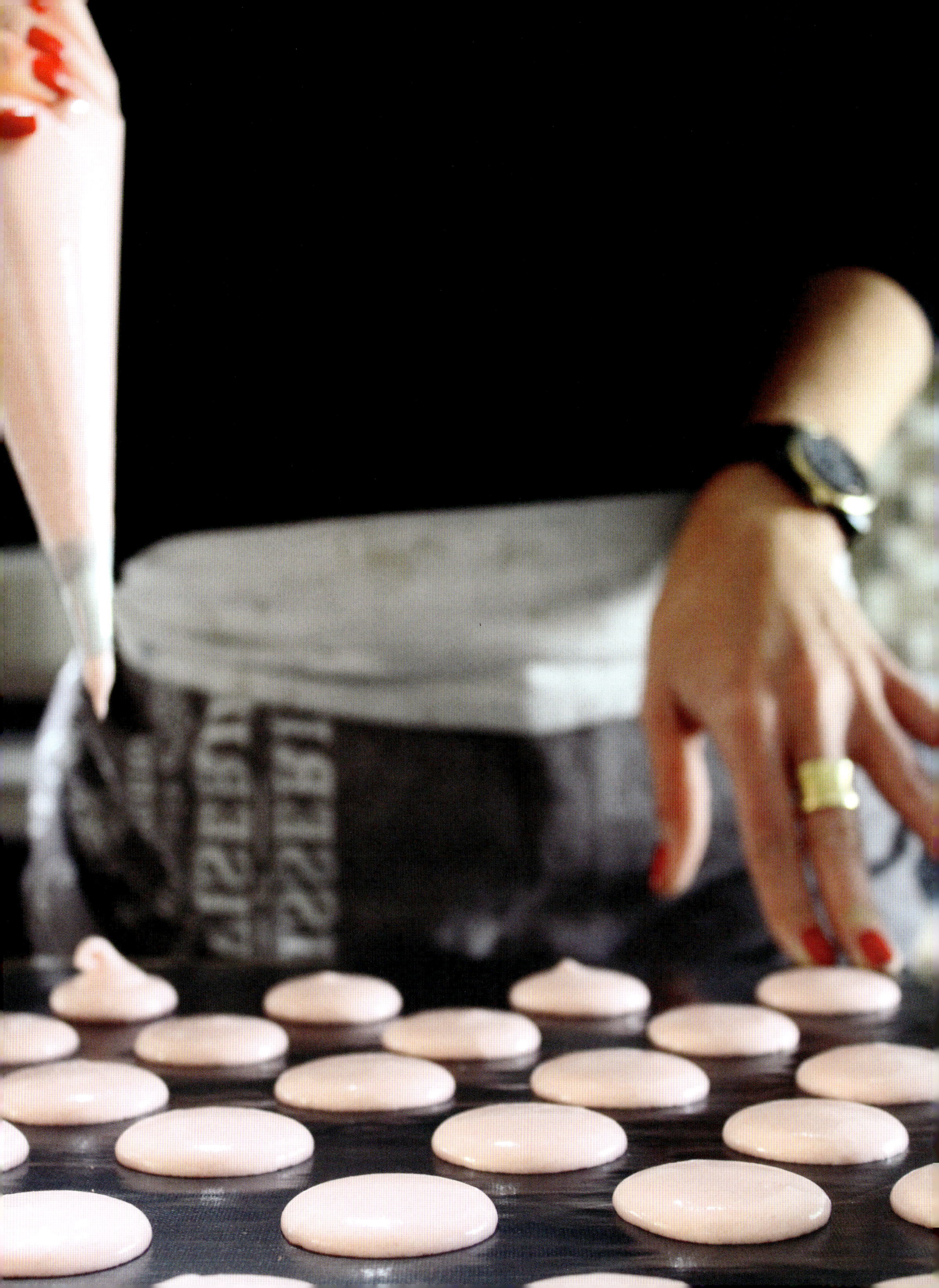

Macarons
basic recipe

makes 30

1 ½ cups (150 gr) almond flour
1⅜ cups (150 gr) powdered sugar
2 egg whites (55 gr)

italian meringue - recipe p. 204
+ ¼ tsp food coloring (optional)

Preheat the oven to 284F / 140C.
Line 2 baking sheets with silicone baking mats. Fit a pastry bag with a Wilton round tip #12.
Place the almond flour in a baking pan in a single layer.
Roast in the oven for 8 minutes or until warm to the touch.
Let cool completely in a mixing bowl before continuing - about 10 minutes.
Pulse the almond flour and powdered sugar in a food processor - about 2 minutes.
Sift through a sieve over a large mixing bowl. Disregard any larger almond pieces.
This will give a smooth texture to the shells.
Mix in the egg whites and food coloring (optional). Set aside.
Make the Italian meringue.
Stir 2 tbsp of the meringue into the almond flour mixture to soften the batter.
Fold in the rest of the meringue with a rubber spatula.
Start in a gentle, slow and circular motion for about 2 minutes or until both mixtures are combined.
Stir faster for 2 minutes or until the batter is smooth and falls off the spatula in a thick ribbon. It is called "faire le ruban"--"to make the ribbon".
Transfer the batter to the prepared pastry bag. Pipe 0.7-in (2 cm) disks on the prepared baking sheets leaving 2 in (5 cm) between each.
Leave at room temperature until dry to the touch - 30 minutes to an hour.
Bake in the preheated oven for 19 minutes. Wait 15 minutes before gently pushing them off the mat from the bottom. Do not pull them off from the top!
Keep the macaron shells in an air tight container in the fridge until needed and up to 2 weeks.

vegetarian | gluten-free

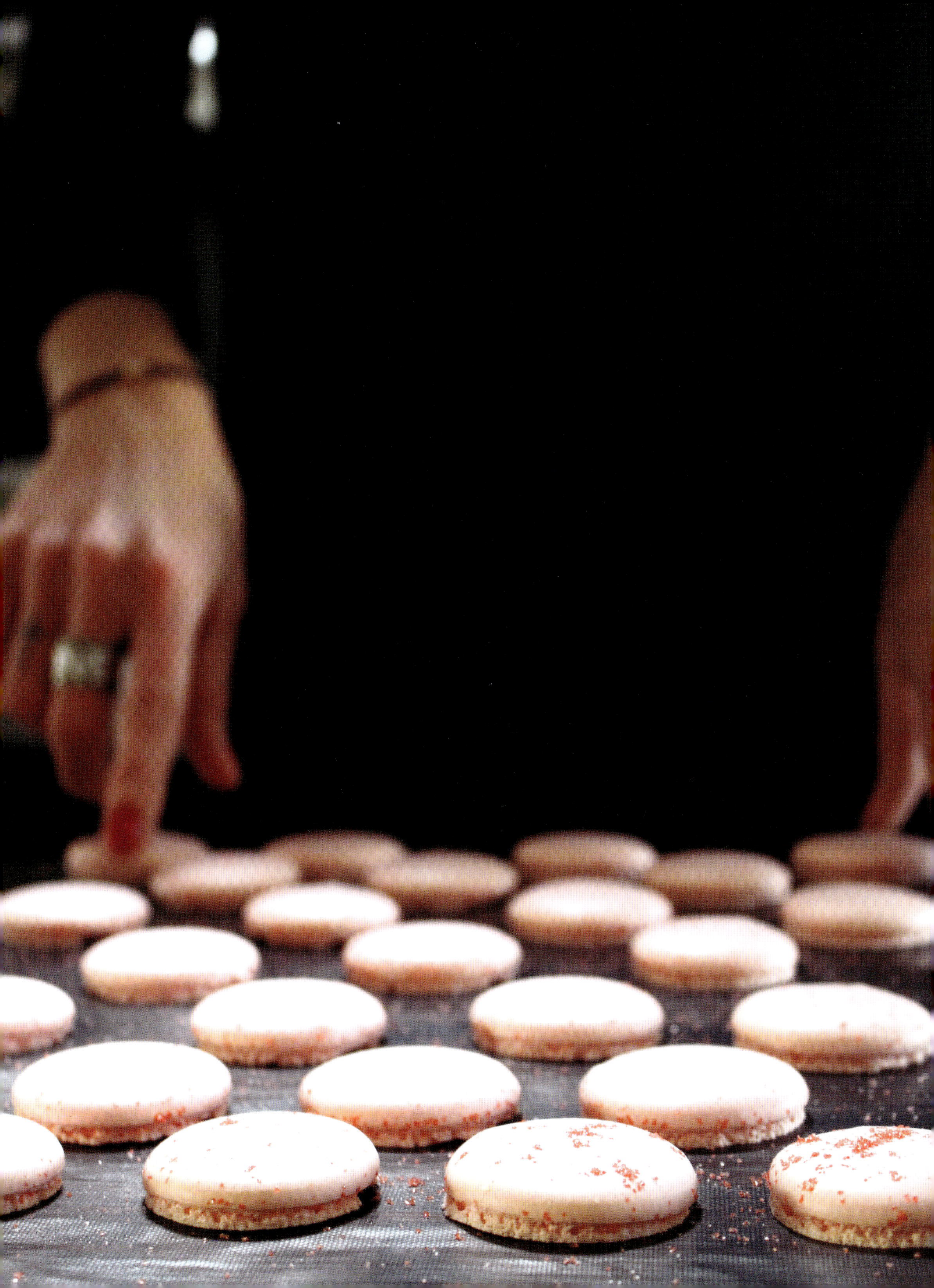

Macarons Nutella®

makes about 30

macaron shells - recipe p. 212
Nutella® mousse - recipe p. 198

Make the Nutella® mousse and refrigerate until needed.
Make the macaron shells using a brown food coloring.
Sort and match into pairs.
To assemble, transfer the Nutella® mousse to a piping bag fitted with a Wilton round tip #12.
Pipe the filling onto one shell, cover with the other shell.
Place the macarons in an airtight container.
Refrigerate overnight before eating - it is a must so that the macarons have the best consistency!
Store in an airtight container in the fridge for up to a week.

vegetarian | gluten-free

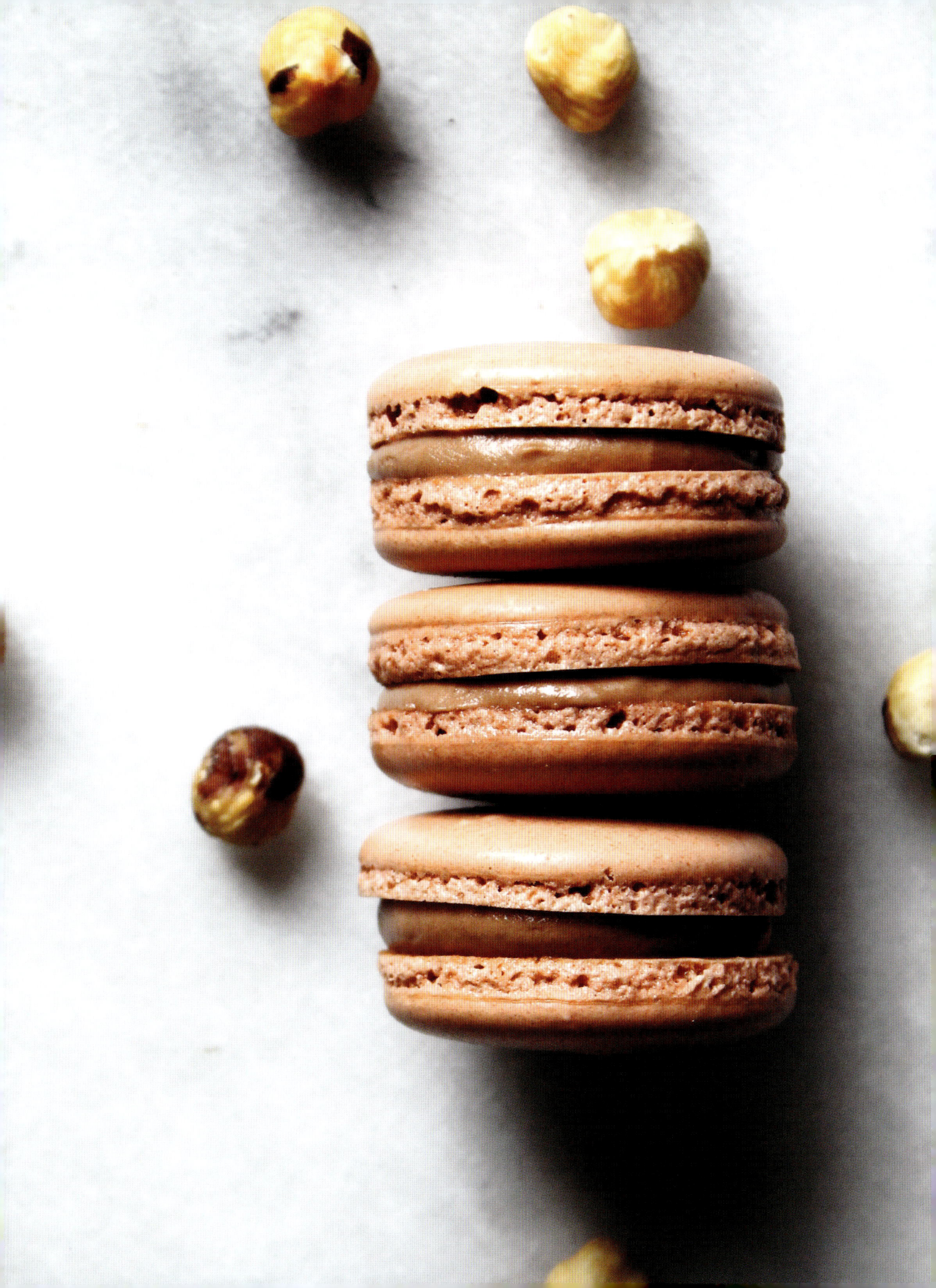

Macarons Fraise

makes 30

macaron shells - recipe p. 212
1 cup (250 gr) organic strawberries - frozen

¾ cup (150 gr) granulated sugar
2 ½ tsp (8 gr) pectin

Place the strawberries in a large pot over medium heat. Bring to a boil. Stir in half of the sugar.
Mix the other half with the pectin. When the sugar has fully dissolved, add the sugar/pectin mixture.
Bring to a boil and count 7 minutes cooking time. Whisk constantly.
Remove from the heat and place in a large bowl. Let cool completely.
Make the macaron shells using a red food coloring.
Sort and match into pairs.
Place the strawberry filling in the bowl of an electric mixer with the whip attachment.
Mix at full speed for 1 minute.
Fit a pastry bag with a Wilton round tip #12 and add the strawberry filling.
Pipe the filling onto one shell, cover with the other shell.
Place the macarons in an airtight container.
Refrigerate overnight before eating - it is a must so that the macarons have the best consistency!
Store the macarons in an airtight container, in the fridge for up to a week.

vegetarian | gluten-free

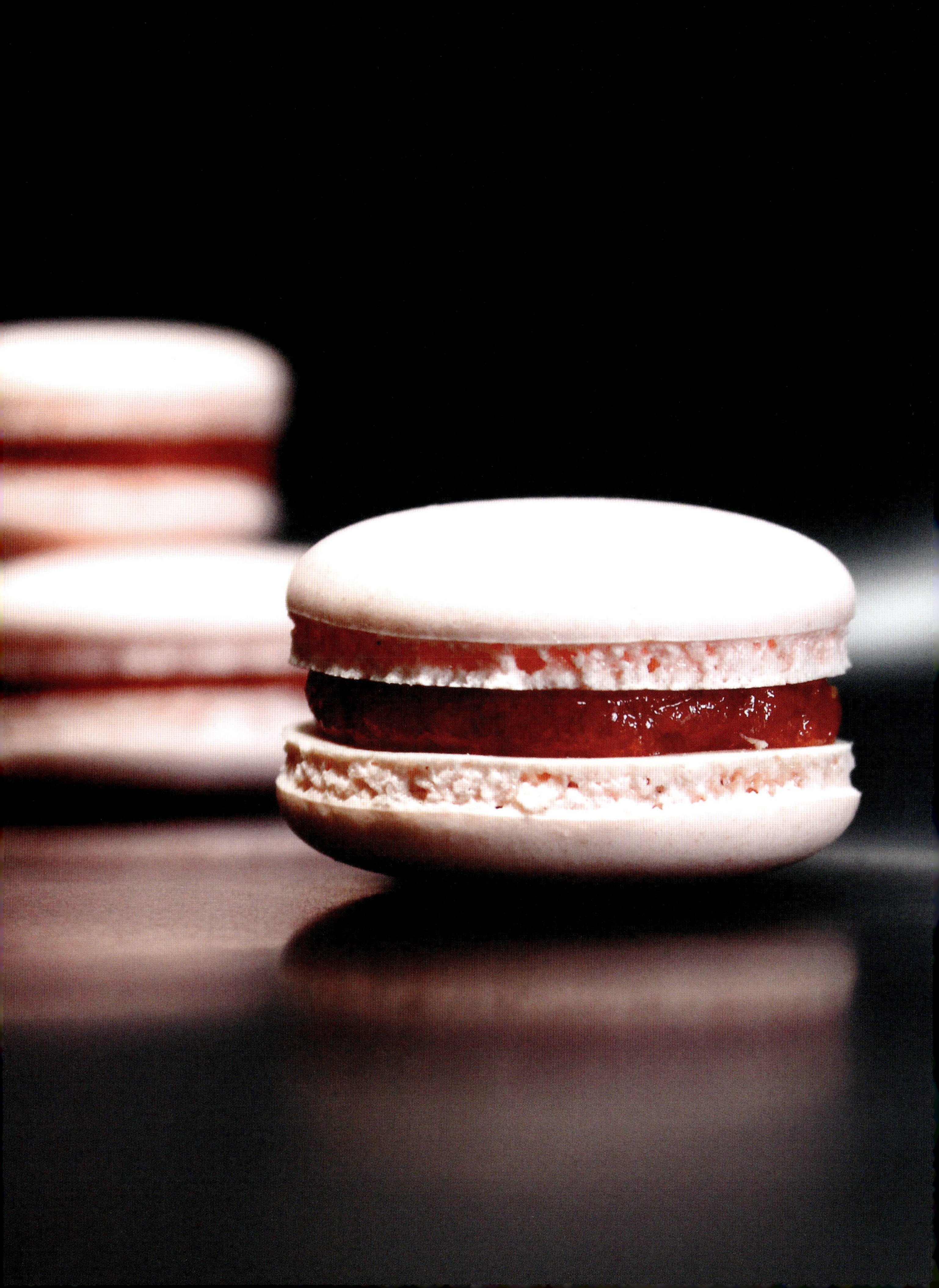

Macarons Pistache

makes 30

macaron shells - recipe p. 212
1 cup (175 gr) white chocolate chips

¾ cup (180 gr) heavy whipping cream
¼ cup (50 gr) pistachio paste

Place the white chocolate chips in a mixing bowl.
Melt over a double-boiler (saucepan with simmering water).
Warm the cream and pistachio paste in a small saucepan over medium heat.
Stir in the melted white chocolate using a rubber spatula.
Use a hand blender for a nice and smooth texture.
Cover and refrigerate for 6 hours or overnight.
Make the macaron shells using a green food coloring. Sort and match into pairs.
Place the pistachio filling in the bowl of an electric mixer with the whip attachment.
Mix at medium to high speed until soft peaks form - about 2 minutes.
Fit a pastry bag with a Wilton round tip #12. Add the pistachio filling.
Pipe the filling onto one shell, cover with the other shell.
Place the macarons in an airtight container.
Refrigerate overnight before eating - it is a must so that the macarons have the best consistency!-
Store the macarons in an airtight container, in the fridge for up to a week.

vegetarian | gluten-free

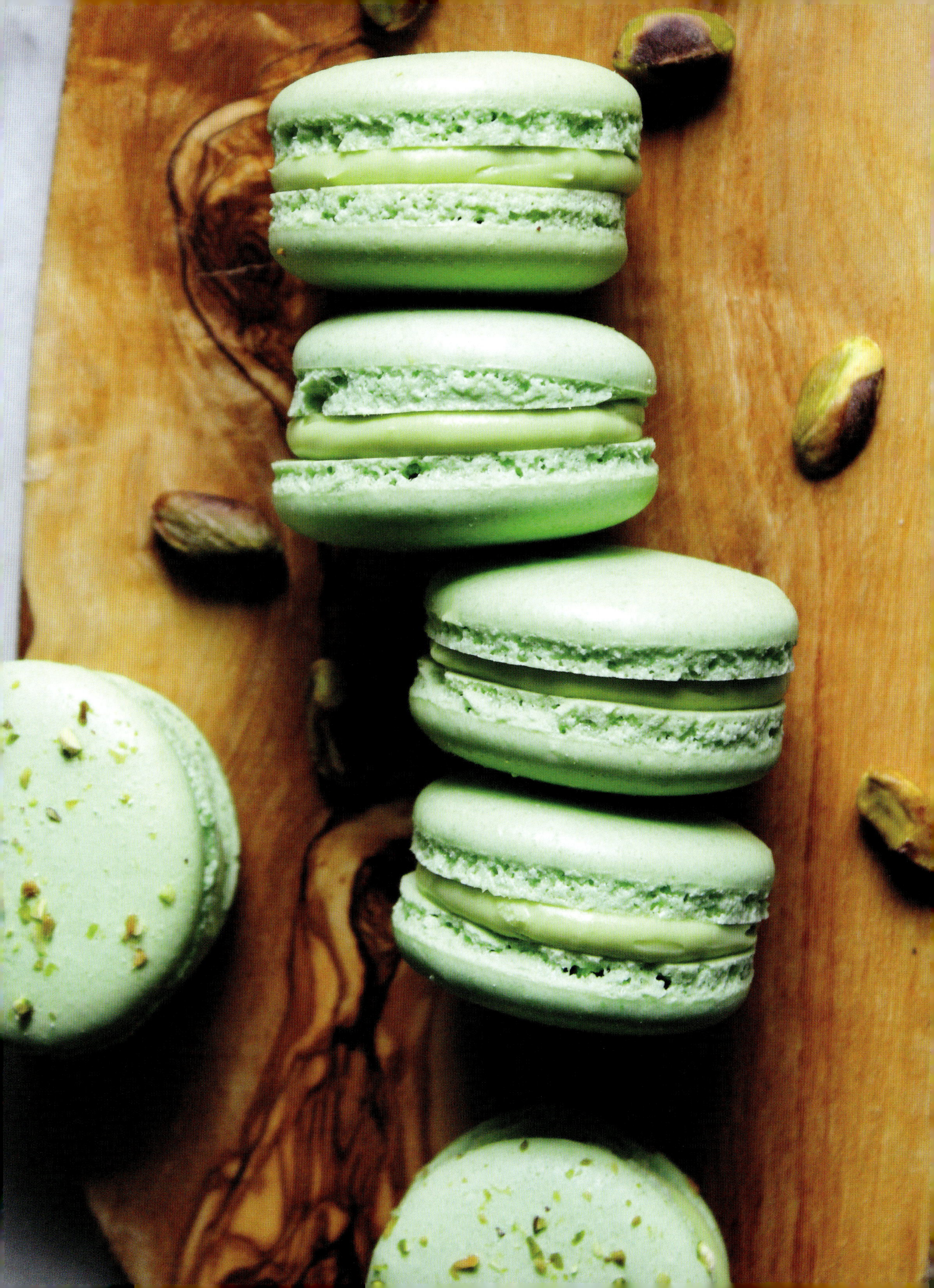

Macarons Vanille

makes 30

macaron shells - recipe p. 212
1 cup (175 gr) white chocolate chips

¾ cup (180 gr) heavy whipping cream
2 vanilla beans

Halve the vanilla beans lengthwise using a small curved knife. Scrape the seeds out and place the seeds and pods in a small saucepan with the heavy cream. Bring to a boil and remove from the heat.
Cover and let infuse for 20 minutes.
Place the white chocolate chips in a mixing bowl.
Melt over a double-boiler (saucepan with simmering water).
Remove the pods from the cream and quickly warm the cream over medium heat.
Stir in the melted white chocolate using a rubber spatula.
Use a hand blender for a nice and smooth texture.
Cover and refrigerate for 6 hours or overnight.
Make the macaron shells. Sort and match into pairs.
Place the vanilla filling in the bowl of an electric mixer with the whip attachment.
Mix at medium to high speed for about 1 minute.
Fit a pastry bag with a Wilton round tip #12. Add the vanilla filling.
Pipe the filling onto one shell, cover with the other shell.
Place the macarons in an airtight container.
Refrigerate overnight before eating - it is a must so that the macarons have the best consistency!
Store the macarons in an airtight container, in the fridge for up to a week.

vegetarian | gluten-free

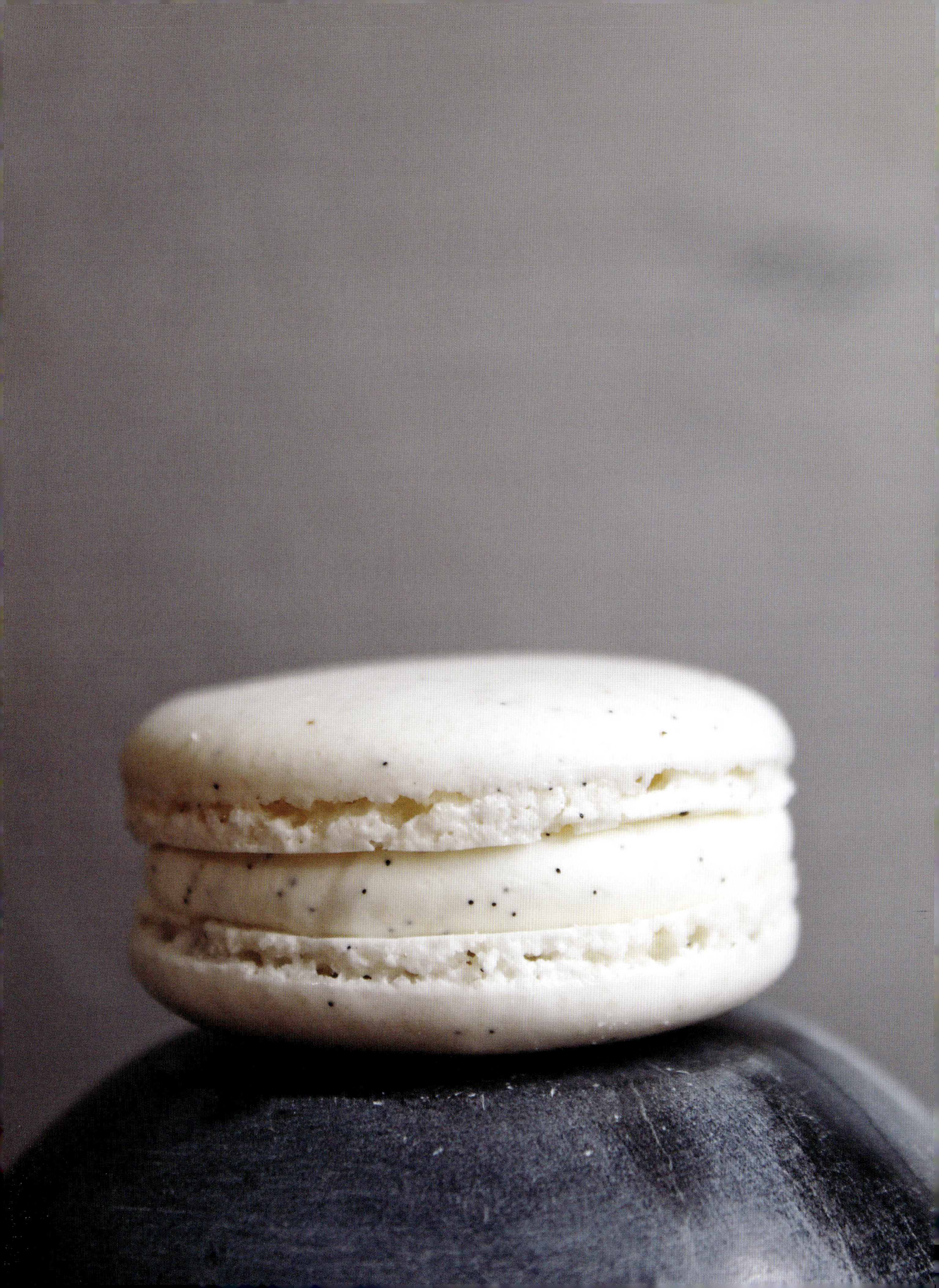

Everything is possible
and everything,
even this day,
is unknown
until you live it.

— MARK NEPO